*How to Use*
# CorelDRAW!

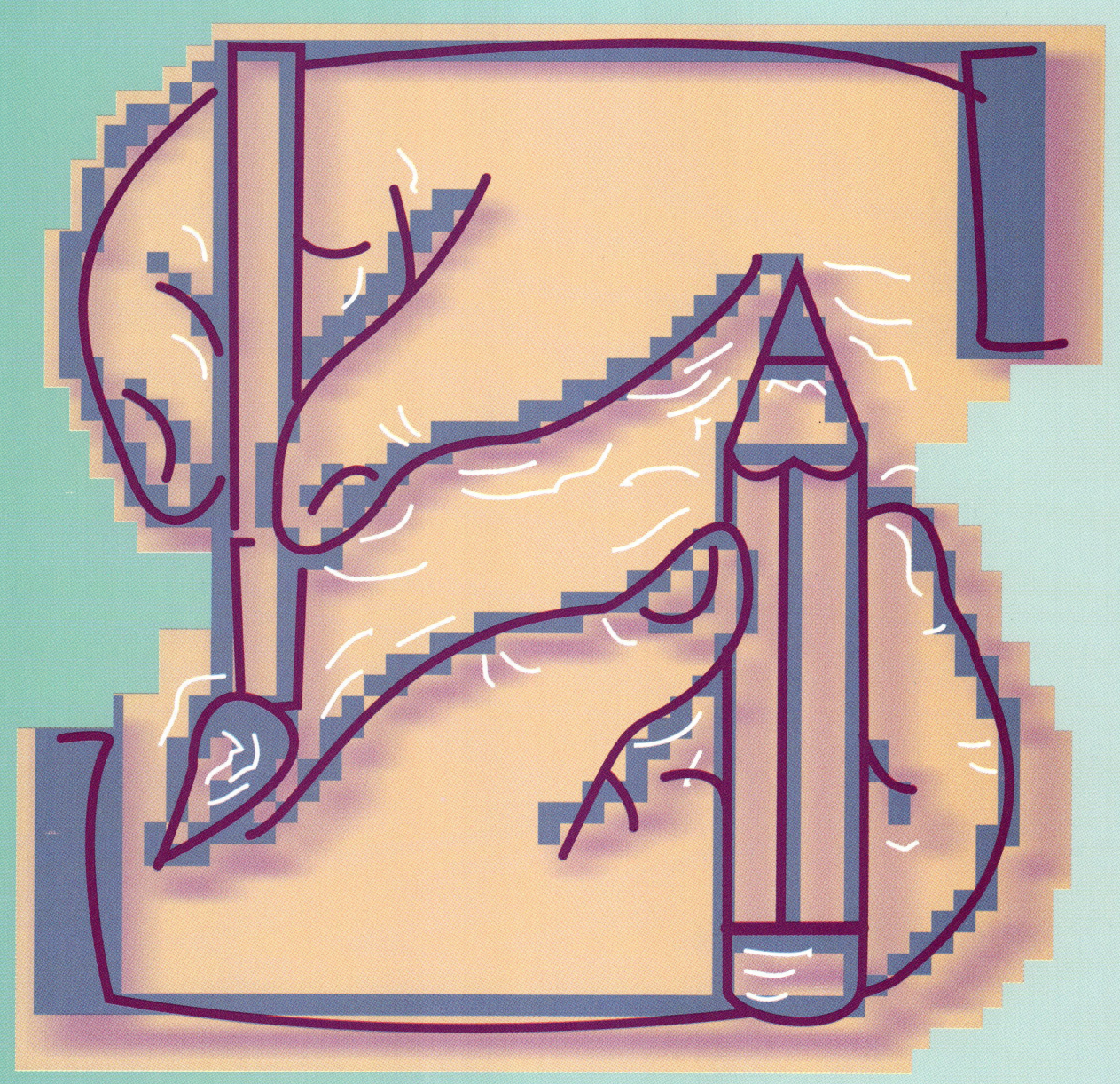

# *How to Use* CorelDRAW!

### Deborah Craig

#### Illustrated by
#### Tony Davis

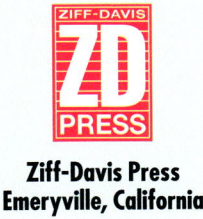

**Ziff-Davis Press**
**Emeryville, California**

| | |
|---|---|
| Copy Editor | Heidi Steele |
| Technical Reviewer | Heidi Steele |
| Project Coordinator | Barbara Dahl |
| Proofreader | Carol Burbo |
| Cover Illustration | Tony Davis |
| Cover Design | Carrie English |
| Book Design | Dennis Gallagher/Visual Strategies, San Francisco |
| Screen Graphics Editor | Dan Brodnitz |
| Technical Illustration | Tony Davis, and Cherie Plumlee Computer Graphics and Illustration |
| Word Processing | Howard Blechman |
| Page Layout | Bruce Lundquist |
| Indexer | Deborah Craig |

Ziff-Davis Press books are produced on a Macintosh computer system with the following applications: FrameMaker®, Microsoft® Word, QuarkXPress®, Adobe Illustrator®, Adobe Photoshop®, Adobe Streamline™, MacLink® *Plus*, Aldus® FreeHand™, Collage Plus™.

If you have comments or questions or would like to receive a free catalog, call or write:
Ziff-Davis Press
5903 Christie Avenue
Emeryville, CA 94608
1-800-688-0448

Copyright © 1994 by Ziff-Davis Press. All rights reserved.
PART OF A CONTINUING SERIES

Ziff-Davis Press and ZD Press are trademarks of Ziff Communications Company.

All other product names and services identified throughout this book are trademarks or registered trademarks of their respective companies. They are used throughout this book in editorial fashion only and for the benefit of such companies. No such uses, or the use of any trade name, is intended to convey endorsement or other affiliation with the book.

No part of this publication may be reproduced in any form, or stored in a database or retrieval system, or transmitted or distributed in any form by any means, electronic, mechanical photocopying, recording, or otherwise, without the prior written permission of Ziff-Davis Press, except as permitted by the Copyright Act of 1976, and except that program listings may be entered, stored, and executed in a computer system.

THE INFORMATION AND MATERIAL CONTAINED IN THIS BOOK ARE PROVIDED "AS IS," WITHOUT WARRANTY OF ANY KIND, EXPRESS OR IMPLIED, INCLUDING WITHOUT LIMITATION ANY WARRANTY CONCERNING THE ACCURACY, ADEQUACY, OR COMPLETENESS OF SUCH INFORMATION OR MATERIAL OR THE RESULTS TO BE OBTAINED FROM USING SUCH INFORMATION OR MATERIAL. NEITHER ZIFF-DAVIS PRESS NOR THE AUTHOR SHALL BE RESPONSIBLE FOR ANY CLAIMS ATTRIBUTABLE TO ERRORS, OMISSIONS, OR OTHER INACCURACIES IN THE INFORMATION OR MATERIAL CONTAINED IN THIS BOOK, AND IN NO EVENT SHALL ZIFF-DAVIS PRESS OR THE AUTHOR BE LIABLE FOR DIRECT, INDIRECT, SPECIAL, INCIDENTAL, OR CONSEQUENTIAL DAMAGES ARISING OUT OF THE USE OF SUCH INFORMATION OR MATERIAL.

ISBN 1-56276-221-4

Manufactured in the United States of America
10 9 8 7 6 5 4 3 2 1

# TABLE OF CONTENTS

*Introduction* x

**CHAPTER 1**
**WHAT YOU CAN DO WITH CORELDRAW!** 1
  *Drawing Shapes and Using Graphics from Other Sources* 2
  *Entering, Editing, and Manipulating Text* 4

**CHAPTER 2**
**GETTING ACQUAINTED WITH DOS AND WINDOWS** 7
  *Getting into Windows from DOS* 8
  *Starting Programs from within Windows* 10
  *Maneuvering with the Mouse* 12
  *Working with the Keyboard* 14
  *Contending with Dialog Boxes* 16

**CHAPTER 3**
**GETTING STARTED IN CORELDRAW!** 19
  *What's on Your Screen* 20
  *Getting Help When You Need It* 22

**CHAPTER 4**
**DRAWING LINES AND SHAPES** 25
  *How to Draw Lines and Curves* 26
  *How to Draw Lines and Curves in Bézier Mode* 28
  *Drawing Squares and Rectangles* 30
  *Drawing Circles and Ellipses* 32

**CHAPTER 5**
**ENTERING TEXT** 35
  *How to Enter Small Blocks of Text* 36
  *How to Enter Larger Blocks of Text* 38
  *How to Enter Special Symbols* 40

**TRY IT!** 42

**CHAPTER 6**
**WORKING WITH FILES** 47
  *How to Save Files* 48
  *How to Open Existing Files* 50
  *How to Clear Your Screen* 52

**CHAPTER 7**
**MANIPULATING TEXT AND DRAWINGS** 55
  *How to Select Text and Shapes* 56
  *How to Move and Copy Objects* 58
  *How to Change Your Mind and How to Repeat Yourself* 60

**CHAPTER 8**
**PRINTING YOUR DRAWINGS** 63
  *How to Print Your Entire File* 64
  *How to Print Just a Portion of a File* 66

**CHAPTER 9**

## DIFFERENT WAYS OF VIEWING YOUR DOCUMENTS  69

*How to Zoom In and Out  70*

*How to Change the Orientation of Your Drawing  72*

*Other Ways of Viewing Your Drawings  74*

**CHAPTER 10**

## COLORING AND FILLING SHAPES  77

*How to Apply Colors the Easy Way  78*

*How to Apply Texture Fills  80*

*How to Apply Fountain (Gradient) Fills  82*

*How to Apply Two-Color Pattern Fills  84*

*How to Apply Full-Color Pattern Fills  86*

## TRY IT!  88

**CHAPTER 11**

## RESHAPING OBJECTS  93

*How to Stretch, Scale, and Mirror Objects  94*

*How to Rotate and Skew Objects  96*

*How to Use the Shaping Tool  98*

**CHAPTER 12**

## REARRANGING OBJECTS  101

*Changing How Objects Overlap  102*

*How to Align Objects  104*

*How to Group Objects Together  106*

**CHAPTER 13**

## EDITING AND ALTERING TEXT  109

*How to Add and Delete Text  110*

*How to Perfect Your Writing  112*

*How to Format Paragraphs  114*

*How to Fit Text to a Path  116*

**CHAPTER 14**

## WORKING WITH OUTLINES  119

*How to Change the Outline Size and Color  120*

*How to Create Different Line Styles and Line Endings  122*

**CHAPTER 15**

## IMPORTING AND EXPORTING FILES  125

*How to Import Files  126*

*How to Export Files  128*

## TRY IT!  130

**APPENDIX**

## THE INSTALLATION PROCEDURE  137

*Installing CorelDRAW!  138*

## Index  140

## ACKNOWLEDGMENTS

Anyone who survives the experience of writing a computer book comes away with a long list of people to thank; I'm no exception.

I'm grateful to Eric Stone, Cheryl Holzaepfel, and Cindy Hudson for their respective roles in providing me with the opportunity in the first place.

To my good fortune, editor par excellence Heidi Steele found time in her hectic schedule to both copy edit my manuscript and check it for technical accuracy. She's conscientious, tactful, and has the eyes of an editorial hawk—nothing gets by her. Plus she was kind enough to bring over her poodle Joss periodically to keep my dogs entertained (writing computer books is *not* their idea of a good time) and to take me running on occasion so I didn't turn into one of those notorious tuberous vegetables.

Illustrators Tony Davis and Cherie Plumlee contributed the colorful designs that adorn just about every page of this book. Thanks to both of you for patience and perseverance while I hemmed and hawed and changed my mind, asking for literally dozens of revisions both large and small.

Barbara Dahl, project editor, managed this book deftly while putting up with more than her share of my whining about the various rules and regulations involved in doing a four-color book. Dan Brodnitz did his usual masterful job on the screens, and made the work load seem lighter by injecting his own version of humor into the process. Kim Haglund inquired about deadlines with more tact than I had thought possible. Howard Blechman, word processor, somehow managed to decipher my handwriting. And Bruce Lundquist did a skillful job on the page layout, enabling me to squeeze the maximum amount of content into a minimum amount of space.

Dino, Greg, Joe, and the other patrons of Woody Woodman's Finger Palace (that musical epicenter of the Western hemisphere) kept me going with weekly doom reports concerning the state of the world, sugar fixes, and music that continually grew curiouser and curiouser. Thanks again guys. Can't wait for that road trip....

Finally, many many thanks to Lisa—my own personal favorite computer book author—for support and encouragement, for making sure I ate my vegetables, and for checking now and then that my writing was in at least a reasonable facsimile of the English language.

# INTRODUCTION

 The book that you have in your hands is for beginners. It doesn't assume that you know the slightest thing about the CorelDRAW! graphics program or even that you know anything about Windows and DOS, the programs that make CorelDRAW! go. It also doesn't bandy about special computer code words or mysterious acronyms. At the same time, this book does not presuppose that you need to be talked down to or that you can proceed, at best, at a slow crawl.

What this book *does* assume is that you're a reasonably intelligent beginner. It starts at the beginning, explaining what CorelDRAW! is and what it can do in a straightforward, no frills manner—tossing in just enough DOS and Windows basics to ensure that you can get started in CorelDRAW!. Once you've read this book, you'll have a firm grasp of the fundamentals. What's more, you'll be comfortable enough with CorelDRAW! concepts and vocabulary to tackle its documentation, work your way through other more advanced books on the topic, and even talk to CorelDRAW! experts, including the support personnel over at Corel Corporation. In short, this book aims to make you as self-sufficient as possible, supplying you with both the skills and the self-confidence to go out and explore the wide world of computer graphics on your own.

If you're a new user—either of computers or of computer graphics programs—you may be wondering what graphics packages are really all about. Simply put, graphics programs are special software for drawing and designing using your computer. Some of the first things you discover in this book are how to draw simple shapes. You'll also learn how to work with colors and textures, how to make a wide range of changes to shapes that you've drawn, and how to modify the outlines around shapes. Although its emphasis is on graphics, CorelDRAW! has impressive text-handling capabilities as well. It provides literally dozens of fonts, and permits you to manipulate text—coloring it, rotating it, and more—in an almost limitless number of ways.

As you've probably noticed by now, this book is a little different from most other computer books you may have had to wrestle with. Rather than being organized around text with pictures thrown in periodically to illustrate a point, it's organized around the pictures themselves. Each section consists of two pages covering a single topic—this way you get information in bite-sized pieces. In addition, each of these two-page spreads is arranged in a series of easy-to-follow numbered steps that revolve around a central graphic—the imagery should make concepts both easier to grasp and easier to retain.

While numbered steps explain the basics about how to carry out each task, "Tip Sheets" in every section furnish somewhat more specialized information. You can skip these tips if you like; they're not essential to the process at hand. However, they do include valuable shortcuts, insights that may help you out in a pinch, and interesting or even amusing asides.

In addition to its 15 chapters, this book contains three strategically located "Try It" sections to help you put your skills to the test. If you haven't been experimenting as you go along (and even if you have), you should try out these exercises. There is absolutely no better way to learn a computer program—or anything else for that matter—than by doing things yourself, doing them again, and then doing them some more. And the very best thing about CorelDRAW! is that you'll have fun while you're at it.

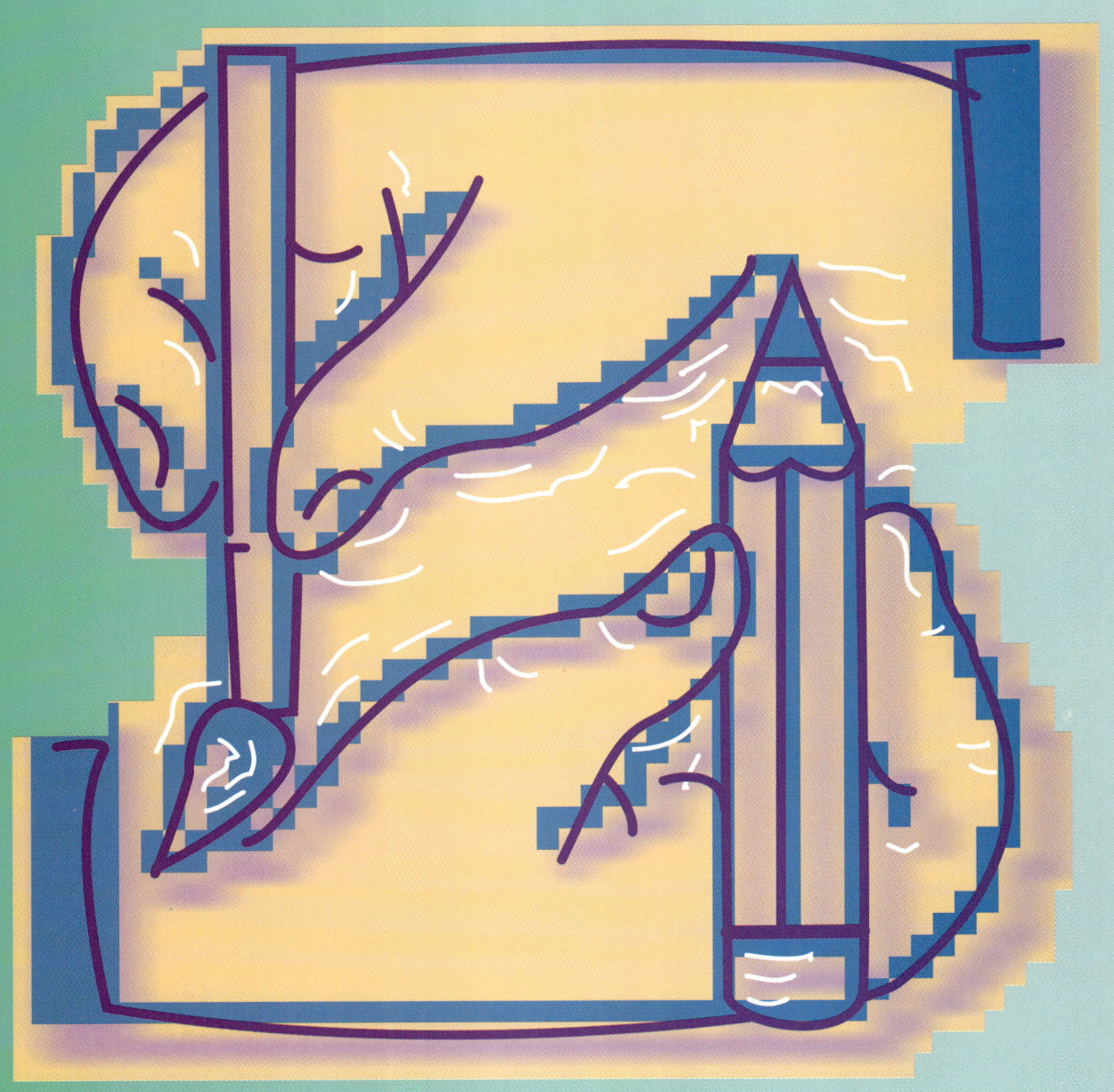

# CHAPTER 1

# What You Can Do with CorelDRAW!

This book is about CorelDRAW! 4.0, a graphics program for IBM-compatible personal computers. In CorelDRAW!, you can draw shapes, enter and manipulate text, import pictures from other programs, and use ready-made images known as "clip art." By combining these elements, you can create extremely sophisticated graphics—everything from flyers to logos to technical illustrations. At the same time, CorelDRAW! is a straightforward program whose basic tools are quite easy to master.

What's the advantage of creating graphics with a computer rather than old-fashioned drawing tools? For one thing, there's no need for an eraser. You can change a drawing to your heart's content, without generating a wastebasket overflowing with failed attempts. And there's none of the mess associated with mixing paints; it takes just a few steps to fine-tune your colors. Because you can see your drawing on the computer screen, you can do what's necessary to adjust its composition, colors, and overall effect—only generating a paper copy when the results look just right.

Before you can use CorelDRAW!, you need to install it onto your computer. Just in case you haven't done so—or someone else hasn't done so for you—the appendix at the end of this book explains the installation procedure.

**2** CHAPTER 1: WHAT YOU CAN DO WITH CorelDRAW!

# Drawing Shapes and Using Graphics from Other Sources

At the heart of CorelDRAW! is a surprisingly modest repertoire of drawing tools for creating lines, curves, rectangles, and ellipses. As you'll discover quickly, however, these simple foundations form the basis for even the most intricate designs.

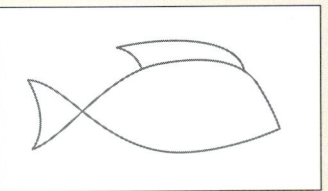

**1** You can easily construct lines, curves, and freehand shapes in CorelDRAW!. Once you master the appropriate tools, only your talent and imagination limit what you can draw.

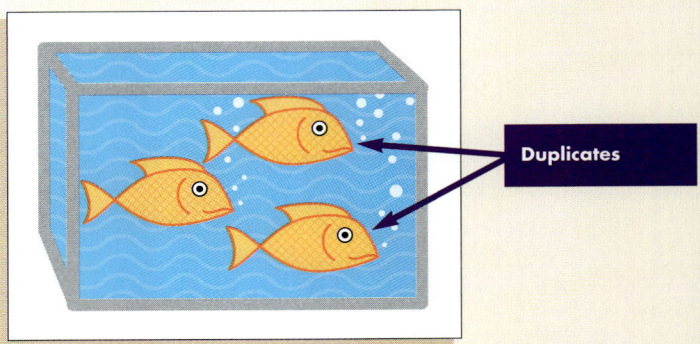

**7** Once you've drawn shapes or garnered graphics from other sources, CorelDRAW! lets you manipulate them in numerous ways. You can move shapes to new locations, duplicate them (as shown here), reshape them, and otherwise alter them to suit your taste.

### TIP SHEET

- **This book covers version 4.0 of CorelDRAW!. If you have a different version, not all the information in this book will apply to you. (The version number is displayed briefly when you start the program, and is also listed on the documentation that came with the software.)**
- **CorelDRAW! includes several extra tools—called add-ons—for tasks such as creating charts, manipulating scanned photographs, and putting together simple animation projects. These features are beyond the scope of this book, but they are covered in detail in the documentation that comes with CorelDRAW!.**

**6** CorelDRAW! provides an extensive clip art library. You can also use all types of computer graphics from outside sources, including additional clip art that you can buy commercially, photographs that you can "scan" to transform into computer files, and drawings or designs that you or someone else may have created in another computer graphics program.

DRAWING SHAPES AND USING GRAPHICS FROM OTHER SOURCES 3

 It's also simple to draw squares and rectangles. You can use these shapes as borders for your newsletters, posters, and flyers. They can also be the building blocks in geometrically oriented drawings—simple floor plans, as just one example.

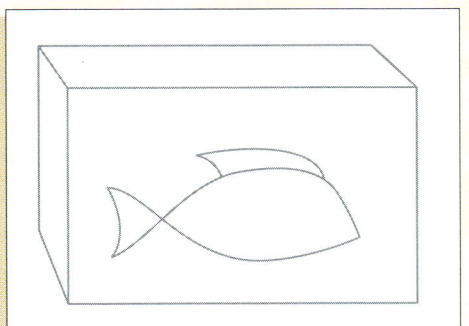

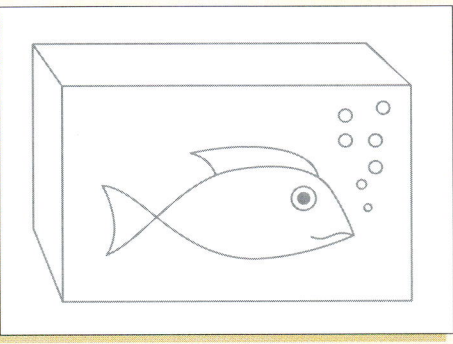

 Circles and ellipses are the third fundamental type of shape you can draw. They can serve as the basis for anything from a simple balloon to a detailed diagram of the solar system.

 All the different shapes that you draw include *outlines*—that is, lines defining the outer edges of the shape. (Simple lines and curves may consist only of an outline, while enclosed shapes such as squares can include outlines plus an inner area that you can fill with patterns and colors.) You can select different line types (dashed and dotted), different line endings (arrows and so on), various line thicknesses, and different colors for these outlines.

 Once you've created enclosed shapes such as rectangles and ellipses, you can fill them with all sorts of patterns and colors. Either use the ready-made fills and colors provided with CorelDRAW!, or devise your own fill patterns and mix custom colors to suit your needs or your fancy.

**4** Chapter 1: What You Can Do with CorelDRAW!

# Entering, Editing, and Manipulating Text

**S**hapes are only part of the picture; Corel-DRAW! is also surprisingly adept with text. It provides a huge number of fonts (styles of type) in a wide range of sizes. It also supplies several features you'd only expect in a word processing program—including word wrap, hyphenation, and both a dictionary and a thesaurus. Perhaps most important, CorelDRAW! permits you to manipulate text much as you can manipulate other shapes—stretching it, rotating it, and even adding perspective to it or wrapping it around shapes. Unlike many word processing programs, CorelDRAW! can treat text as a work of art, to be poked, prodded, reshaped, and reimagined.

### TIP SHEET

▸ Consult Chapters 5 and 13 for details on how to enter text and how to edit and otherwise manipulate text in CorelDRAW!.

▸ If at all possible, you should avoid using too many fonts on a page; the results will most likely look cluttered and be hard to read.

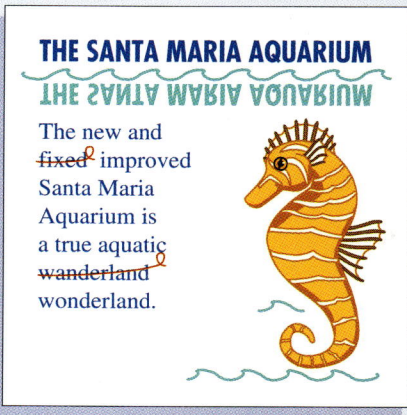

▸**1** You can type small or large amounts of text. It's also easy to go back and change what you've written—adding and deleting text, and in general fine-tuning your writing.

**6** You can also manipulate text much as you can modify any other shape or object in CorelDRAW!. For instance, you can move text, stretch it, rotate it, change its color, create mirror images, and much more. You can even wrap text around a shape, as shown here.

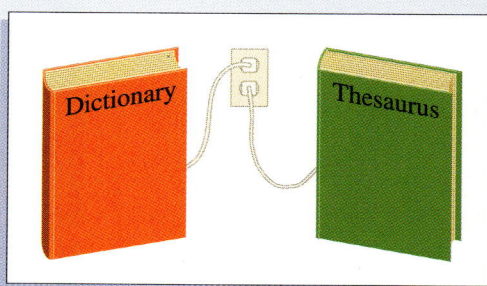

**5** You can takes steps to ensure the accuracy and interest of your text. Use the Spell Checker to double-check your spelling, and take advantage of the Thesaurus to look up alternative words when you find that you're repeating yourself.

ENTERING, EDITING, AND MANIPULATING TEXT 5

**2** For a different look, you can select a new font and size for your text. CorelDRAW! provides literally dozens of fonts (hundreds if you're using the CD-ROM version) in an almost unimaginable range of sizes.

# Here is a large font.

Here is a small one.

**Use bold for emphasis.**

*Italic is more subtle*

32-point Futura Condensed Bold type

36-point Times Roman type

Mirror image text

# THE SANTA MARIA AQUARIUM

**3** For emphasis, you can change the style of the text that you enter—choosing bold or italic, for example. Note, however, that not all fonts come in all styles; for instance, some fonts offer a bold version but no italic version.

## Gala Ball to Celebrate Our Grand Reopening!

40-point Technical Bold Oblique type

*Come One Come All!*

Slanted (skewed) text

Blue text

20-point Times Roman type

Date: October 31, 1995

Place: The S.M. Aquarium
       1234 Otter Lane
       Downtown Santa Maria

Time: 8:00 P.M.

Dress: Black Tie

### "Friends of the Aquarium"

Welcome to "Friends of the Aquarium," our brand new monthly newsletter } concerning all creatures aquatic, large and small, from mammals to shellfish…

 **4** When entering large amounts of text, you may want to divide it into columns. This approach is particularly well-suited to newsletters.

**CHAPTER 2**

# Getting Acquainted with DOS and Windows

 DOS and Windows are specialized programs that let you run other programs on your computer. Some programs only need DOS to run, but Windows-based programs such as CorelDRAW! need both DOS and Windows.

DOS means *disk operating system*—all computers need some sort of operating system to do any useful work. Although operating systems are programs, they're different from *application programs,* which let you do things such as type documents or create drawings. Instead, operating systems provide a link between the software (the programs) and the hardware (the actual machinery in your computer). DOS enables you to install application programs by copying them from their original floppy disks onto your computer's hard disk. Equally critical, DOS permits you to load application programs into your computer's memory each time you want to work with them.

Windows performs many of the same functions as DOS, but in a more "friendly" and graphical manner, providing plenty of visual cues in the form of icons and menus. These programs also look and behave quite similarly, so once you master the terrain in a single Windows-based program, it is that much easier to learn another one.

DOS starts automatically when you turn on your computer. However, in most cases you need to start Windows yourself, and Windows has to be running before you can use CorelDRAW!. This chapter unravels the mysteries of how to get into Windows, and how to make your way around once you're there.

**8** CHAPTER 2: GETTING ACQUAINTED WITH DOS AND WINDOWS

# Getting into Windows from DOS

When you turn on your computer, some of its first signs of life are a series of cryptic messages on the screen. The last line you'll see is called the *DOS prompt;* this is DOS's way of saying "tell me what to do now." At this point, you can type any number of DOS *commands*—to copy or delete files, to take inventory of the files on a disk, or even to change the way the DOS prompt looks. Most relevant at the moment, you can tell DOS to start programs, including Windows itself.

▶ **1** Turn on your computer. You may be able to flip a single main switch, or you may have to turn on several components individually, including the computer itself (the box), the monitor (the screen), and the printer. You'll hear a certain amount of whirring and grinding, messages will flash past on the screen, and, finally, you'll see either a message asking for specific information, or a DOS prompt indicating that DOS is at your beck and call.

### TIP SHEET

▶ **When you turn on your computer, there's some chance that you'll be dumped directly into Windows instead of placed at the DOS prompt. In this case, you should see the words "Program Manager" somewhere on the screen, and can begin working within Windows, as described in the rest of this chapter.**

▶ **Your computer may be set up to place you in the DOS Shell instead of at the DOS prompt. (The DOS Shell is a program designed to make it easier to work in DOS.) If so, you'll see the words "DOS Shell" at the top of the screen. To get to the DOS prompt from here, hold down the Alt key while typing F, and then type X when the menu appears. Now you can start Windows as described here.**

▶ **It's also possible that your computer has a custom *menu system*, tailor-made to help you perform your job. If you see a menu (a list of choices) instead of a DOS prompt when you turn on your computer, look for a choice such as Windows or Windows 3.1 on the menu. Then press the ↓ key until that choice is highlighted, and press the Enter key to start Windows. If you run into trouble, consult your office's resident computer expert.**

**5** If you got a message such as "Bad command or file name" when you typed **win** at the DOS prompt, try again with **c:\windows\win**. If that doesn't work either, try **d:\windows\win**. If you're still having no luck, there could be any number of problems, from large to small (not the least of which is that Windows may not be installed!). See if you can find some more computer-literate friend or colleague to bail you out, or call up the technical support department at Microsoft, the manufacturer of Windows.

GETTING INTO WINDOWS FROM DOS  9

**2** If necessary, type in any requested information and press Enter. You may be asked to supply the date and time, or to provide your name and a password if you're working on a network (a *network* is simply several computers linked together so that you can share information or programs between them). Pressing Enter is a critical piece of the equation: You need to press this key before DOS can interpret a command.

Don't forget to press Enter.

Ready when you are!

**3** After you satisfy any preliminary demands for information, you should be rewarded with a DOS prompt. Remember, this is DOS's way of asking what you want to do next. The DOS prompt has many guises, but most often it looks something like C:\>. (It may also include the date or time, the name of a directory, or even some plain-English text such as "Tell me what to do now.") No matter what the DOS prompt looks like, it is from here that you start Windows.

**4** Now just type **win** and press the Enter key. You should see a Windows logo and then an hourglass. With luck, next you'll see the words "Program Manager" on the screen. This means that Windows is running and ready to go. Most likely, this Program Manager screen will consist of some configuration of "windows" (boxes) or icons (symbols) within a larger window labeled "Program Manager." If your computer does not seem to be cooperating, read the next step.

The DOS prompt

# Starting Programs from within Windows

When you start Windows, you should automatically end up in the *Program Manager*. This program comes with Windows and enables you, among other things, to start and install other Windows-based programs. Since the Windows environment is almost infinitely customizable, your screens might look different than the ones shown here.

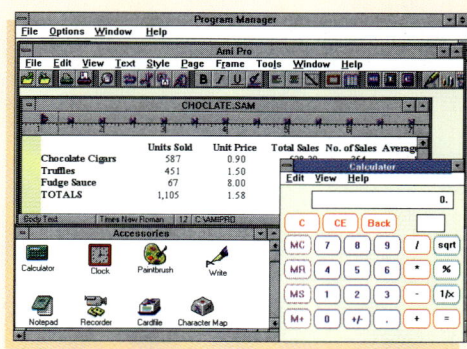

▶ ① The Windows program presents information as a series of *windows*—one or more boxes displayed in various configurations on the screen. Most Windows-based programs feature both an *application window* and *document windows*. The application window is simply the window associated with the program as a whole, and document windows are subwindows. Here you can see three application windows (Program Manager, Ami Pro, and Calculator) and two document windows (CHOCLATE.SAM and Accessories).

### TIP SHEET

▶ In case you don't like or don't own a mouse, you can use the keyboard to open a program group window and start any of the programs within it. Just press the Alt key, type W to pull down the Window menu, and then type the number to the left of the program group in question. Once you've opened the program group window, you can start a program by pressing the arrow keys until the program's name is highlighted and then pressing the Enter key.

▶ Windows lets you open more than one program at once. If one program is running, you can press Alt+Esc to return to the Program Manager without closing the open program. Then you can open another program using the methods described on this page. When you have two or more programs running at a time, you can switch between them by pressing Alt+Esc.

▶ When you're done working with a document window, you can close it by double-clicking on the Control Menu box—the dash in the window's upper-left corner. You can also double-click on an application window's Control Menu box to exit the program. Two other ways to exit from programs when you're done are to choose the Exit command from the File menu or to press Alt+F4.

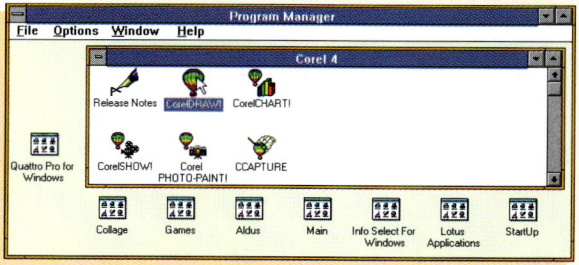

⑥ Now, to start a program, just track down its program item in the program group window, move the mouse until the arrow pointer is directly over that program item, and again double-click.

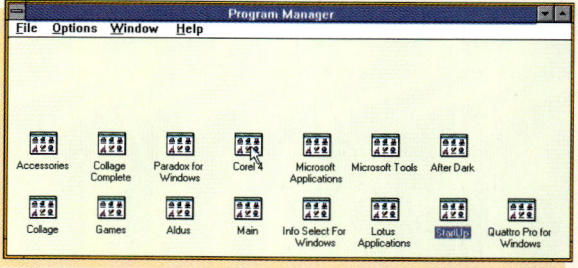

⑤ To start a program from within the Program Manager, first open the program group containing its program item. To open a program group, move your mouse until the arrow pointer is directly over the program group; then double-click the left mouse button. You'll learn about mouse techniques on the next page.

STARTING PROGRAMS FROM WITHIN WINDOWS 11

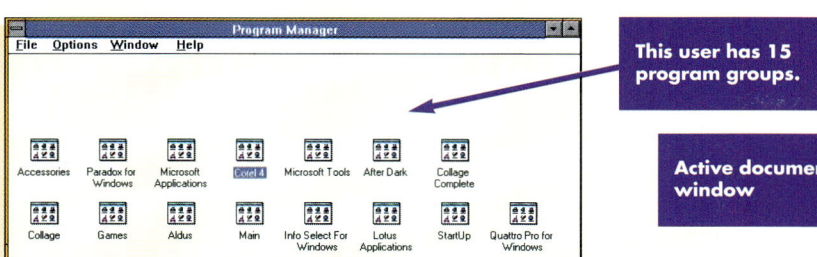

This user has 15 program groups.

Active document window

**2** Application windows include a number of common features, including a *title bar* that tells you the name of the program (Program Manager, in this case) and a *menu bar* that enables you to pull down menus from which you can issue commands. The Program Manager application window also includes *program groups,* which may appear either as icons that look a bit like little waffles (as here) or as document windows within the Program Manager window. Program groups contain sets of related programs. For instance, one program group might include all of your computer games.

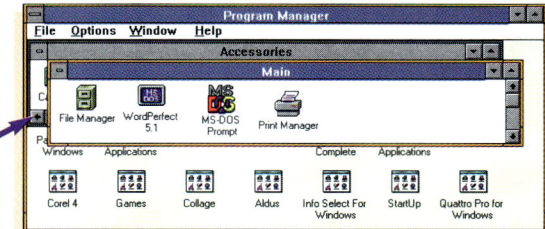

**3** You can open more than one document window at a time. However, only one of these windows can be *active*—that is, affected by any actions you take or commands you issue. Like application windows, document windows have title bars, but these display the document rather than the application name. The title bar of the active document window is highlighted to distinguish it from any other open document windows that may be displayed.

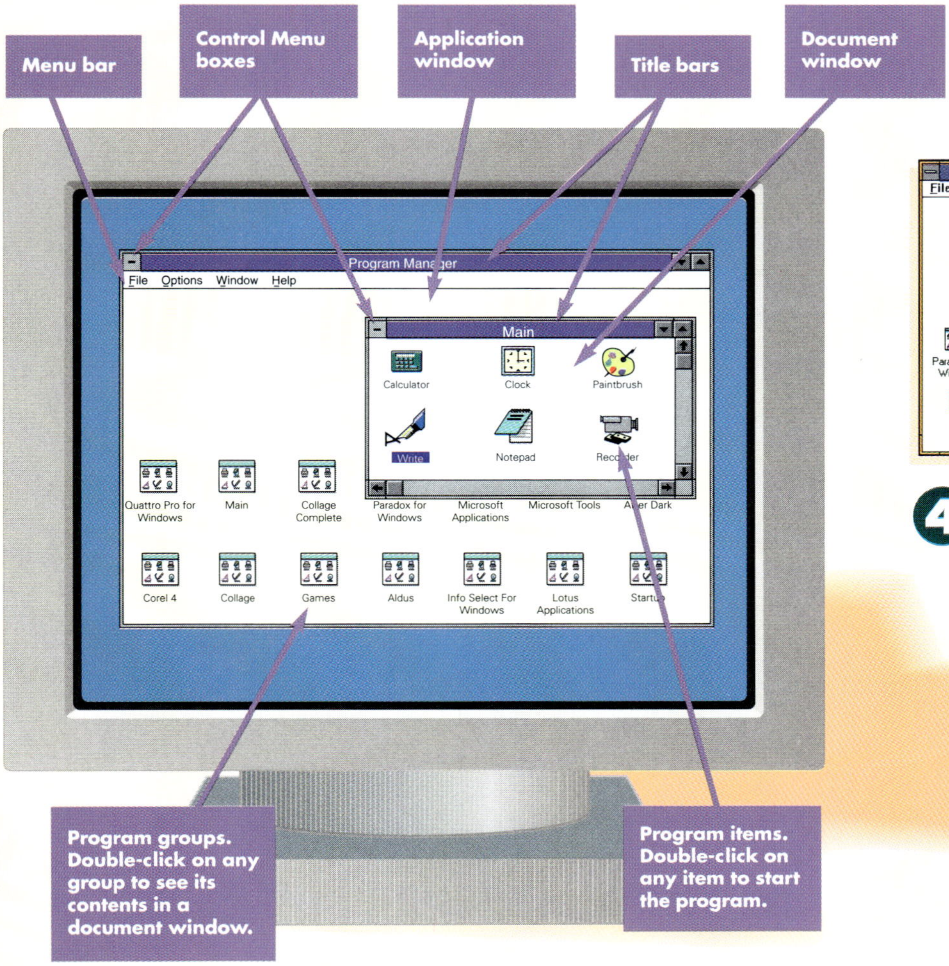

Menu bar

Control Menu boxes

Application window

Title bars

Document window

The Corel 4 document window contains nine program items.

Program groups. Double-click on any group to see its contents in a document window.

Program items. Double-click on any item to start the program.

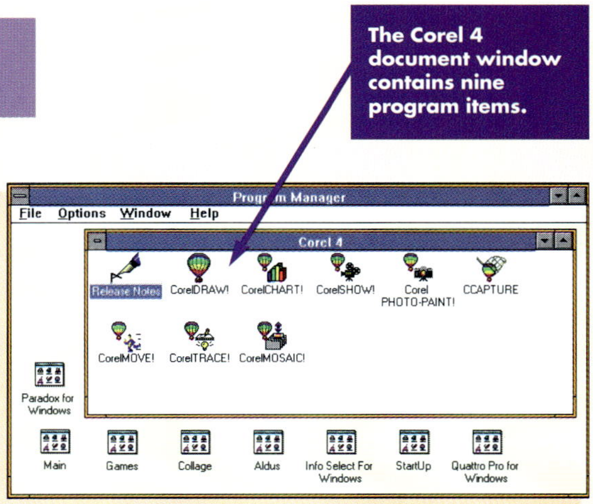

**4** You might find the term "document window" confusing. In word processing programs, document windows contain documents such as memos and letters—that much makes sense. In programs like CorelDRAW!, however, document windows are more likely to contain shapes and drawings. And in the Program Manager, document windows contain *program items*—that is, little icons that symbolize the programs available in that program group. For this reason, these document windows are often called *program group windows.*

# Maneuvering with the Mouse

To make the best use of Windows-based programs, you need to familiarize yourself with the *mouse*, a rodent-sized device that is attached to your computer with a tail of a cord. Like the keyboard, the mouse is an *input device* that you use to carry on communications with your computer. Although the mouse cannot replace the keyboard as a method of entering text or characters, it is fast becoming a favored method for issuing commands and manipulating objects on the screen. Windows-based programs let you perform most tasks with the keyboard if you prefer, but they offer a host of shortcuts and techniques that you'll miss out on if you don't acquire and acquaint yourself with a mouse.

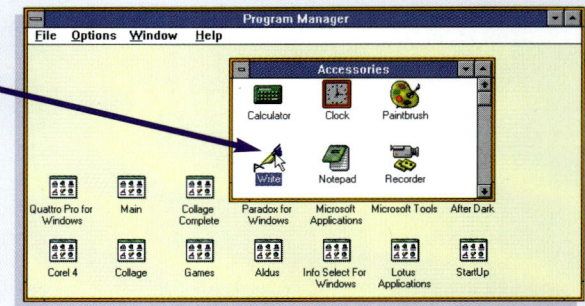

The mouse pointer is on the Write program item.

**1** When you move the mouse on your desk, a *mouse pointer* moves correspondingly on the screen. In the Program Manager, this pointer will usually be shaped like an arrow, but in other programs the mouse pointer can take on a wide variety of shapes, depending on the task you're performing. Placing the tip of the mouse pointer directly over an object on your screen is called *pointing* to that object. By itself, pointing doesn't do anything; it's just that you often need to point to something before initiating an action with the mouse.

### TIP SHEET

▶ The mouse techniques described here all make use of the *left* mouse button. Many mice also sport a right button and some even have a third button, but these buttons are only infrequently used. For this reason, you should use the left mouse button unless instructed to do otherwise.

▶ Just in case you don't like or don't own a mouse, you can turn to the next page, which covers many common keyboard techniques.

▶ The mouse pointer only moves when you move your mouse on your desk; it doesn't move when you pick your mouse up off the desk and place it in another location. So, if you've rolled your mouse all the way to the edge of your desk but the mouse pointer hasn't yet reached the desired location, just pick up your mouse, move it back a bit, put it down again, and resume rolling it in the same direction.

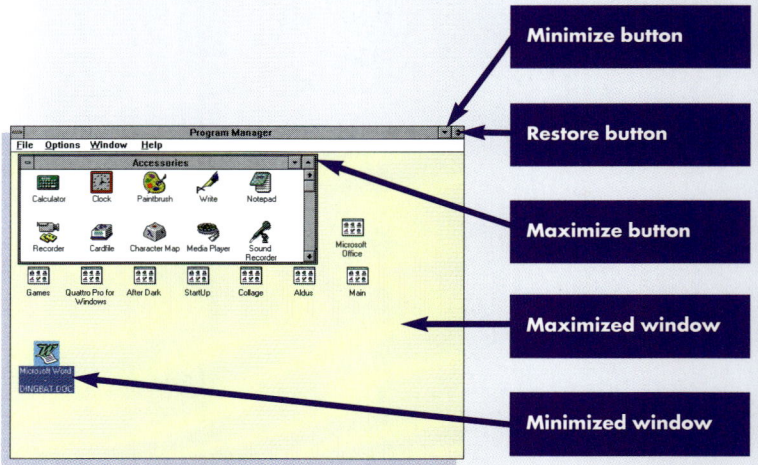

Minimize button
Restore button
Maximize button
Maximized window
Minimized window

**6** There are a number of mouse techniques for changing a window's size. You can *maximize* a window by clicking on the maximize button in the window's upper-right corner. When you maximize an application window, it fills the entire screen; when you maximize a document window, it fills the entire application window. You can then click on the restore button to *restore* the maximized window to its original size. (In a maximized window, the maximize button changes into the restore button.) Finally, you can *minimize* a window, reducing it to an icon with an accompanying title. To restore minimized windows to their original size, simply double-click on them.

## MANEUVERING WITH THE MOUSE    13

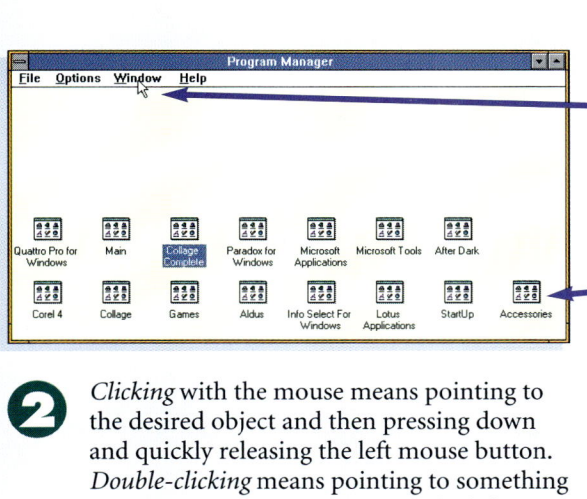

**Click here to pull down the Window menu. Then click on a command to select it. To close the menu without issuing a command, click outside the menu.**

**Double-click here to open the associated program group window.**

**❸** *Dragging* with the mouse means pointing, *holding down* the left mouse button, moving the mouse, and then releasing the mouse button. Most often, you drag to select items in preparation for performing some action that affects them; you also can drag items to move them around on the screen.

**❷** *Clicking* with the mouse means pointing to the desired object and then pressing down and quickly releasing the left mouse button. *Double-clicking* means pointing to something and then pressing and releasing the left mouse button twice in quick succession. Remember, you double-click on a program item to start the associated program.

**Drag across a word to select it. Then press the Delete key to delete it.**

**Point to this scroll arrow and hold down the left mouse button to scroll down through the document.**

**Vertical scroll bar**

**Horizontal scroll bar**

**Drag the scroll box along the scroll bar to see other parts of the document.**

**❹** When a document window is not big enough to display its entire contents, it will have *scroll bars* at the right edge and sometimes at the bottom. These let you "scroll" through your document so you can view it in its entirety. One way of scrolling is to point to the *scroll arrows* at the top or bottom (or right or left) end of the scroll bars and hold down the left mouse button. This lets you see more information in the direction of the arrow.

**❺** You can also scroll by dragging the square *scroll box* to a new position on the scroll bar. The position of the scroll button indicates your position in the document. For example, dragging the scroll box to the middle of the scroll bar places you more or less in the middle of your document. Particularly in longer documents, this technique is handy for moving through your document in larger leaps.

# Working with the Keyboard

In Windows-based programs, you can do almost everything with the mouse except type text. However, it's well worth your while to learn some of the keyboard alternatives for issuing commands and making your way through the program. If you're already typing, you won't have to interrupt what you're doing by removing your fingers from the keyboard. In addition, knowing keyboard techniques can be a lifesaver if and when your mouse dies an untimely death.

 As on a typewriter, the Shift key only works in combination with other keys; you can hold it down while typing to generate upper-case letters and other special characters. Similarly, the Alt and Ctrl keys only have an effect if you use them along with certain other keys. Which keys you use them with depends on the program you're running, although many Windows-based programs use some of the same "key combinations."

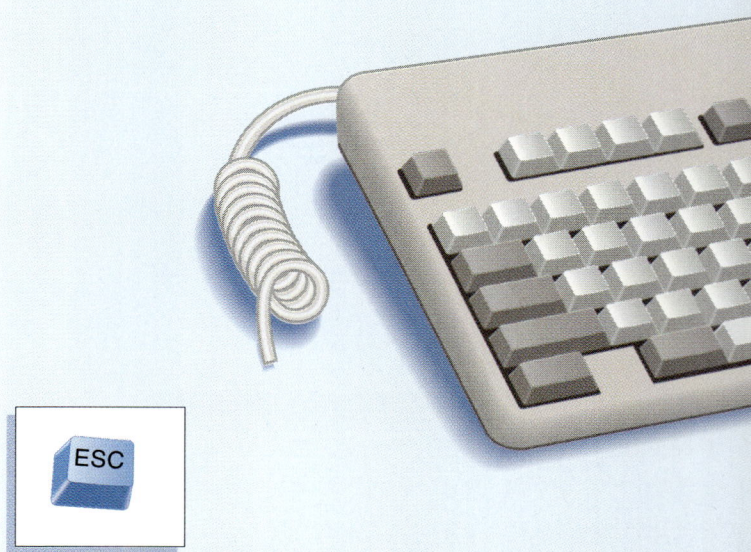

**6** Get to know the Escape key (it's usually labeled Esc). When you press the wrong key, issue a command unintentionally, or otherwise fall asleep at the wheel of your PC, this key may give you a reprieve. Among other things, you can use the Escape key to close menus without going ahead with a command (in this case press Esc twice), or to remove dialog boxes from the screen without making any changes to your document. (Dialog boxes are covered in a moment.) Regardless of the program you're using, the Escape key will often provide just the escape hatch you need.

### TIP SHEET

- These key combinations are used in many Windows programs: PgUp and PgDn scroll the display up and down one screenful at a time; Ctrl+Home moves you to the top of the document; and Ctrl+End moves you to the end of the document.
- If you have an older keyboard, the function keys may be located along the left side of the keyboard instead of across the top. It's also possible that you have 10 rather than 12 function keys.
- If you're familiar with the number keys on a calculator, you may want to press the Num Lock key so you can use the numeric keypad to enter numbers; you can use the other set of arrow keys to navigate. Especially if you're typing many numbers, this should speed up data entry.

## Working with the Keyboard

**2** It's very common to use Shift, Alt, and Ctrl with the function keys to issue commands. (The *function keys* are generally labeled F1 to F12 and located across the top of your keyboard.) As one example, in many Windows programs pressing Alt+F4 (that is, holding down the Alt key while pressing and then releasing the F4 key) closes the program. Many of the function keys also have an effect when used without Shift, Ctrl, or Alt.

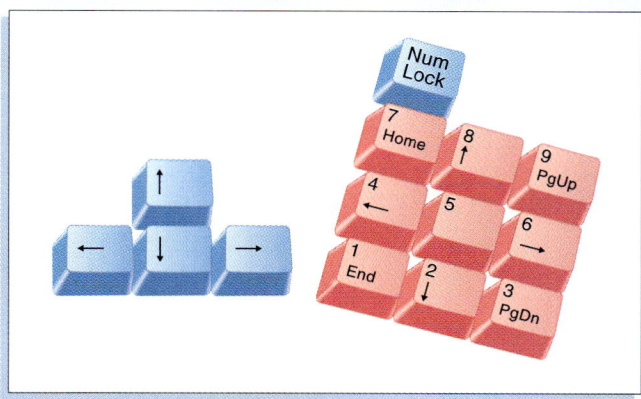

**3** Instead of using the mouse to scroll to another location in your window, you can use the ↑, ↓, ←, and → keys. Depending on your keyboard, you may actually have two sets of arrow keys: one just to the right of the main keyboard area and one on the numeric keypad at the far right edge of the keyboard. (If the arrow keys on the numeric keypad aren't cooperating, try pressing the Num Lock key.)

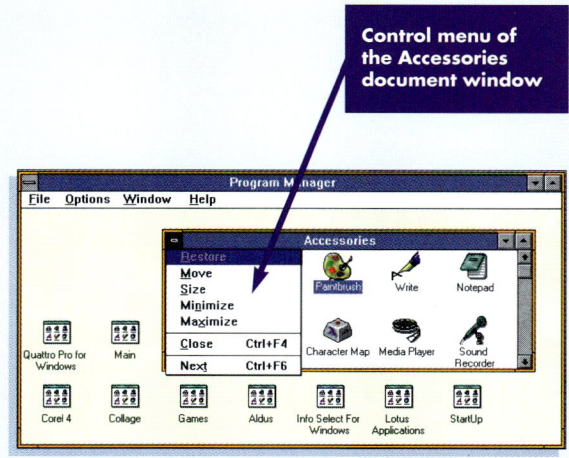

**Control menu of the Accessories document window**

**4** If you want to minimize, restore, or maximize windows without a mouse, just press Alt+spacebar to open an application window's Control menu, or Alt+hyphen to open a document window's Control menu. Then press ↓ until the command you want to issue is highlighted, and press Enter. Note that you can also close a window by using the Control menu.

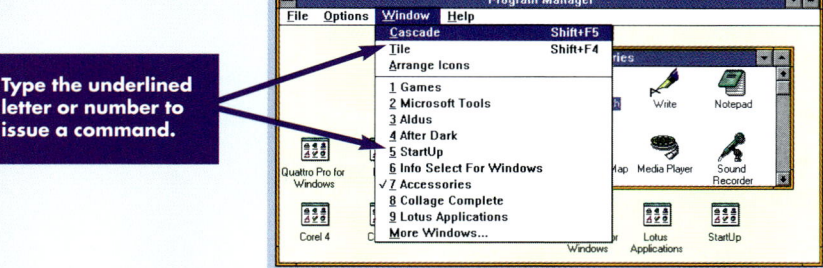

**Type the underlined letter or number to issue a command.**

**5** To open one of the menus on the menu bar, press Alt in combination with the underlined character in the menu's name. (For example, press Alt+W to open the Window menu.) Once you've pulled down a menu, just type the underlined letter in a command name to execute that command.

# Contending with Dialog Boxes

All Windows programs let you issue commands by means of menus that you pull down from the menu bar. You can carry out many commands just by selecting them from their menus, but certain commands need to know more before they can proceed. This is where dialog boxes come in: They are simply windows requesting additional information. For example, if you decide to print a file, you'll most likely choose a Print command from the File menu. Then you'll be presented with a dialog box that, among other things, asks you how many copies to print, which printer to print them on, and so on—engaging you in a dialog with your computer.

### TIP SHEET

- It's easiest to navigate in dialog boxes using the mouse. If you prefer the keyboard, however, you can generally choose options by holding down the Alt key while typing the underlined letter in the option name. Alternatively, press the Tab (or Shift+Tab) key to move between options. Then use these techniques: To either mark or clear check boxes, press the spacebar. To mark the desired option button, use the arrow keys. To open a drop-down list box, use the ↓ key, use the arrow keys to highlight your choice, and then press Tab. To edit within a text box, use Delete, Backspace, the arrow keys, and type as you would normally. And, finally, to select a command button, make certain that it's highlighted (it will acquire a thick dark border) and press the Enter key.
- Sometimes dialog boxes get in the way. If so, you can almost always move them to the side by dragging on the title bar.
- Don't be put off by the fact that CorelDRAW!'s option buttons are diamond shaped; they work just like any other Windows option buttons.

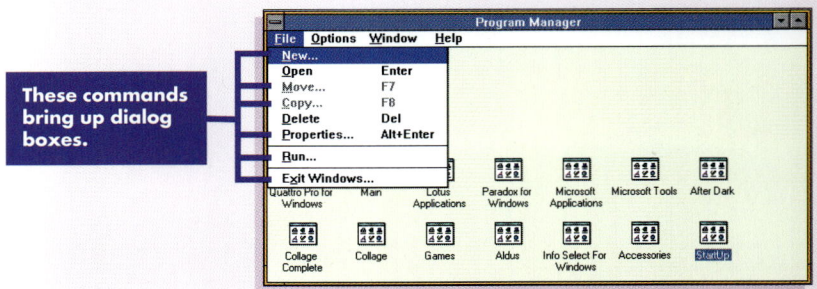

▶ **1** In Windows, all menu options whose names are followed by ellipses (...) lead to dialog boxes. There are a number of ways to feed information to a dialog box, as described next.

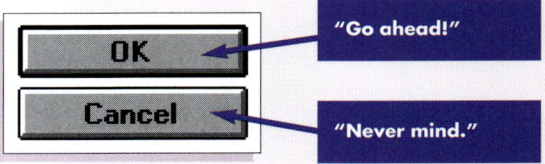

**6** When you're all done making selections and entering text in a dialog box, click on the OK button to go ahead with the command. (You may instead need to click on a button labeled something like Print or Find Next.) If you need to close a dialog box without issuing a command, you can click on the Cancel button or press the Escape key. OK and Cancel are *command buttons*—buttons that carry out some action—and are featured in nearly every dialog box. Some dialog boxes include additional command buttons for performing other actions, or, in some cases, for going on to yet another dialog box.

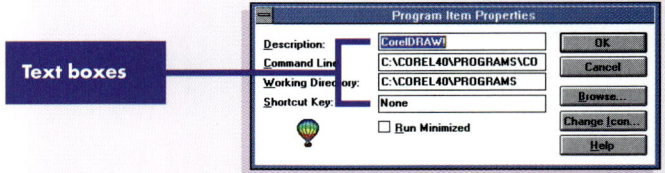

**5** *Text boxes* let you type in text rather than choosing from a list of selections. To enter text into a text box, click within it and then just type away. If you need to delete or modify existing text, use the arrow keys to position the insertion point before you type additional text, and use the Backspace and Delete keys to delete text. (The insertion point is a flashing vertical bar that indicates where your text will be inserted or deleted.)

## CONTENDING WITH DIALOG BOXES 17

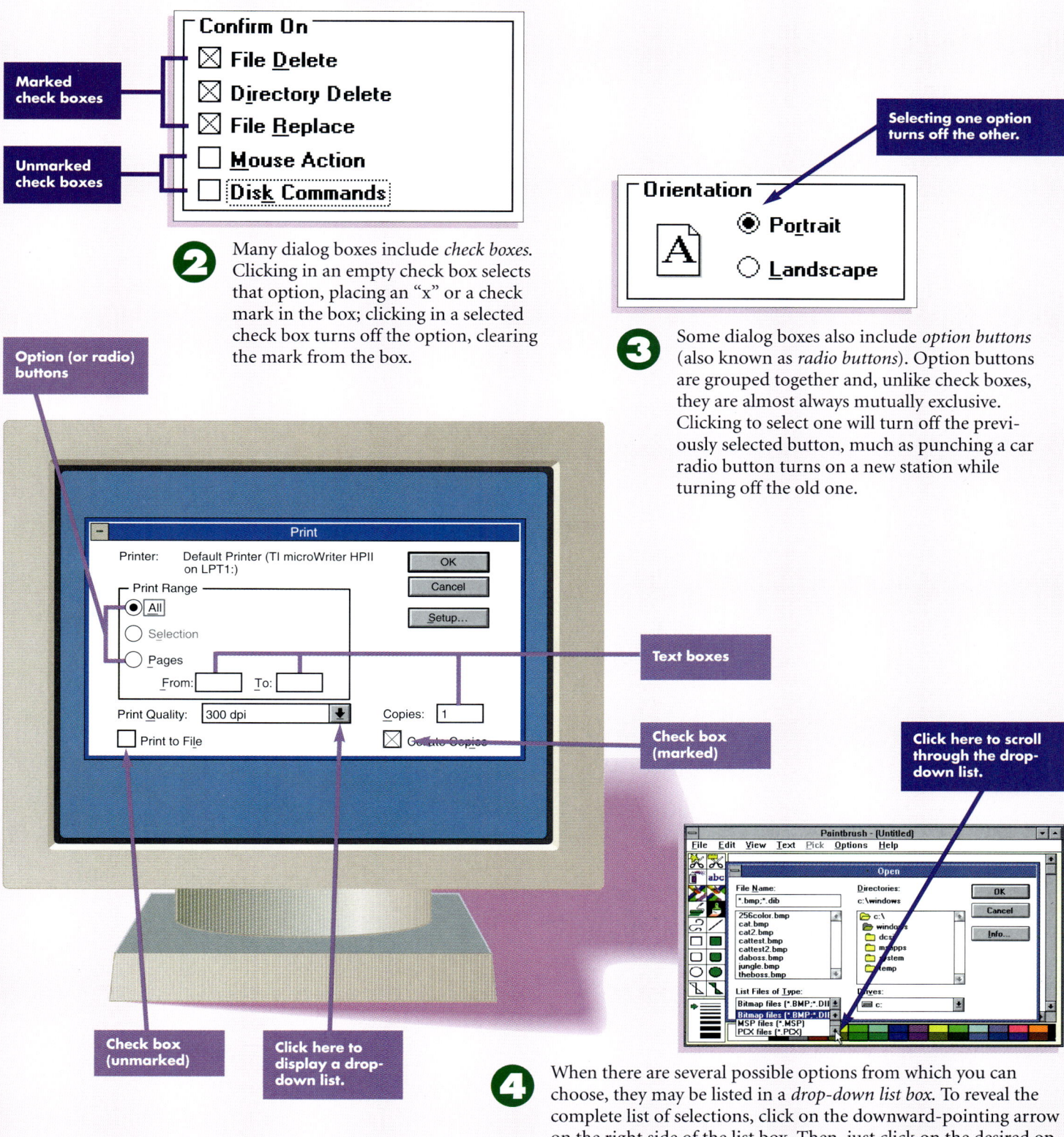

**Marked check boxes**

**Unmarked check boxes**

**Selecting one option turns off the other.**

**②** Many dialog boxes include *check boxes*. Clicking in an empty check box selects that option, placing an "x" or a check mark in the box; clicking in a selected check box turns off the option, clearing the mark from the box.

**Option (or radio) buttons**

**③** Some dialog boxes also include *option buttons* (also known as *radio buttons*). Option buttons are grouped together and, unlike check boxes, they are almost always mutually exclusive. Clicking to select one will turn off the previously selected button, much as punching a car radio button turns on a new station while turning off the old one.

**Text boxes**

**Check box (marked)**

**Check box (unmarked)**

**Click here to display a drop-down list.**

**Click here to scroll through the drop-down list.**

**④** When there are several possible options from which you can choose, they may be listed in a *drop-down list box*. To reveal the complete list of selections, click on the downward-pointing arrow on the right side of the list box. Then, just click on the desired option to select it. You may also encounter regular *list boxes*, which reveal multiple options at all times, rather than dropping down a list at your request. Both types of list boxes will acquire scroll bars if they include too many items to display at once.

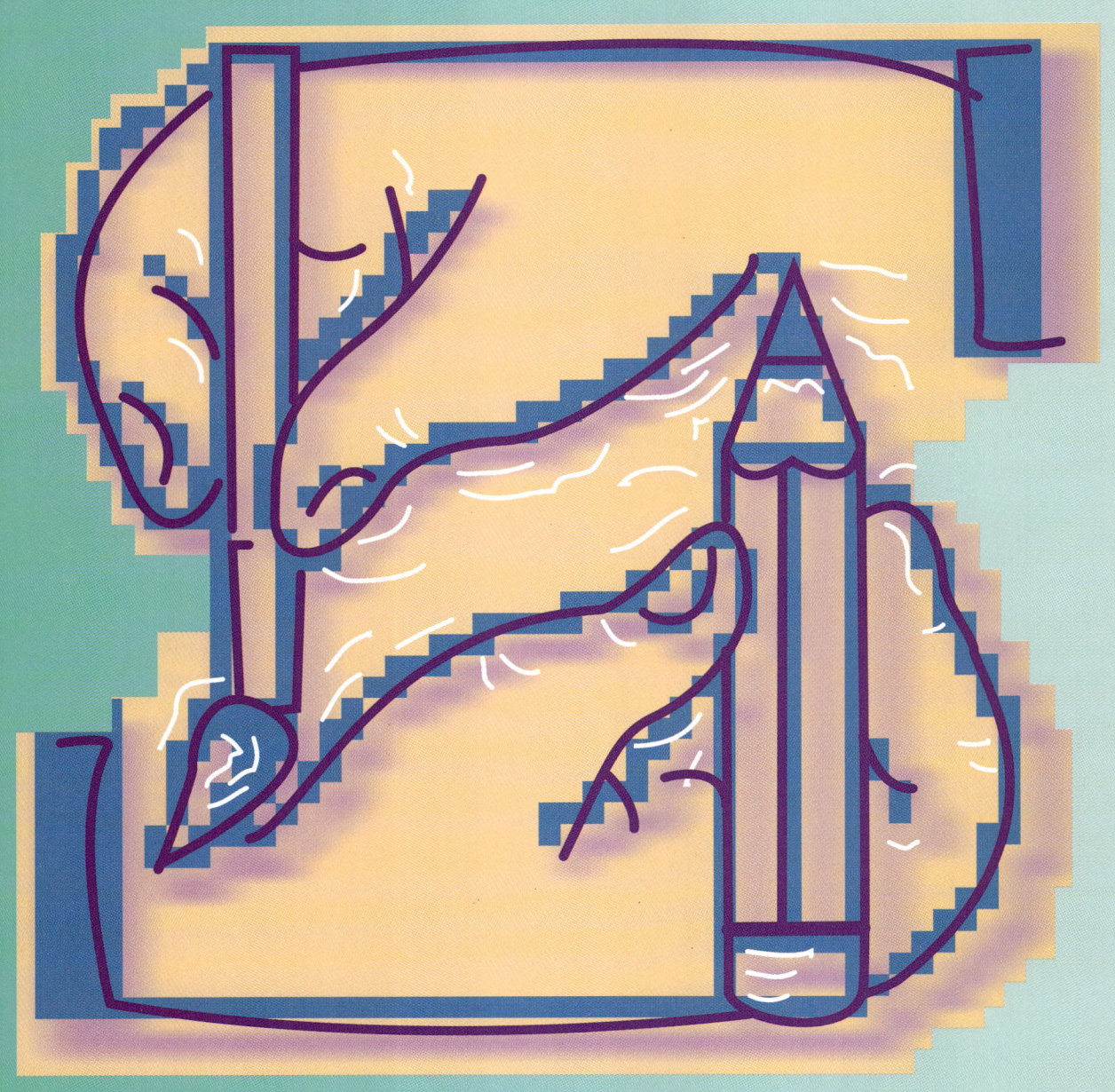

**CHAPTER 3**

# Getting Started in CorelDRAW!

When you start CorelDRAW!, you are greeted with the electronic equivalent of a blank sheet of paper. At the same time, the screen itself is far from empty. On your left is a group of tools for drawing, entering text, coloring and filling objects, and manipulating objects on the screen. At the bottom of the screen is a palette of ready-mixed colors that you can apply to text and shapes. And at the top of the screen is the menu bar, which gives you access to CorelDRAW's system of menus and dialog boxes for issuing commands.

    This chapter maps out the CorelDRAW! landscape. You'll learn a bit about how to recognize and how to use the various tools you now have at your fingertips. Don't be put off by what may seem like a parade of foreign objects; most of these items are fairly straightforward and easy to master. Also, don't feel compelled to memorize every bit of information that sails your way. The second half of the chapter introduces CorelDRAW!'s on-line help system, which you can always call upon if you have a memory lapse. This feature is also indispensable if you run up against the proverbial brick wall, or simply want to do a bit of exploring on your own.

# What's On Your Screen

When you start CorelDRAW!, you will see a screen similiar to the one shown here. Before you get started, you should familiarize yourself with what's on this screen—much as you would consult a road map before setting off on a voyage. Once again, try not to be intimidated: The CorelDRAW! program actually has far fewer tools and clutter than most, and soon these items will come to seem like old friends.

### TIP SHEET

▶ When you start CorelDRAW!, the application window may not fill the entire screen. If you'd prefer that it did, simply click on the maximize button (the upward-pointing triangle) in the window's upper-right corner. If the window is maximized and you'd prefer that it not be, click on the restore button (the two triangles) in the window's upper-right corner. See Chapter 2 or a Windows text for more details on changing a window's size.

▶ If you prefer a less cluttered screen, you can remove the status line, the rulers, or the color palette from view. Just pull down the Display menu and then choose Show Rulers, Show Status Line, or Color Palette from the menu that appears. When you choose Color Palette, you need to choose No Palette from the submenu that appears. To return any of these items to view, just repeat the preceding steps.

▶ Some of the items in the toolbox are actually several tools wrapped up in one. For example, clicking on the Zoom tool displays a *flyout menu* that provides additional tools for changing the display of your drawing. In addition, the Outline and Fill flyout menus let you open the Pen and Fill *roll-up windows*—*roll-ups*, for short. These are special dialog boxes that you can keep displayed on the screen while you work, saving you the trouble of repeatedly having to go through the menu system. CorelDRAW! provides over a half dozen of these roll-ups, which you'll learn about as needed.

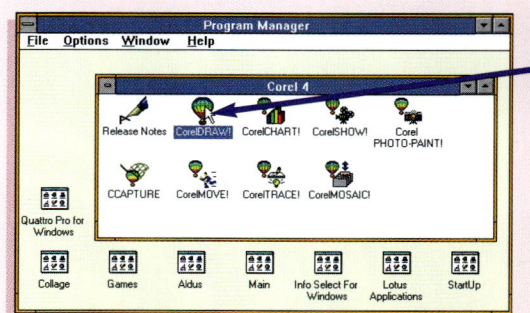

 **1** If CorelDRAW! is not already started, you'll need to start it now. To do so, get into Windows, open the program group that contains CorelDRAW! (it's probably called Corel 4), and double-click on the CorelDRAW! icon. (See "Starting Programs from within Windows" in Chapter 2 if you need help.) This brings up the main CorelDRAW! screen like the one shown here.

**7** The *color palette* at the bottom of the screen provides you with a quick way to apply colors to text and drawings. Note that you can click on the arrows at either end of the color palette to bring additional colors into view. CorelDRAW! also lets you choose from different palettes and enables you to mix custom colors, as explained in greater detail in Chapter 10.

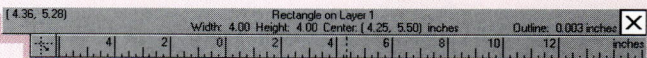

**6** The *status line* directly underneath the menu bar indicates the location of the mouse pointer within the drawing window. It may also include information such as the width and height of the selected object. For example, the status line here shows that the selected object is a rectangle that is 4 inches wide and 4 inches high. Use the status line to keep tabs on where you are and what you're doing. You can also use the *rulers* at the top and left side of the screen to track your location on the screen. (Choose Show Rulers from the Display menu to turn on the rulers if they're not already displayed.)

**5** The large white area occupying the main portion of the screen is called the *drawing window*. The rectangular area in the center of the drawing window represents the *printable page;* although you can draw outside the bounds of this rectangle, only the portion of your drawing within this area will actually be printed. You might drag a portion of your drawing off the printable page if you don't want to print it at the moment, but are not ready to get rid of it altogether.

WHAT'S ON YOUR SCREEN  **21**

**②** Note that the title bar includes the name of the application plus the name of the file you're currently working on. When you start CorelDRAW!, the program opens a blank document and calls it UNTITLED.CDR. In Chapter 6, you'll learn how to give your own names to files—you do this when you save files so you can come back to them later. As you can see, the title bar includes a Control Menu box, a minimize button, and either a maximize or restore button. See Chapter 2 if you need the details on these Windows features.

**③** Like all Windows-based programs, CorelDRAW! includes a menu bar through which you gain access to its many commands. As you can see here, CorelDRAW! provides nine menus. Remember that you can pull down a menu by clicking on it or by holding down the Alt key while typing the underlined letter in the menu name. Try pulling down some of CorelDRAW!'s menus, if you like. To close a menu without issuing a command, just click anywhere outside it or press the Escape key twice. You'll learn about the various menus and menu options as they become relevant.

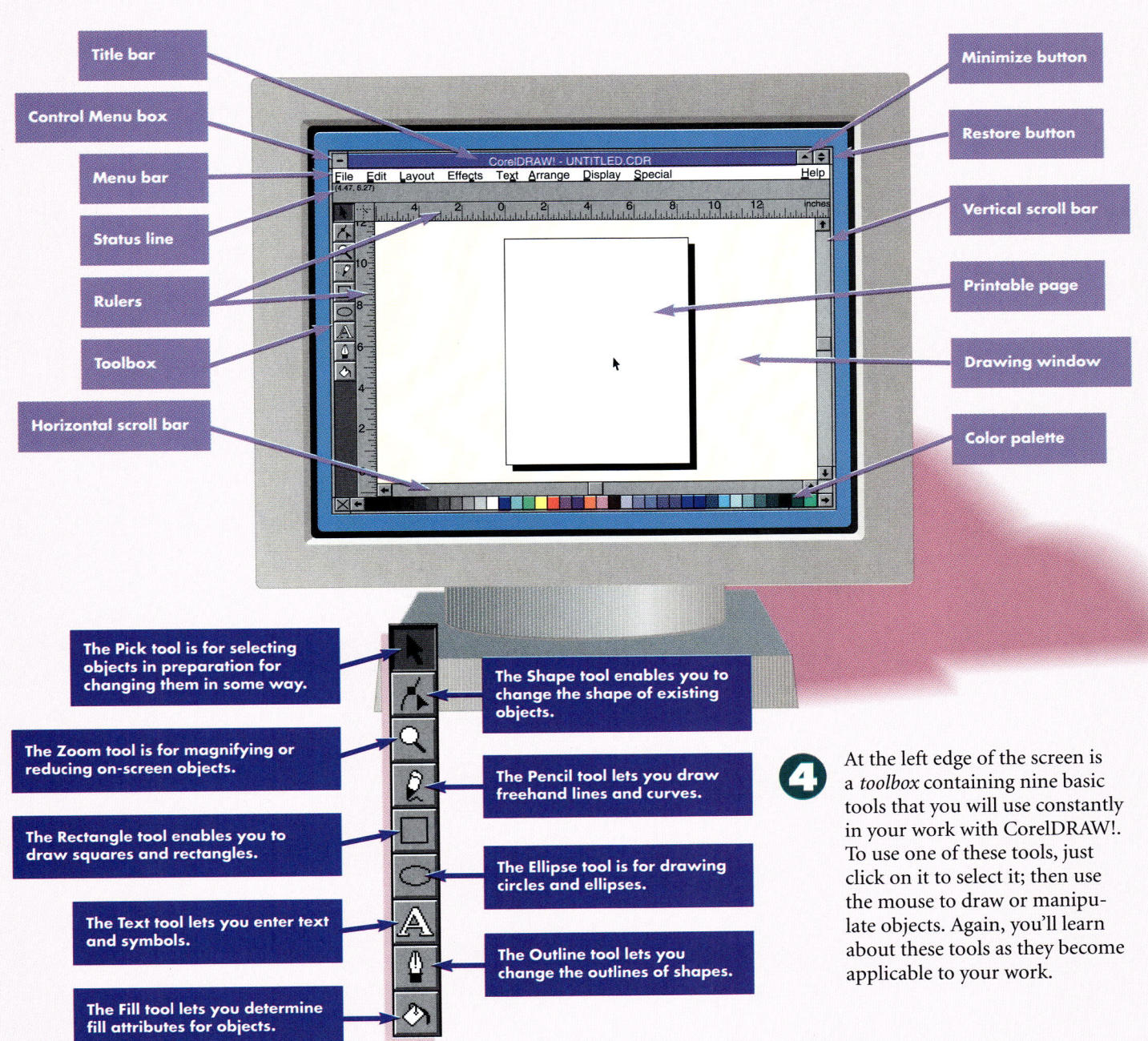

**④** At the left edge of the screen is a *toolbox* containing nine basic tools that you will use constantly in your work with CorelDRAW!. To use one of these tools, just click on it to select it; then use the mouse to draw or manipulate objects. Again, you'll learn about these tools as they become applicable to your work.

# How to Get Help When You Need It

Like most programs these days, CorelDRAW! comes complete with an *on-line help system* to supplement (or even stand in for) its printed manuals. If you're stranded, suffering from amnesia about how a feature works, or just curious about a procedure you've never tried before, this should be one of the first places you go. In many ways, an on-line help system is like an electronic manual that you can display on your computer screen; if you're lucky, you'll find the information you need without cracking a book or even removing your fingers from the keyboard. What's more, there are any number of approaches to obtaining on-line help, as you'll learn here. This lets you hunt for information in a way that suits both your temperament and your needs.

### TIP SHEET

- ▶ Often when you get into trouble, what you need is not the help system but the Undo feature, which can reverse one or more of your previous actions. The Undo feature is covered in Chapter 7.
- ▶ If you want to return to your drawing but keep the help screen displayed, you can choose Always on Top from the help system's Help menu. Then you can shrink the help screen to the desired size, and click within your drawing to reactivate CorelDRAW! without removing the help screen from view.
- ▶ Click on the History button to display a list of the help screens you've visited during your current help session. Then double-click on the name of a help screen if you want to return to it. This feature is invaluable if you take a wrong turn in the help system and want to backtrack.

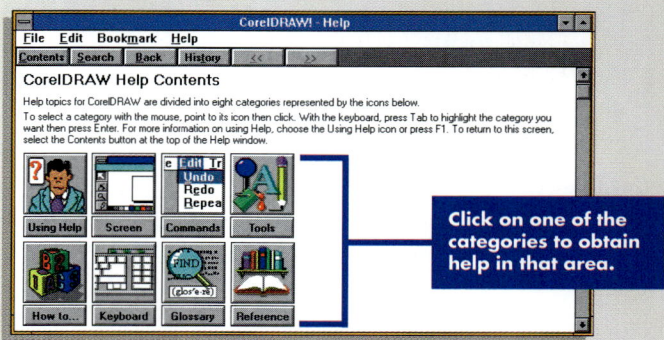

 The help system table of contents screen gives you an overview of the types of help available in CorelDRAW!. Come here to get to know the help system. To display this screen, choose Contents from the Help menu at the far right end of the menu bar, or press F1 when no menus or dialog boxes are displayed. Then click on a category that seems appropriate and go on from there. For example, click on the Tools button and then click on the Rectangle tool to display a description of that tool. The Help Contents screen can also lead you to information about commands, keyboard shortcuts, and much more. At any point, you can click on the Contents button at the top of the help window to return to the Help Contents screen.

 When you're done using the help system, you need to choose Exit from the File menu or press Alt+F4 to return to the main CorelDRAW! screen. Don't confuse the help system with a dialog box, which you can leave just by pressing Esc; instead, it's actually a separate program that you have to leave as you'd leave any other program.

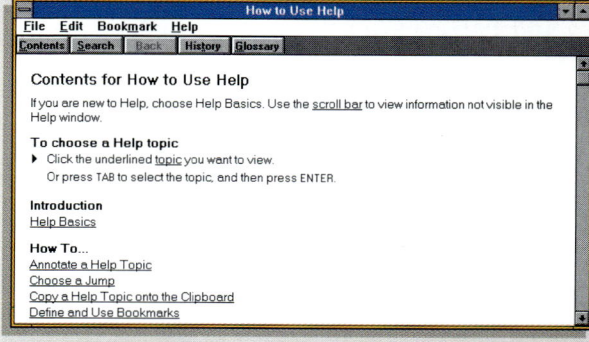

 If you need help getting your bearings in the help system, try choosing How To Use Help from the Help menu. (You can also click on the Using Help button from the Help Contents screen.) Then click on jumps to find the information you need. For example, you could click on the topic Choose a Jump under How To to display a screenful of information on what jumps are and how they work.

HOW TO GET HELP WHEN YOU NEED IT  23

**2** Pressing F1 while a menu option is selected or a dialog box is open brings up *context-sensitive help*—that is, help on exactly what it is you're doing at the moment. For instance, if you open the Display menu and then press F1, you'll see a help screen on the Show Rulers command (the first menu option in the Display menu). Context-sensitive help is like an express train that gives you a quick ride straight to the information you need.

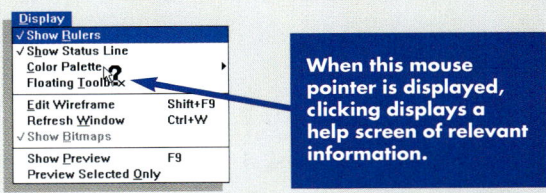
When this mouse pointer is displayed, clicking displays a help screen of relevant information.

**3** There's an additional strategy for obtaining quick help on screen items and menu options: Choose Screen/Menu Help from the Help menu or press Shift+F1. The mouse pointer acquires a question mark, and you can now click on any item you're wondering about. For example, to discover more about the color palette, press Shift+F1 and then click on the color palette. You can also learn about menu options by pressing Shift+F1, clicking to pull down the desired menu, and then clicking on the option in question, as shown here. (If you decide not to seek help, simply press Shift+F1 again; the mouse pointer will return to normal.)

**4** If you're hunting for help on a particular topic, turn to the help system's Search dialog box. To activate this feature, choose Search For Help On from the Help menu or press Ctrl+F1. (If you're already in the help system, just choose the Search button.) Once you've opened the Search dialog box, either type in a topic or select one from the list. When you see a topic that looks promising, click on it to select it and then click on Show Topics to display a list of related topics at the bottom of the dialog box. Now select the desired topic and click on Go To to display a help screen of information on the subject.

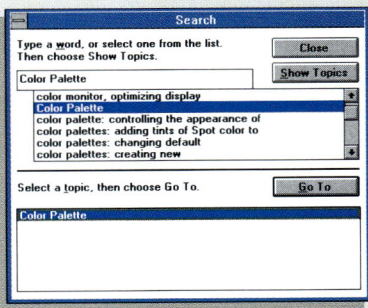

**5** Many help screens include underlined terms or phrases called *jumps*—cross-references that you can click on to "jump" directly to a help screen of information on a related topic. If you change your mind after leaping to a new topic, click on the Back button to jump back to your previous position. Some help screens also contain words or phrases with dashed underlining; you can click on these words to display their definition. (Click again or press Esc to remove the definition from view.) When you point to a jump or a definition, the mouse pointer changes into a hand with an extended index finger, meaning "click here for additional information."

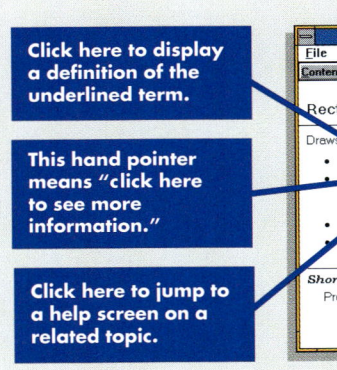
Click here to display a definition of the underlined term.

This hand pointer means "click here to see more information."

Click here to jump to a help screen on a related topic.

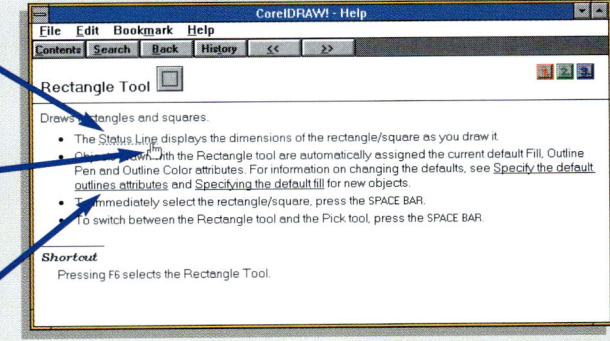

**CHAPTER 4**

# Drawing Lines and Shapes

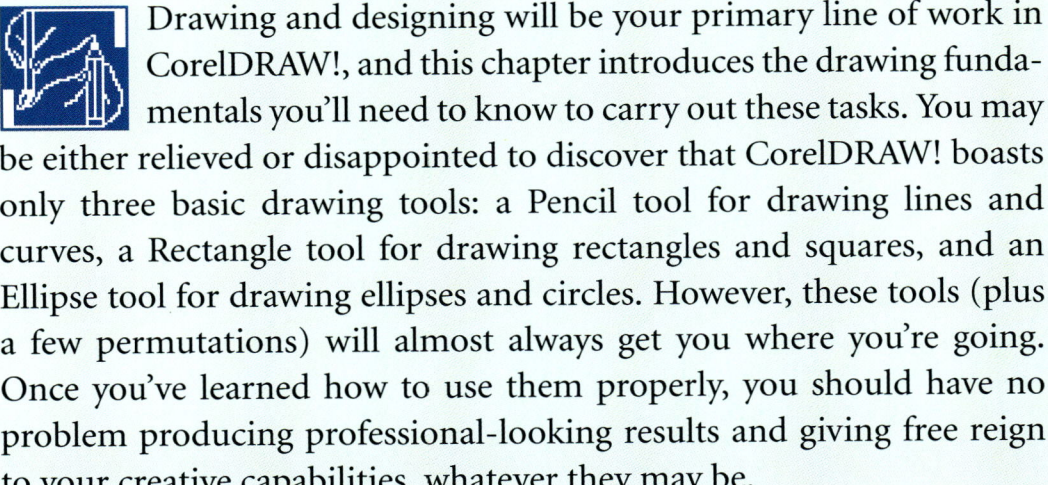Drawing and designing will be your primary line of work in CorelDRAW!, and this chapter introduces the drawing fundamentals you'll need to know to carry out these tasks. You may be either relieved or disappointed to discover that CorelDRAW! boasts only three basic drawing tools: a Pencil tool for drawing lines and curves, a Rectangle tool for drawing rectangles and squares, and an Ellipse tool for drawing ellipses and circles. However, these tools (plus a few permutations) will almost always get you where you're going. Once you've learned how to use them properly, you should have no problem producing professional-looking results and giving free reign to your creative capabilities, whatever they may be.

As you grapple with these basic drawing tools and techniques, constantly keep in mind that your first drawing efforts needn't be perfect, or even anywhere close to it. In fact, you'll have a much easier time of it if you think of your first attempt as a rough sketch that you can refine farther on down the road. CorelDRAW! provides plenty of tools for polishing and fine-tuning your drawings, and these tools are the topic of most of the second half of this book. For the moment, just draw as best you can, concentrate on learning the inner workings of these potentially very powerful drawing tools, and don't worry too much if your initial results more closely resemble those of a preschooler than a Rembrandt or a Picasso.

# 26 CHAPTER 4: DRAWING LINES AND SHAPES

# How to Draw Lines and Curves

**A**ll shapes consist of a combination of straight lines and curves, and in CorelDRAW! you will use the Pencil tool to draw every conceivable shape except for rectangles and ellipses. Actually, you can use the Pencil tool to draw in one of two modes—Freehand mode and Bézier mode—as well as to draw dimension lines. *Freehand mode,* the more intuitive drawing mode, is explained here. *Bézier mode,* covered on the next pair of pages, lets you draw with much greater precision. When you're first learning, you may find it easiest to stick with Freehand mode and then perfect your drawing after producing a rough sketch.

### TIP SHEET

- **In Freehand mode you can constrain straight lines to particular angles by holding down Ctrl while moving your mouse. (The default is 15-degree increments; to establish a new setting, choose Preferences from the Special menu and enter a new value under Constrain Angle.) This applies to straight lines that you draw by clicking, not to curves that you draw by dragging.**

- **You can use the three additional tools in the Pencil flyout menu to draw dimension lines, which display measurements and are especially suitable for technical or architectural drawings. Although the dimension tools are beyond the scope of this book, they are covered in your CorelDRAW! documentation.**

- **Anytime you draw, whether in Freehand or Bézier mode, CorelDRAW! inserts *nodes* (small squares) where lines begin and end, as well as along the path of curves that you draw. You can use these nodes to manipulate shapes after the fact, as you'll learn in Chapter 11.**

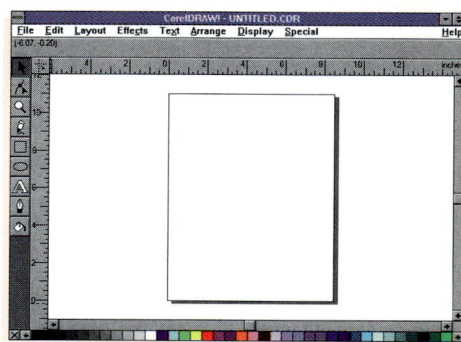

**1** Start CorelDRAW! if you haven't already (see Chapter 2 for details if you're not sure how to do this). You should see the main CorelDRAW! screen, with an empty rectangle in the center of the screen representing the printable page, and the toolbox at the left side of the screen. This chapter is where you begin to get to know the tools in this toolbox. By the end of this book, you should have at least a working knowledge of all nine of these tools.

**6** You can delete a line or curve that you've just drawn simply by pressing the Delete key. In fact, you can use this method to rid your screen of rectangles, ellipses, and all the other shapes you'll learn to draw here. However, if you've drawn some other shapes in the interim, you can't just press Delete to erase a shape you drew earlier. In Chapter 6, you'll learn strategies for clearing everything from your screen; in Chapter 7, you'll learn how to delete selected portions of your drawing.

**5** You'll have no trouble creating curves in Freehand mode if you ever finger painted as a toddler—and your first results might not look much better! Make sure the Pencil tool is selected and check that you're in Freehand mode. Then place the mouse pointer where you want to begin the drawing and drag with the mouse to draw. As long as you hold down the mouse button, you'll generate a line that follows the trajectory of your mouse pointer. Release the mouse button if you want to end the line, and resume dragging to start a new line. Although you won't achieve great accuracy using Freehand mode to draw curves, you can generate preliminary sketches that will be easy to refine later, as you'll learn in Chapter 11.

How to Draw Lines and Curves  27

**2** To use a tool, first select it by clicking on it. Click on the Pencil tool; it will look as though it has been pressed in, and the mouse pointer will change into a crosshair (a large plus sign with the middle missing) when you move it into the drawing window. (If your Pencil tool looks different from the one shown here, press and hold down the mouse button over the Pencil tool and then choose the leftmost tool from the flyout menu that appears.)

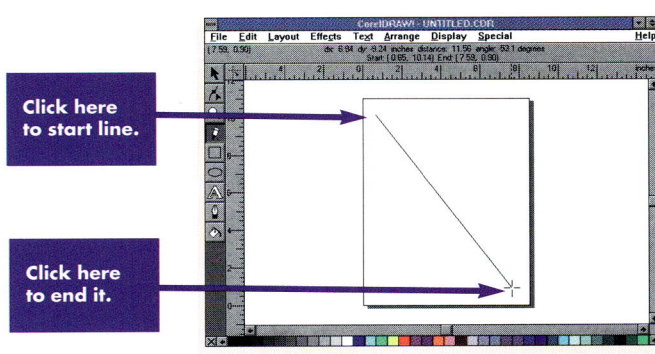

Click here to start line.

Click here to end it.

**3** To draw a straight line, place the mouse pointer where you want the line to start, click once, and release the mouse button. Then begin to move the mouse pointer, noting that a line now stretches from the spot where you first clicked to the current mouse pointer position. (Do *not* hold down the mouse button as you move the mouse, or you'll draw a curve instead of a line.) Place the mouse pointer where you want the line to end and click a second time to lock the line into position. Note that you can monitor the angle and length (distance) of the line as you draw by keeping an eye on the status line.

Your lines will look a bit rough when you draw in Freehand mode.

 If you want to draw a line or shape containing many segments, get the mouse pointer into position and click once to establish the starting point for your first line. Then move the mouse pointer and double-click where you want the first line segment to end and the next one to begin. Continue moving the mouse pointer and double-clicking to add additional line segments. To end the final line segment, move the mouse pointer to the desired spot and click a single time. If this procedure seems complicated, just keep in mind these two simple rules: Single-click to begin or end a shape; double-click to end a line segment but continue creating a shape.

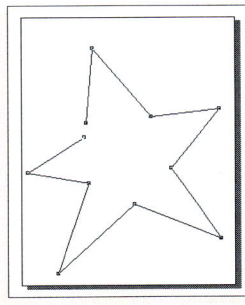

**28** CHAPTER 4: DRAWING LINES AND SHAPES

# How to Draw Lines and Curves in Bézier Mode

As mentioned, CorelDRAW! provides a second way of drawing lines and curves, called Bézier mode. This drawing method is quite a bit more complicated than Freehand mode, and is guaranteed to take some getting used to. However, Bézier mode permits you to draw with significantly greater precision, letting you construct sophisticated curves that you position precisely between two or more points. Once you've learned how to build Bézier curves, your drawings will never again resemble the clumsy attempts of a two-year-old. Note that Bézier mode is introduced only briefly here; you should consult your CorelDRAW! documentation or a more advanced text on CorelDRAW! for complete information.

### TIP SHEET

- ▶ Whether you draw in Freehand or Bézier mode, CorelDRAW! introduces nodes to mark the beginning and ending of lines, and also to plot the path of curves. You can drag on these nodes—as well as their associated control points—to reshape your lines and curves, as described in Chapter 11.
- ▶ Control points are only associated with nodes on curves; they are not associated with the nodes you find on straight line segments.
- ▶ When you draw in Bézier mode, the two control points move correspondingly when you drag one of them with your mouse. There are other types of nodes whose associated control points behave differently; you'll learn a bit about this in Chapter 11. For a more in-depth discussion of nodes and control points, consult your documentation or a more comprehensive book on CorelDRAW!.

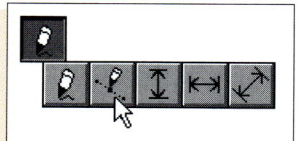

▶ **1** Press and hold down the mouse button over the Pencil tool to display the flyout menu shown here. Click on the second tool from the left in the flyout menu, noticing that the flyout menu is tucked back in, the new Pencil tool shows up in the toolbox, and the status line indicates that you are in Bézier mode.

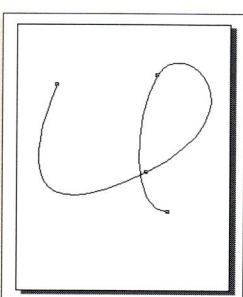

**6** To attach additional curve segments to the shape you're drawing, just continue in this manner, adding as many nodes as you like simply by moving the mouse pointer to a new location, pressing and holding down the mouse button, and dragging to position the control points and set the shape of the curve. As you draw, notice the smoothness of the curve—as opposed to the ragged and amateurish curves you produced in Freehand mode.

**5** Press and again *hold down* the mouse button where you want the curve (or curve segment) to end, noticing that CorelDRAW! inserts a curve between the two nodes. Now you can drag with your mouse to manipulate the control points for the second node in order to determine the shape of the curve.

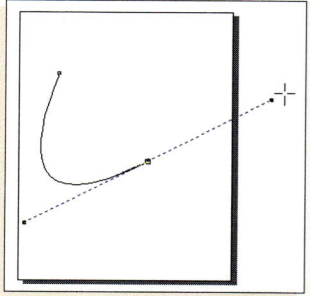

How to Draw Lines and Curves in Bézier Mode    29

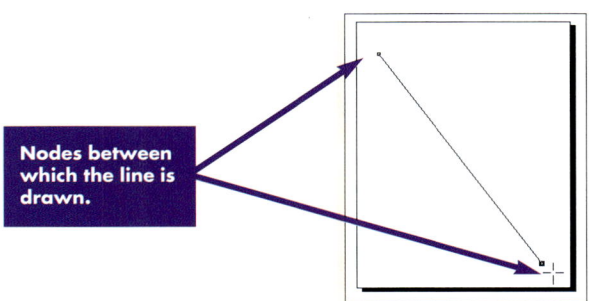

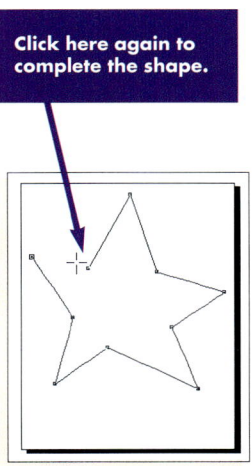

**②** To draw simple lines in Bézier mode, click where you want the line to begin and again where you want it to end, as when drawing freehand. Note, however, that lines only appear on the screen after you have marked out two points—called *nodes*—between which the line is to be drawn. (Remember that in Freehand mode you can see the line you're drawing as you move your mouse pointer.) The status line even tells you how many nodes there are.

**③** To draw multisegment lines in Bézier mode, just move the mouse and click again to add additional line segments. (There's no need to double-click, as you do in Freehand mode.) If you click on the starting point of a shape, CorelDRAW! assumes you are done drawing that particular shape. To draw two or more lines that are not connected, press the spacebar twice before drawing each new line.

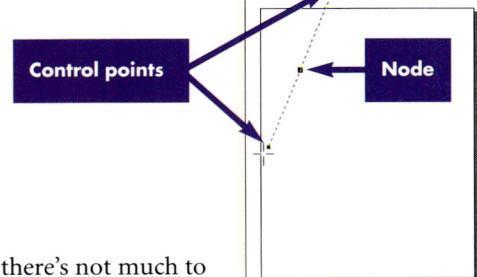

**④** When you're drawing straight lines, multisegment lines, or polygons, there's not much to recommend Bézier mode over Freehand mode. When you're drawing curves, however, it's a different story. To draw curves in Bézier mode, you have to insert nodes to indicate where the curve (or curve segment) will begin and end, and you also manipulate *control points* at each node to determine the slope and height or depth of the curve between the two nodes. Press and *hold down* the mouse button to insert a node (it looks like a black square). Keeping the mouse button held down, move the mouse away from the node. You'll see two control points (smaller black squares) attached to the node with dashed lines. The angle of the control points establishes the curve's slope, and their distance from the node determines the depth or height of the curve. Release the mouse button to freeze the control points of the first node into position.

**30** CHAPTER 4: DRAWING LINES AND SHAPES

# How to Draw Squares and Rectangles

Theoretically, you could draw rectangles and squares using the Pencil tool. To draw precisely, however, you'd have to spend an undue amount of time monitoring the status line to keep your angles right and your lines where you want them. Fortunately, CorelDRAW! provides the Rectangle tool, which does much of this work for you. After you've experimented with the Pencil tool, the Rectangle tool will seem easy. Although its function is more limited, you'll be surprised how often you need this tool—for everything from ornamental borders to architectural drawings to aquariums. And don't forget that you can revamp your rectangles to a certain extent after the fact, as you'll learn in Chapters 7, 11, and 12.

 Using your mouse, point to the Rectangle tool in the toolbox at the left side of your screen and then click. (You can also press F6 to select the Rectangle tool.) Notice that the Rectangle tool looks as though it has been pressed in, and the mouse pointer changes into a crosshair when you move it into the drawing window. The status line provides an additional reminder that the Rectangle tool is selected.

### TIP SHEET

▶ If you want to learn how to change a rectangle's outline, consult Chapter 14; to find out how to change a rectangle's fill pattern or color, refer to Chapter 10.

▶ Besides using the grid, you can use nonprinting guidelines to align objects with greater precision. To do so, click on the vertical or hoizontal ruler and then drag into the drawing window to introduce a vertical or horizontal guideline, releasing the mouse button where you want the guideline to go. You can add as many guidelines as you like; CorelDRAW! will save them with your drawing. You can even move or remove guidelines later by dragging them across the drawing window. In addition, you can request that objects snap to these guidelines by choosing Layout, Snap To, and then choosing Guidelines.

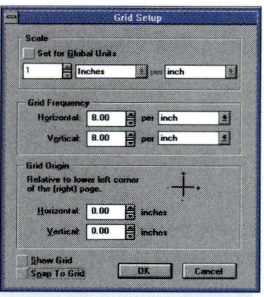

 If you're having trouble positioning your rectangles exactly where you want them, here's one tactic you can try: Choose the Grid Setup command from the Layout menu; you'll see the dialog box shown here. Click on both Show Grid and Snap To Grid to select them, and then click on OK. You'll be returned to the main CorelDRAW! screen, which will now will be filled with a series of faint dots at regular intervals. The Show Grid option displays these nonprinting dots—representing a grid—which can help you draw with greater precision. The Snap to Grid option causes the grid to behave a bit like a magnet, attracting any rectangles that you draw to the closest grid marker.

# How to Draw Squares and Rectangles 31

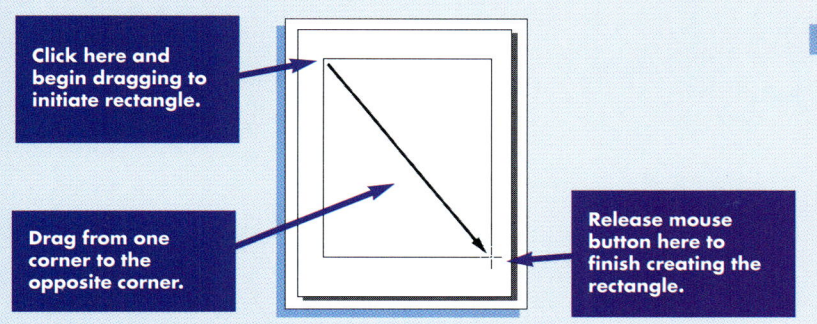

**Click here and begin dragging to initiate rectangle.**

**Drag from one corner to the opposite corner.**

**Release mouse button here to finish creating the rectangle.**

**3** As you draw, you can monitor the width and height of the rectangle by keeping an eye on the status line. (You can also check the dashed lines on the rulers, if your rulers are displayed.) As long as you hold down the mouse button, you can change the rectangle's height and width; the one thing you can't change is its point of origin—the place where you clicked initially. When you release the mouse button, the rectangle's size and shape is fixed, although as you'll learn later, it's easy to move, change, and delete shapes.

**2** The point you initially clicked on becomes one corner of the rectangle, and as you drag you'll generate a rectangle on the screen, as you can see here. Release the mouse button when the rectangle looks the way you want it to.

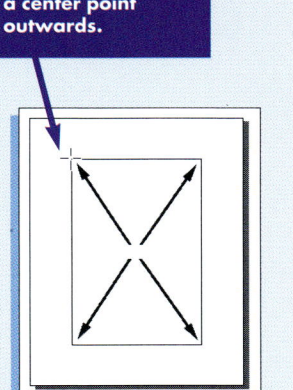

**Perfect square**

**This rectangle is being drawn from a center point outwards.**

**5** CorelDRAW! lets you draw starting from the center and moving outwards. This method works well if you know where you want the exact center of your rectangle. To draw a rectangle from the center outwards, make sure the Rectangle tool is selected, place the mouse pointer where you want the center of rectangle to be, hold down the Shift key, and then drag with your mouse. Hold down both Ctrl and Shift while dragging to create a square from the center outwards.

**4** To draw perfect squares instead of rectangles, simply hold down the Ctrl key while you drag with the mouse. (The Ctrl key is also known as the *constrain key*.) Notice that now you cannot drag in one direction without your rectangle increasing size in the other direction—this way it remains a perfect square. When you're done drawing, release the mouse button as usual. In this case, however, make certain to let go of the mouse *before* releasing the Ctrl key.

# How to Draw Circles and Ellipses

The Ellipse tool operates much like the Rectangle tool, but instead enables you to draw circles and ellipses of all sorts and sizes. Like the Rectangle tool, the Ellipse tool permits you to create only a limited range of shapes. But perfect ellipses and circles would be nearly impossible to construct using the Pencil tool. Besides, you'll undoubtedly have occasion to use ellipses or circles in your work—whether you're creating the sun, the moon, or a batch of bubbles.

 Click on the Ellipse tool in the toolbox. (You can also activate the Ellipse tool by pressing F7.) The tool will look as though it has been pressed in, and the mouse pointer will change into a crosshair when you move it into the drawing window. The status line also tells you that the Ellipse tool has been selected.

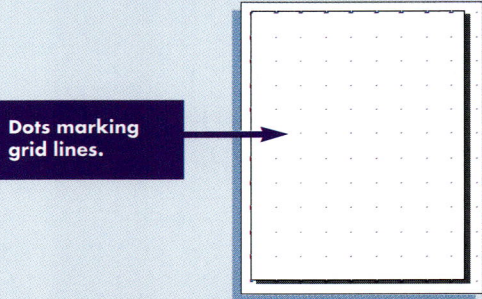

Dots marking grid lines.

**6** If you have a hard time positioning your ellipses exactly where you want them, try this: Choose the Grid Setup command from the Layout menu to display the Grid Setup dialog box, click on both Show Grid and Snap To Grid to select them if they're not already selected, and then click on OK. You'll be returned to the main Corel-DRAW! screen, which will now will be filled with a series of faint dots at regular intervals, as you can see here. The Show Grid option displays these nonprinting dots—representing a grid—which can help you draw with greater precision. The Snap to Grid option makes the grid behave something like a magnet, attracting any ellipses that you draw to the closest grid marker. (As mentioned, the "snap to" effect is subtle, but turning this option on can make it easier to start drawing at a specific spot.)

## TIP SHEET

▶ For details on changing an ellipse's outline, read Chapter 14; for information on changing an ellipse's fill pattern or color, see Chapter 10.

▶ As when drawing rectangles, you can use the rulers, the grid, or guidelines to position ellipses more exactly. If the rulers are not already displayed, you can display them by choosing Show Rulers from the Display menu. To create guidelines, remember that you can simply drag from either the horizontal or vertical ruler; if you like, specify that objects you draw "snap" to these guidelines by selecting Snap To from the Layout menu and then selecting Guidelines from the submenu that appears.

**HOW TO DRAW CIRCLES AND ELLIPSES** 33

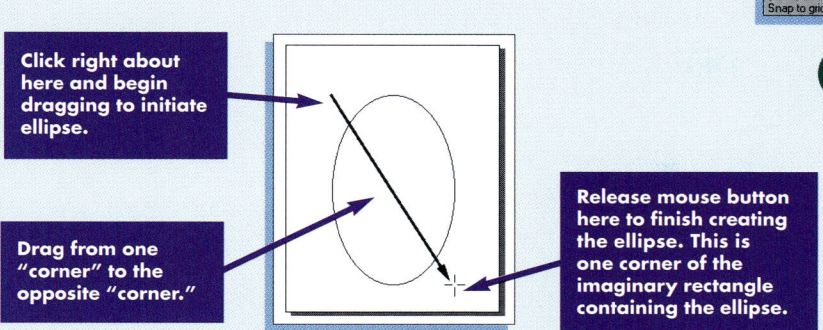

**Click right about here and begin dragging to initiate ellipse.**

**Drag from one "corner" to the opposite "corner."**

**Release mouse button here to finish creating the ellipse. This is one corner of the imaginary rectangle containing the ellipse.**

**2** When drawing an ellipse, you are actually tracing an imaginary rectangle that will enclose the ellipse. The spot where you first clicked is one corner of that rectangle, and the spot where you release the mouse button is the opposite corner.

**3** As you draw, you can keep tabs on the width and height of your ellipse by watching the status line. (You can also monitor the dashed lines on the rulers.) While the mouse button is held down, you can change the height and width of the ellipse; the only thing you can't change is its point of origin—the place where you clicked initially. But when you release the mouse button, the ellipse's size and shape are fixed. As when drawing rectangles, don't be too concerned about the exact size or position of your ellipses, since it's very simple to move, change, and delete them later.

Come visit us at the Santa Maria Aquarium.

**Perfect circle**

**4** To draw perfect circles instead of ellipses, hold down the Ctrl key while you drag with the mouse. While you hold down the Ctrl key, you cannot drag in one direction without your ellipse also increasing size in the other direction; this is CorelDRAW!'s way of ensuring that your ellipse remains a perfect circle. When you've finished drawing, release the mouse button as usual, but this time make sure to let go of the mouse *before* releasing the Ctrl key.

**5** CorelDRAW! lets you draw ellipses starting from the center and moving outwards. Use this technique if you know which spot you want to designate as the exact center of your ellipse. To draw an ellipse from the center outwards, check that the Ellipse tool is selected, position the mouse pointer at the center of the ellipse, hold down the Shift key, and then drag. If you like, you can even hold down both the Ctrl and Shift keys while dragging to create a perfect circle from the center outwards.

**This ellipse is being drawn from the center outwards.**

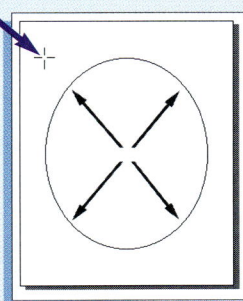

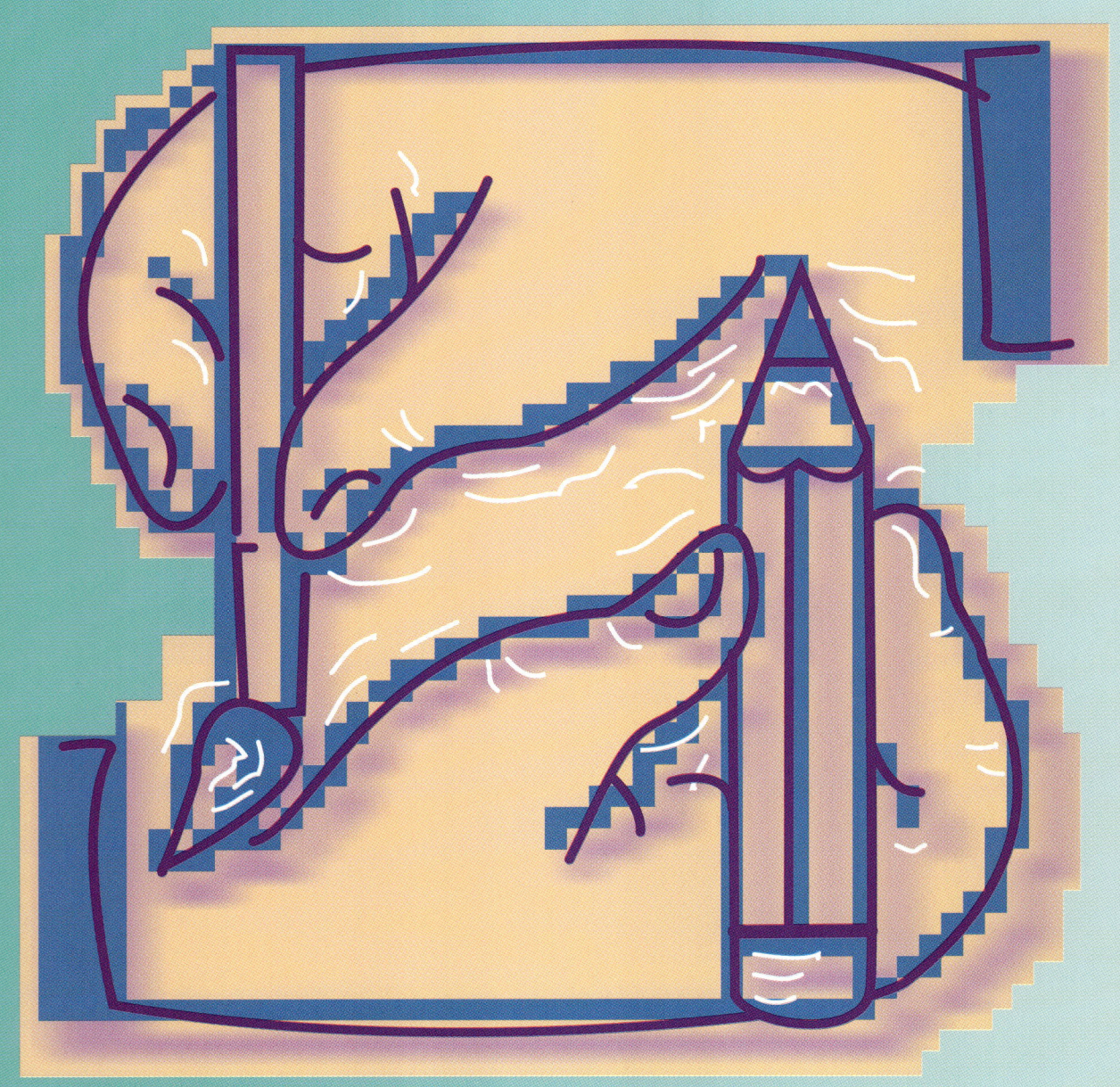

**CHAPTER 5**

# Entering Text

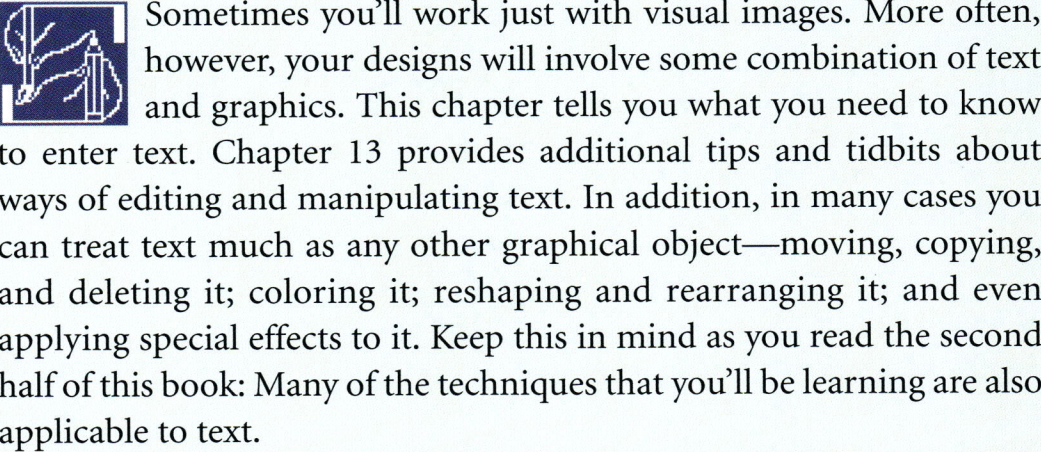Sometimes you'll work just with visual images. More often, however, your designs will involve some combination of text and graphics. This chapter tells you what you need to know to enter text. Chapter 13 provides additional tips and tidbits about ways of editing and manipulating text. In addition, in many cases you can treat text much as any other graphical object—moving, copying, and deleting it; coloring it; reshaping and rearranging it; and even applying special effects to it. Keep this in mind as you read the second half of this book: Many of the techniques that you'll be learning are also applicable to text.

You can actually enter two types of text in CorelDRAW!: *artistic text* and *paragraph text*. As you'll learn in a moment, you use artistic text for small amounts of text, and paragraph text for larger blocks of text. CorelDRAW! also features a Symbols Library—an enormous collection of symbols that you can use to spice up your work.

# How to Enter Small Amounts of Text

When you're entering small amounts of text such as titles, captions, and headings, you should enter it as artistic text. Although these "text strings" can only include up to 250 characters, you can enter as many of them as you want in a single drawing. When typing artistic text, always keep in mind that it does not *word wrap*—that is, text does not move to the next line automatically when you reach the end of the page. If you want to end one line of text and begin another, you have to press the Enter key. You also cannot use features such as columns, hyphenation, and tabs with artistic text. At the same time, you have more freedom to manipulate and apply special effects to this type of text.

### TIP SHEET

- **When you begin to enter text, it may seem surprisingly small. This is because your screen normally displays an entire page. By default, the point size is 24, which is actually fairly large. (Much of the type that you read every day is only 10 or 12 points.) In Chapter 9, you'll learn how to change your display—either to enlarge or reduce the printable page.**

- **If you like, you can enter and edit text in the text entry area at the top of the Artistic Text dialog box. As when entering text on the screen, use the arrow keys to move the insertion point, and then either type to insert text or press Delete or Backspace to delete characters.**

- **Many word processing programs feature an overtype mode, in which new characters you type overwrite existing characters instead of pushing them to them right. There is no overtype mode in CorelDRAW!; if you want to replace characters, you need to delete them and then type in the new text.**

 **1** Click on the Text tool to select it. (You can also press F8 to select this tool.) The tool will look as though it has been pressed in, the status line should point out that you're now ready to enter text, and the mouse pointer will change into a crosshair when you move it into the drawing window. (If your Text tool doesn't look like the one shown here, press and hold down the mouse button over the Text tool, and then click to choose the leftmost tool—the letter "A"—from the flyout menu that appears.)

**7** It's refreshingly easy to adjust the spacing between the letters, words, and lines of your text. Click on the Spacing command button in the Artistic Text dialog box to bring up the Spacing dialog box. Enter a value under Character to increase the amount of space between characters (generally there is none). Change the value under Word to modify the spacing between words; the default setting is 100, or one complete space. If you've entered several lines of text, you can also adjust the spacing between lines. When you're done, click on OK twice to return to the main screen and put your changes into effect.

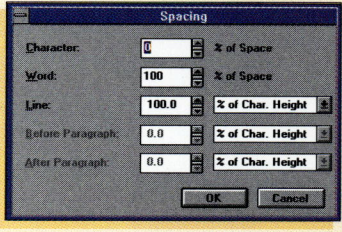

**6** You can use the alignment option buttons in the Artistic Text dialog box to change the alignment of artistic text, but if you're used to word processing this process may be baffling at first. Artistic text is aligned with respect to the *insertion point that you set when you first entered the text*. However, it may be easier just to enter your text, and change its position on the screen using the techniques for moving objects that are covered in Chapter 7.

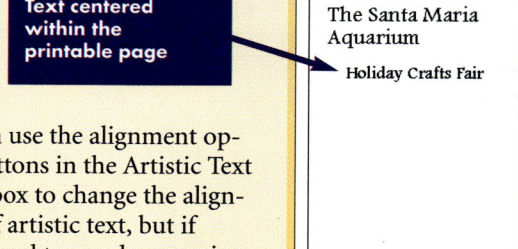

Text centered within the printable page

How to Enter Small Amounts of Text  37

**2** Place the crosshair pointer where you want to begin entering text, and then click. You'll see a vertical line called the *insertion point* (sometimes called the *text cursor*). This line indicates where text you type will be inserted; it also points out where text will be deleted. Essentially, the insertion point tells you where the action is.

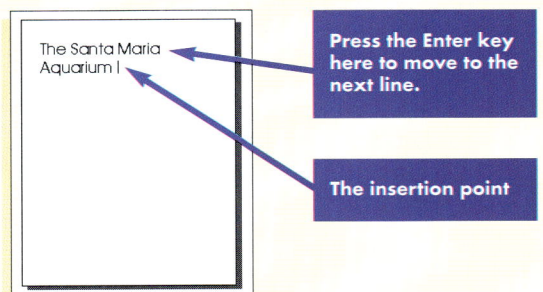

### Holiday Crafts Fair!
#### *Come One Come All!*

**50 stalls filled with exciting merchandise**

**Dolphin Pendants
Lobster Caps
Crab Potholders
Whale Whistles
Octopus Slippers
and much, much more!**

**Entertainment provided by
the world-renowned
Nuclear Whales Saxophone Quartet**

December 16th and 17th
The S.M. Aquarium
1234 Otter Lane
Downtown Santa Maria

**3** Now you can type away to insert text. Remember that you can only enter up to 250 characters in one shot, and that text will not wrap when you reach the edge of the printable page, or even the edge of the drawing window. You need to move text to the next line manually by pressing the Enter key. If you make a mistake, you can press the Backspace key to delete the character just to the left of the insertion point, or the Delete key to erase the character just to the right of the insertion point. (You can reposition the insertion point with the arrow keys if you need to backtrack to add or delete something.) And if you want to enter another text string of up to 250 characters in a different place, simply move the mouse pointer and click again to introduce a new insertion point.

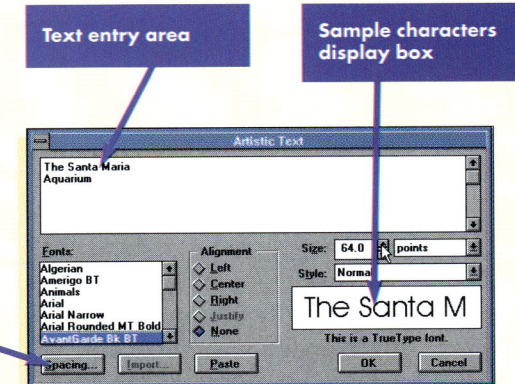

**5** You can also choose a different font and type style through the Artistic Text dialog box. Scroll through the Fonts list box until you find a font you like, and then click on it to select it. If applicable, you can pick a different style for the selected font by pulling down the Style drop-down list box and choosing between bold, italic, or bold-italic. You can see a sample of the selected font and style in the sample characters display box on the right side of the dialog box.

 Once you've entered some text, it's easy to make it larger or smaller by choosing a new point size. (A *point* is a typographical measurement equal to $1/72$ of an inch; a 72-point letter would be one inch high.) You can specify a point size anywhere from 0.7 to 2160 points (that's 30 inches high!), and you can enter fractional values such as 6.5 points. To change the point size of a text string, make sure your insertion point is in the text; then choose Edit Text from the Text menu (the shortcut is Ctrl+T). You'll see the Artistic Text dialog box shown here. Click on the up arrow or down arrow in the Size selection box to increase or decrease the point size, or type directly in the Size box.

# How to Enter Larger Amounts of Text

**W**hen working with larger blocks of text—the contents of a newsletter or brochure, for example—you should enter it as paragraph text. Entering this brand of text is much more like word processing: Text wraps at the end of a line, you can divide text into columns, and you can justify text so that it lines up evenly both on the left and the right sides. In addition, paragraphs can include up to 4,000 characters, and you can enter multiple paragraphs in a single file. When entering paragraph text, you first mark out a frame for the text. As you'll see in a moment, this is like setting your own margins, within which text is wrapped and alignment is determined.

### TIP SHEET

- ▶ You can enter and edit text in the text entry area at the top of the Paragraph Text dialog box. This enables you to alter or add to your text while you're selecting a font or type size. As when entering text on the screen, use the arrow keys to move the insertion point, and then either type to insert text or press Delete or Backspace to delete characters. You can even press the Enter key from here to generate a new paragraph.

- ▶ There are many other features that you can use with paragraph text. Among other things, CorelDRAW! provides a spell checker and a thesaurus. In addition, you can take advantage of the Paragraph dialog box to turn on hyphenation, set tabs and indents, and create bulleted lists. You'll learn more about these features in Chapter 13.

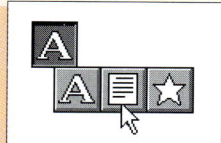

▶ **1** Place your mouse pointer over the Text tool and hold down the mouse button until you see the flyout menu shown here. Then select the middle Text tool—the one that looks like a sheet of paper containing a paragraph of text. The flyout menu will be tucked away, and the Text tool will show its new face in the toolbox.

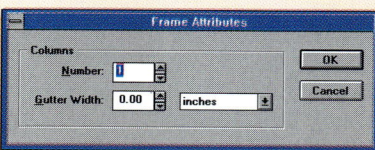

 You can divide paragraph text into up to eight columns. To do so, choose Frame from the Text menu to display the Frame Attributes dialog box. Under Number, select the number of columns for your text; under Gutter Width, choose how much space you want between columns. (You should change this setting to at least 0.2 or 0.3 so your columns don't run together.)

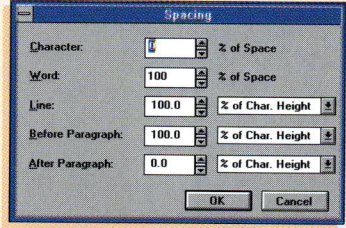

**6** If you choose the Spacing button in the Paragraph Text dialog box, CorelDRAW! displays the Spacing dialog box. Notice that the Before Paragraph and After Paragraph options are now available, enabling you to increase or decrease the amount of space between paragraphs. These values are cumulative, so if you enter 100 (or 100 percent of the type size) under After Paragraph and leave the setting at 100.0 under Before Paragraph, you'll have an extra line between paragraphs.

**HOW TO ENTER LARGER AMOUNTS OF TEXT** 39

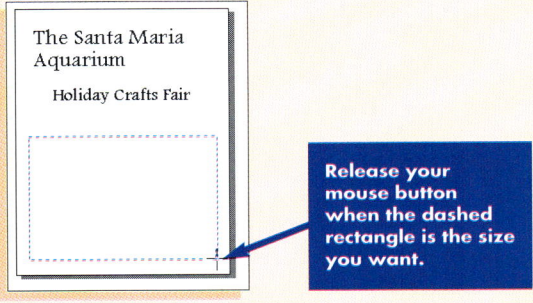

**2** Move the crosshair pointer into the printable page and drag to draw a frame in which you can enter text. As you drag, a dashed rectangle indicates how large the text frame will be when you release the mouse button. (You can click within the printable page to create a frame that occupies, and is centered within, most of the page.) These text frames *will not print;* they are visual aids to help you enter text. In addition, note that if you type more text than fits within the frame, the text will be cut off.

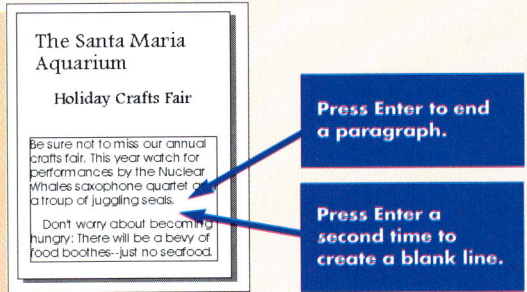

**3** Once you've inserted the text frame, you can type away. You can enter up to 4,000 characters per paragraph, and text will wrap to the next line when you reach the edge of the frame. As before, if you make a mistake, use Backspace or Delete to erase the character immediately to the right or left of the insertion point.

## THE SANTA MARIA AQUARIUM AQUATIC NEWSLETTER

Don't miss our fabulous crafts fair—the time and place to do all your holiday shopping in one fell swoop! Overcome by the holiday season? Already tired of the incessant barrage of Christmas carols? Come to our fair. We will feature the Nuclear Whales Saxophone Quartet playing only the best jazz and hip hop. Juggling seals and dancing dolphins will provide delightful entertainment for children of all ages.

There will be over 50 stalls at the crafts fair, where you'll find everything from crab potholders to whale tapes to octopus slippers to dolphin pendants, as well as the perennially popular lobster caps.

Don't worry about becoming hungry; there will be a bevy of food booths—just no seafood.

Come early. The first 20 shoppers will receive a free rainbow trout refrigerator magnet.

For the very first time this year's crafts fair will include a game arcade, providing entertainment for both children and adults. Play Pin the Tail on the Dolphin, Whale of Fortune, the aquatic version of Trivial Pursuit and much, much more. Have fun, and win fabulous prizes. This year's grand prize winner will receive a trip to Marine World. For further details call 1-800-DOLPHIN.

**Date:** December 16th & 17th
**Place:** The S.M. Aquarium, 1234 Otter Lane, Downtown Santa Maria

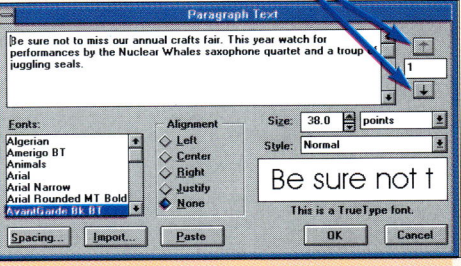

**4** You can modify paragraph text in the Paragraph Text dialog box, which you open by choosing Edit Text from the Text menu or by pressing Ctrl+T. Here you see only (and can change only) one paragraph at a time in the text entry area at the top of the dialog box. To modify your text, make sure the paragraph to be changed is showing in the text entry area; choose the desired font, point size, and type style; and then click on OK as usual.

**5** To select a new alignment for your paragraph text, choose the appropriate option button under Alignment, and click on OK to align your text between the left and right edges of the frame. The paragraph text in this announcement has been justified, so that text lines evenly up at both the left and right borders of the frame.

# How to Enter Special Symbols

CorelDRAW! provides a huge number of symbols that you can use for everything from bullet characters to whimsical background patterns. The Symbols Library includes over 5,000 symbols, in such diverse categories as animals, computers, food items, musical symbols, and plants. As an added bonus, you are free to edit and alter these symbols using CorelDRAW!'s standard techniques for moving, copying, reshaping, and rearranging objects.

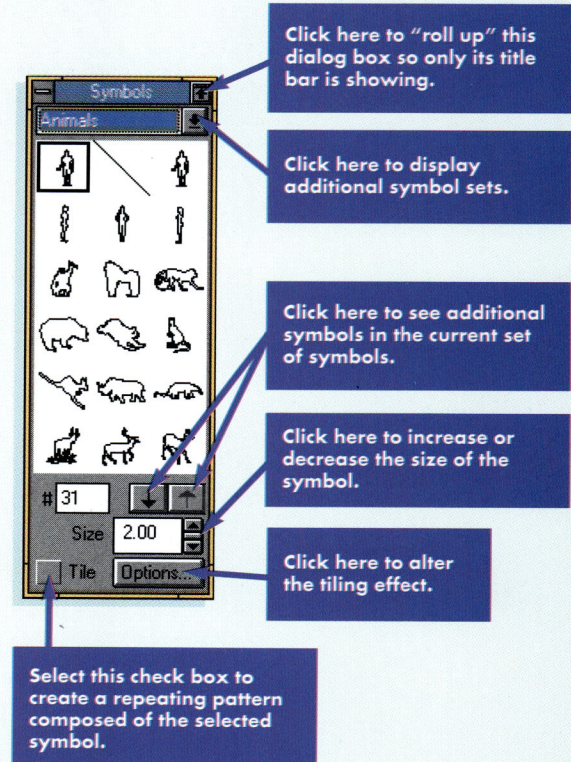

Click here to "roll up" this dialog box so only its title bar is showing.

Click here to display additional symbol sets.

Click here to see additional symbols in the current set of symbols.

Click here to increase or decrease the size of the symbol.

Click here to alter the tiling effect.

Select this check box to create a repeating pattern composed of the selected symbol.

**▶ 1** Select the symbol tool (it's shaped like a star) from the Text flyout menu. You'll see the Symbols roll-up menu shown here. Don't be intimidated if you've never encountered a roll-up before; it's just a special form of dialog box that stays on screen while you continue to work within the drawing window. As with any other window, you can move a roll-up by dragging on its title bar. In addition, you can "roll it up"—much as you'd roll up a shade—by clicking on the up arrow in its upper-right corner. When you do this, only the roll-up's title bar remains visible. To pull the roll-up back down, click on the down arrow on the right end of its title bar.

## TIP SHEET

▶ If you like, you can create symbols of your very own and add them to the symbol set of your choice. Simply draw a shape, promptly choose Create Symbol from the Special menu, choose the symbol category to which to add your creation, and click on OK. The new symbol will show up in the Symbols roll-up, and you'll be able to insert it into your drawings as described on this page.

▶ If you (or whoever installed CorelDRAW!) did not install the Symbols Library while installing CorelDRAW!, the symbol sets will not be available to you. If you have the program disks, you can install the Symbol Library using the CorelDRAW! setup program. For more details, consult your CorelDRAW! documentation or the appendix at the end of this book.

HOW TO ENTER SPECIAL SYMBOLS  41

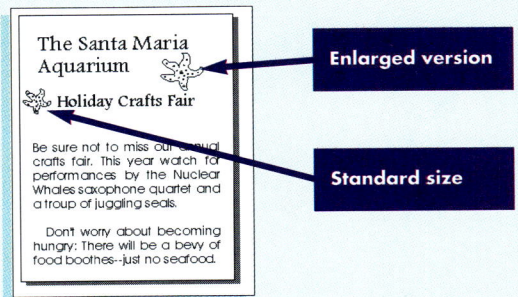

**List of available symbol sets**

**More symbols in same symbol set**

**Enlarged version**

**Standard size**

**2** To insert a symbol into your drawing, simply drag it from the roll-up to the desired location on the drawing. To hunt for additional symbols in the current symbol set, click on the large down or up arrow just below the list of symbols. If you want to see a different set of symbols, make a new selection from the drop-down list box at the top of the roll-up.

**3** You can enlarge or reduce the size of symbols that you insert into your drawing. Just increase or decrease the Size setting at the bottom of the Symbols roll-up before dragging a symbol onto the drawing window (this is inches by default). Note that you can also change a symbol's size after the fact—much as you can alter the size of any other object—by using the techniques for stretching and scaling that are covered in Chapter 11.

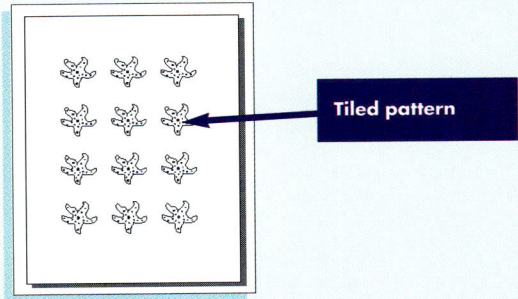

**Tiled pattern**

**4** If you like, you can create a pattern of symbols by choosing the Tile check box in the lower-left corner of the Symbols roll-up. With this check box selected, drag the desired symbol onto the page, noticing how it proliferates immediately. You can also increase or decrease a symbol's size, as just described, before using it in such a tiled pattern.

**5** CorelDRAW! lets you modify the spacing between symbols before you create a tiled pattern. To do so, click on the Options button in the lower-right corner of the Symbols roll-up; you'll see the Tile dialog box shown here. The Horizontal option lets you specify the horizontal distance between symbols, and the Vertical option lets you determine the vertical distance between symbols. Select the Proportional sizing check box to lock in the Horizontal and Vertical settings—so they always match each other.

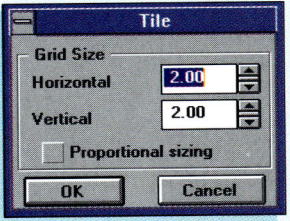

# TRY IT!

In the first five chapters of this book, you've been exposed to quite a few concepts and have picked up a number of skills. This is your first chance to roll up your sleeves and put into practice some of your new abilities. (Provided that you haven't already been dabbling on your own!) Follow these instructions to put together the flyer shown here. Along each step of the way, chapter numbers help remind you where these topics were covered in detail, so you can flip back if necessary to refresh your memory. Also, don't worry too much if your results don't exactly match the ones shown here: It's possible that you or someone else has (inadvertently or intentionally) changed the defaults for such things as fonts and line thickness.

 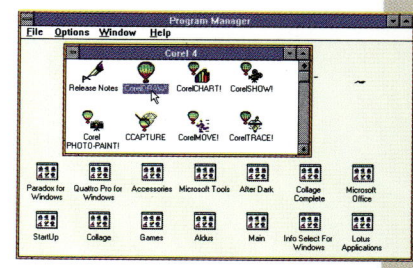

If you need to, turn on your computer, start Windows (Chapter 2), and then start CorelDRAW! (Chapter 2). If you need to clear your screen, choose New from the File menu and choose No when asked whether to save the current changes. (You'll learn more about clearing the screen and saving files in the next chapter.)

## Join Now!

### The Santa Maria Aquarium Membership Drive

Now is the time to join the Santa Maria Aquarium. Our basic membership is a low $35. Members in this category receive a free subscription to our calendar of events, as well as a 10% discount on all items in our gift shop. For $65, you'll be the proud recipient of our famed Aquarium T-shirt. You'll also get first crack at tickets for popular events. At $100, the deluxe membership guarantees you a place at our black tie fundraising ball, complete with free valet parking.

TRY IT! 43

 **2**

Choose Grid Setup from the Layout menu (Chapter 4).

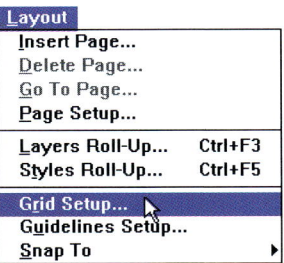

 **3**

In the Grid Setup dialog box that appears, click on the Show Grid and Snap To Grid check boxes to select them, and then click on OK (Chapter 4). This should help you line up objects as you draw.

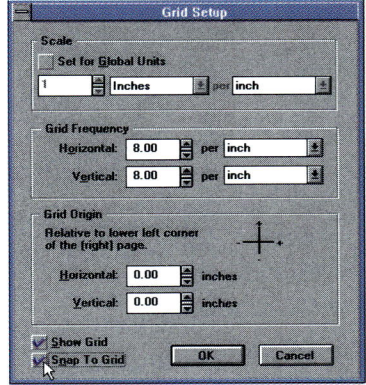

 **4**

Click on the Rectangle tool, move the mouse pointer into the printable page, and draw a rectangle that begins about ½ inch from the edges of the printable page, as shown here (Chapter 4). If your rectangle doesn't turn out as planned, just press Delete and try again. (If your rulers aren't displayed, display them by choosing Show Rulers from the Display menu, as described in Chapter 3.)

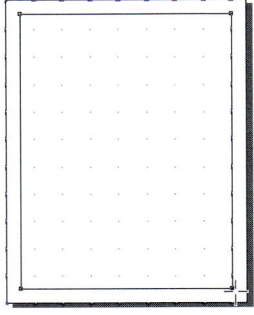

 **5**

Place the mouse pointer over the Text tool, press and *hold down* the mouse button, and choose the symbol tool (the star) from the Text flyout menu (Chapter 5).

 **6**

In the Symbols roll-up, make sure Animals is selected as the symbol set and click twice on the large down arrow just below the list of symbols. You'll see a new crop of animals that includes reptiles and fish (Chapter 5).

 **7**

Still in the Symbols roll-up, click on the upward-pointing triangle in the Size box, holding down the mouse button until the symbol size reaches 4.00 (Chapter 5). If you overshoot your mark, just click on the downward-pointing triangle until you get back where you want to be.

Continue to next page ▶

**44** TRY IT!

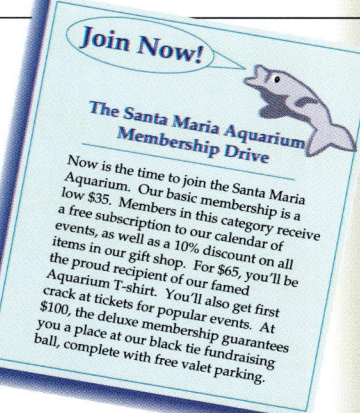

**TRY IT!**

**Continue below**

Click on the fish in the lower-left corner of the Symbols roll-up; you should see the number 82 in the # box. Then drag the selected fish into the upper-right corner of the printable page, just below the rectangular border (Chapter 5). (If the fish doesn't end up in the right place, you can always press the Delete key and try again.)

Double-click on its Control Menu box to close the Symbols roll-up (Chapter 5).

Make sure the Text tool for entering artistic text is selected. If not, choose it from the Text flyout menu (Chapter 5).

To the left of your fish, enter the text **Join Now!** (Chapter 5).

Press Ctrl+T or choose Edit Text from the Text menu (Chapter 5).

In the Artistic Text dialog box, choose Times New Roman under Fonts, choose Bold under Style, and increase the point size to 52. Then click on OK (Chapter 5).

Click on the Ellipse tool to select it, and draw an ellipse around the text that you just entered (Chapter 4).

Click on the Pencil tool, making sure you're in Freehand mode rather than Bézier mode (Chapter 4).

# Try It! 45

Draw two lines to transform the ellipse into a "bubble" indicating that the fish is delivering a special message (Chapter 4). Remember to click once to begin or end a line, and to double-click to both end one line and begin the next.

Select the Text tool again, and place the insertion point below the fish, at 4.25 inches on the horizontal ruler. Then enter **The Santa Maria Aquarium**, press Enter, and type **Membership Drive** (Chapter 5). Don't worry if the alignment looks off; we'll fix it in the next step.

Press Ctrl+T or choose Edit Text from the Text menu. Choose the Times New Roman font, select the point size 32, and choose Center under Alignment. Then click on OK (Chapter 5).

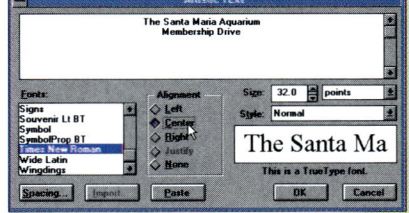

Display the Text flyout menu and choose the tool for entering paragraph text (Chapter 5).

Place the mouse pointer underneath the text you just typed and drag to create a frame filling most of the lower portion of the printable page (Chapter 5). Remember that this frame won't print.

Type the paragraph shown here.

Press Ctrl+T or choose Edit Text from the Text menu. Then choose the Times New Roman font, select a point size of 28, and click on OK (Chapter 5).

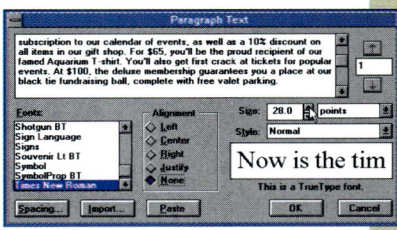

If you want to be able to return to your flyer later, you'll need to save it. Saving is covered in the beginning of the next chapter.

**CHAPTER 6**

# Working with Files

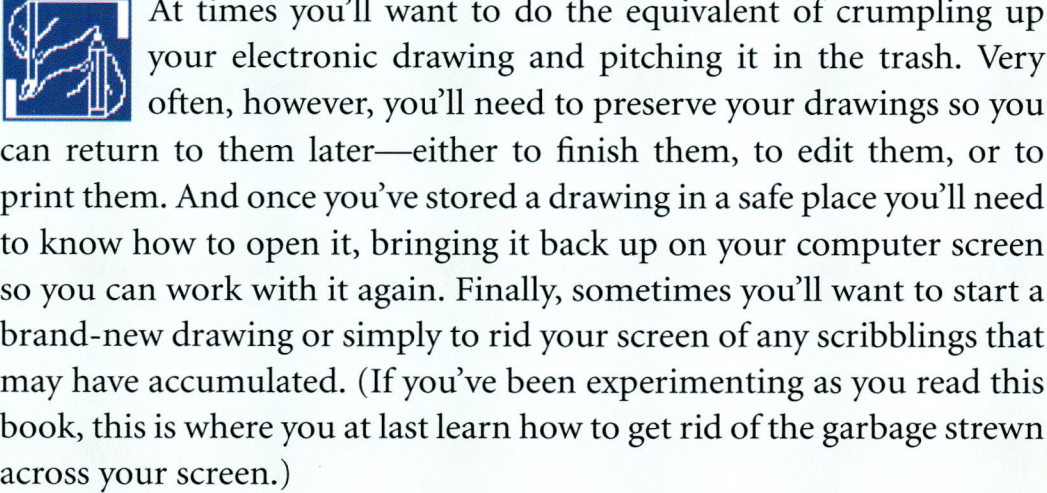 At times you'll want to do the equivalent of crumpling up your electronic drawing and pitching it in the trash. Very often, however, you'll need to preserve your drawings so you can return to them later—either to finish them, to edit them, or to print them. And once you've stored a drawing in a safe place you'll need to know how to open it, bringing it back up on your computer screen so you can work with it again. Finally, sometimes you'll want to start a brand-new drawing or simply to rid your screen of any scribblings that may have accumulated. (If you've been experimenting as you read this book, this is where you at last learn how to get rid of the garbage strewn across your screen.)

You'll discover how to accomplish all of these tasks in this chapter. For the most part, you'll learn how to create and work with files; in computerspeak, a *file* is a named collection of information (in this case a drawing or design) stored on a disk. You must learn certain fundamentals about managing files to do any useful work in CorelDRAW! (If you don't know where your drawings are stowed away, you of course won't be able to put them to any use.) Here you'll learn how to save files, how to open existing files that you saved earlier, and how to create new files so that you can begin a fresh drawing project.

# How to Save Files

When you create a drawing in CorelDRAW!, the information in that drawing is stored temporarily in your computer's memory. However, that memory is like a slate that is wiped clean each time the computer goes off. So, if you turn off your computer, if there's a power outage, or if someone kicks your power cord inadvertently, all your hard work is instantly vaporized. Unless you've saved it, that is. *Saving* a drawing simply means recording it on disk—either a hard disk or a floppy—so you can come back to it later.

### TIP SHEET

- **Although you can use any file name that meets the specifications mentioned here, it's best to create recognizable file names as much as possible. That way, you—and others—will have an easier time tracking down your files later. (As you can imagine, it's tougher to remember what the file 11QRX#%.CDR contains than what NEWSLETT.CDR contains.)**

- **All disks or drives on your computer have a single-letter name. Generally, your floppy drive is called drive A (if you have two floppy drives, the bottom or rightmost drive will be called drive B), your hard drive is called drive C, and any other drives (including network drives or other areas of your hard disk), will have the letters D, E, and so on.**

- **You use the Save command to name and save a file initially, or to save the newest version of a file without changing the file's name (this overwrites the old version of the file with the new). If you instead want to save an extra *copy* of your file with a different name and/or in a different location, you should use the Save As command in the File menu. This brings up the Save Drawing dialog box, and from here you can rename your file and/or choose a new location for it, as described on this page.**

- **It's a simple matter to discard drawings that you decide not to save, as described under "How to Clear the Screen" later in this chapter.**

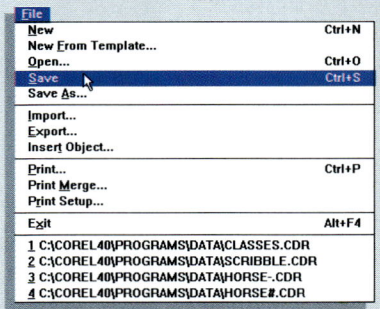

 After having invested a fair amount of time in a drawing, choose Save from the File menu or press Ctrl+S. At what point you decide to save your drawing is really up to you; make sure to save before it would be impossible—or even quite unpleasant—to reconstruct your drawing from scratch.

 As you continue working on a drawing or design, you should save it at regular intervals using the Save command. Otherwise, everything that you've drawn since the last time you saved could evaporate in an instant if there's a power failure or some other mishap occurs. (As a rule of thumb, save whenever you think you'd be miserable if you had to re-create what you've drawn. It's also a good idea to save if you are going to step away from your computer for more than just a minute or two.) Note that after you've saved a file initially, invoking the Save command does not bring up a dialog box. Instead, it just saves the new and improved version of your drawing with the same name and on the same drive and directory.

After you save a file, its assigned name shows up in the title bar.

 Click on OK to go ahead with the save operation. (Or, if you change your mind, click on Cancel or press Esc to close the dialog box without saving the file.) Your drawing is now stored on disk, but also stays on screen so you can continue to work with it. Notice that the file name you entered shows up in the title bar (which before read UNTITLED.CDR).

How to Save Files 49

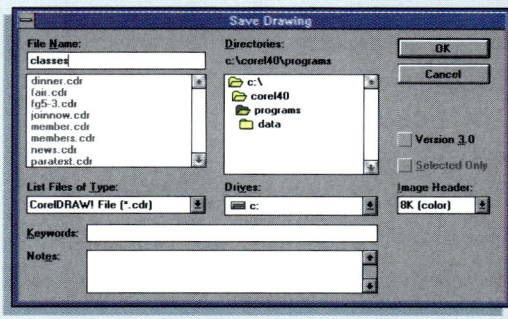

**2** In the Save Drawing dialog box, type a name for your drawing in the File Name text box. File names can be up to eight characters long, and, if you like, can be followed by a period and an *extension* of up to three characters. (If you leave off the extension, CorelDRAW! adds the .CDR extension for you.) Extensions are like last names that typically indicate the file type and/or the program in which it was created. You can include letters, numbers, and certain special characters such as %, #, and - in your file names, but you cannot include spaces or the characters ? * . " / | [ ] : < > + = .

**3** Inspect the entry right underneath Directories. This tells you where your file will be stored on disk. (A *directory* is a place for stashing a group of files on a disk. Placing files in different directories is much like filing them away in labeled file folders, so you can more easily find and retrieve them later. Directories usually contain related program or data files, but to a certain extent they may be as organized or as disorderly as you are.) If the listed directory seems OK, you can skip the next two steps.

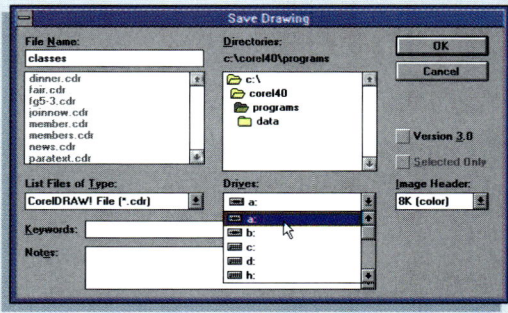

**4** If you want to store your file on a different drive, pull down the Drives dropdown list box and choose a new drive from the list that appears. One of the most common reasons to do this is to save your files on a floppy disk.

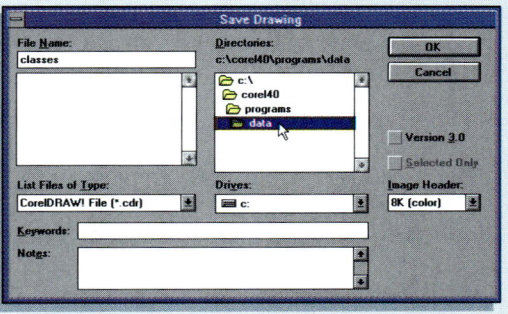

**5** To store your file in a different directory, track down that directory in the Directories list and double-click on it. You may need to scroll to find the directory you want. If necessary, double-click on any directory name to see all of its subdirectories. (For example, to see all subdirectories of the COREL40 directory, double-click on corel40.)

# How to Open Existing Files

The whole point of saving files on disk is so that you can come back to them later. If you want to retrieve a design that you created earlier, you need to *open* it. This displays the drawing in the state it was in when you last saved it. Once you open a file, you can continue working on your drawing as before—adding shapes or text to it, editing it, or printing it. (You'll learn about printing in Chapter 8; you'll find out how to edit your drawings in much of the second half of this book.)

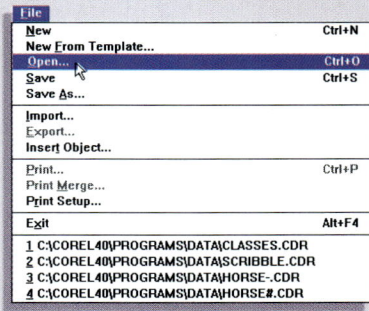

 Choose File from the menu bar and then click on the Open command. (You can also just press Ctrl+O.)

## TIP SHEET

▶ If you modify a file that you've opened, make sure to save your changes by choosing the Save command from the File menu, as discussed on the previous page. (If you decide not to save your changes, by contrast, just choose No at the prompt.)

▶ There's a handy shortcut for reopening one of the four files that you've opened most recently. Just choose File from the menu bar and then choose the name of your file from the list at the bottom of the File menu.

▶ By default, the File Name list includes all files with the .CDR extension in the selected drive and directory. If you're searching for a file with a different extension, you can make a selection from the List Files of Type drop-down list box in the lower-left corner of the dialog box. Or, you can enter a different *file name specification* under File Name. (This is simply a way of telling CorelDRAW! which files to list.) For example, you could enter *.* under File Name to have CorelDRAW! list all files in the current drive and directory.

▶ Unlike many other Windows programs, CorelDRAW! only lets you open one file at a time.

 Click on OK to open the drawing, noting that its name is displayed on the title bar. You can now add to this drawing, edit it, or print it, as you please. (Incidentally, once you see the desired file name under File Name in the Open Drawing dialog box, you can just double-click on it to open the file if you're sure that it's the right one.)

How to Open Existing Files 51

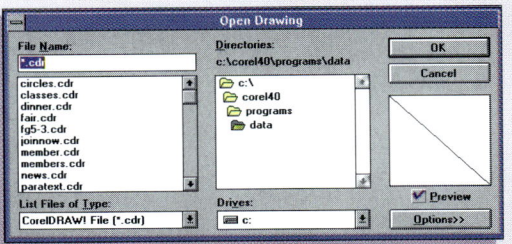

**2** If you already have a file open, you may be asked whether to save any changes to it. Choose Yes to save those changes, No to discard them, or Cancel to return to the currently open file. (Choosing either Yes or No automatically closes the file you were working with.)

**3** In the Open Drawing dialog box that appears, examine the Directories entry. This is where CorelDRAW! is searching for files by default. If the file you're looking for is on the drive and directory listed here, you can bypass the next two steps.

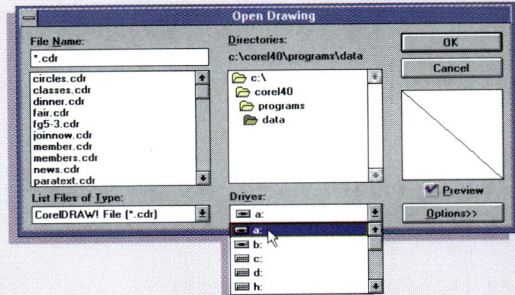

**4** If the file you want to retrieve is on a drive other than the one listed under Directories, pull down the Drives drop-down list box and choose a drive from the list that appears. You might need to choose a different drive, for example, to retrieve a file from a floppy disk that someone has given you.

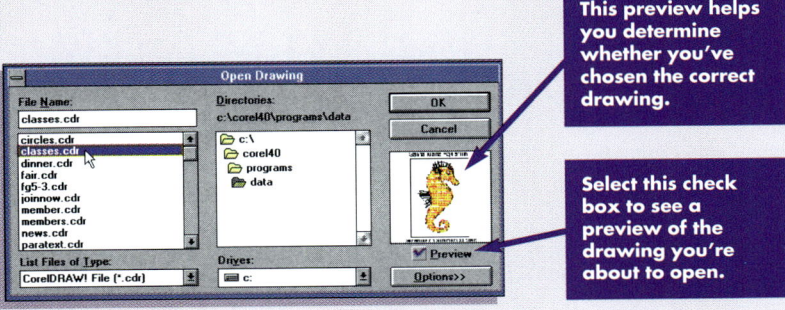

This preview helps you determine whether you've chosen the correct drawing.

Select this check box to see a preview of the drawing you're about to open.

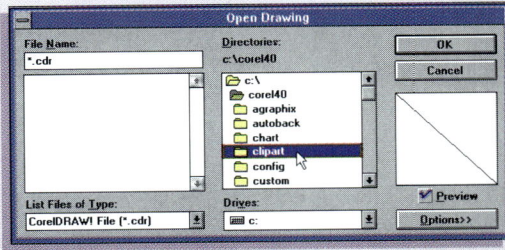

**5** The file you need to open may also be in a directory other than the one originally listed under Directories. If so, track down the desired directory in the Directories list and double-click on it. You may need to scroll to find the directory you want. If necessary, double-click on any directory name to see all of its subdirectories. (To see all subdirectories of the COREL40 directory, for instance, you would double-click on corel40.)

**6** Once you've selected the drive and directory containing the file to be opened, hunt down that file in the File Name list at the left side of the Open Drawing dialog box (you may need to scroll) and click on it to select it. If you like, you can select the Preview check box to see a thumbnail sketch of your drawing before you open it. This is a good way to confirm that you've picked out the right drawing.

# How to Clear the Screen

Sometimes you'll want to toss out everything you've done and start with a clean slate. One way of doing this is to erase everything in your current drawing (the equivalent of erasing your entire drawing from a given sheet of paper). However, another solution is to begin a completely new drawing (the equivalent of discarding one sheet of paper and getting a fresh start on a clean sheet of paper). A third alternative is to add a new page to your current design project.

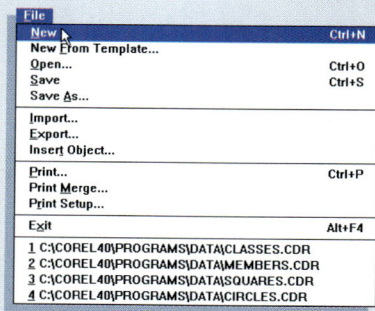

**1** You can clear your screen by creating a new file altogether. To do this, choose New from the File menu or press Ctrl+N.

### TIP SHEET

- Another way to switch between pages in a multiple-page drawing is to choose Go To Page from the Layout menu or click on the page counter itself to display the Go To Page dialog box.

- Sometimes you can clear what's on your screen by using the Undo command on the Edit menu to reverse the effects of one or more previous actions. This command is covered in greater detail in the next chapter.

- If you've drawn just a single item, you can always remove it from the screen by pressing the Delete key.

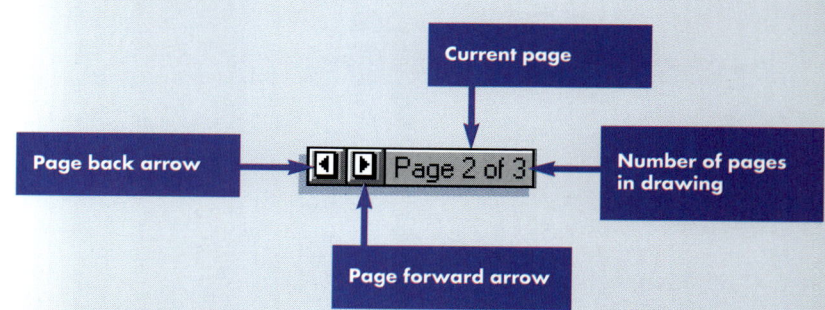

**7** Drawings that contain more than a single page include a *page counter* in the lower-left corner of the screen, just above the color palette. This page counter tells you what page you're on and how many pages your drawing contains. You can also click on the page forward arrow to move forward one page at a time, or the page backward arrow to move backwards one page at a time. If you're on the first or last page of your drawing, one of these arrows changes into a plus sign, which you can click on to display the Insert Page dialog box that was just described.

# How to Clear the Screen 53

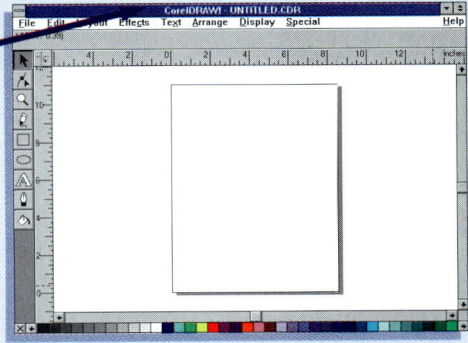

**Brand-new files that you create are untitled at first.**

**2** If you had another drawing on the screen, you may be asked to save any changes to it, as when you're opening an existing file. As you did before, choose Yes to save those changes, No to discard them, or Cancel to return to the currently open file. (Choosing either Yes or No automatically closes the file you were working with.)

**3** At this point, you'll see a blank screen that in all likelihood will be identical to the one you saw when you started CorelDRAW! for the day. (Notice that the file name in the title bar is UNTITLED.CDR.) From here you can start a new drawing, putting into practice all of the skills you have acquired so far.

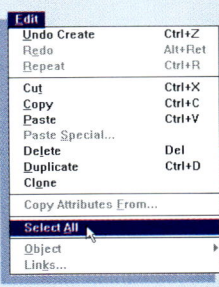

**4** You can also clear your screen by doing the equivalent of erasing everything on the page. (One disadvantage of this technique is that you're not asked whether to save the material you're deleting.) First choose Select All from the Edit menu.

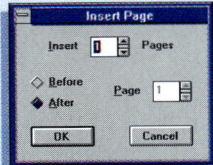

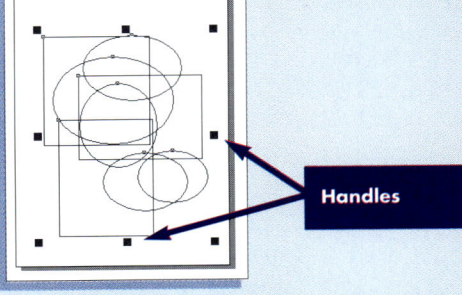

**Handles**

**5** All the objects in your drawing will be enclosed within eight square *handles* that together make up a *highlighting box*. (You'll learn more about selecting items in the next chapter.) At this point, you can simply press Delete to clear everything from the screen.

**6** A third way to clear your screen is analogous to adding a new sheet of paper to your drawing. To do this, just choose Insert Page from the Layout menu. In the Insert Page dialog box that appears, choose how many pages to insert, choose whether to insert them before or after the current page, and, if your drawing already includes multiple pages, choose which page to insert pages before or after. Then click on OK.

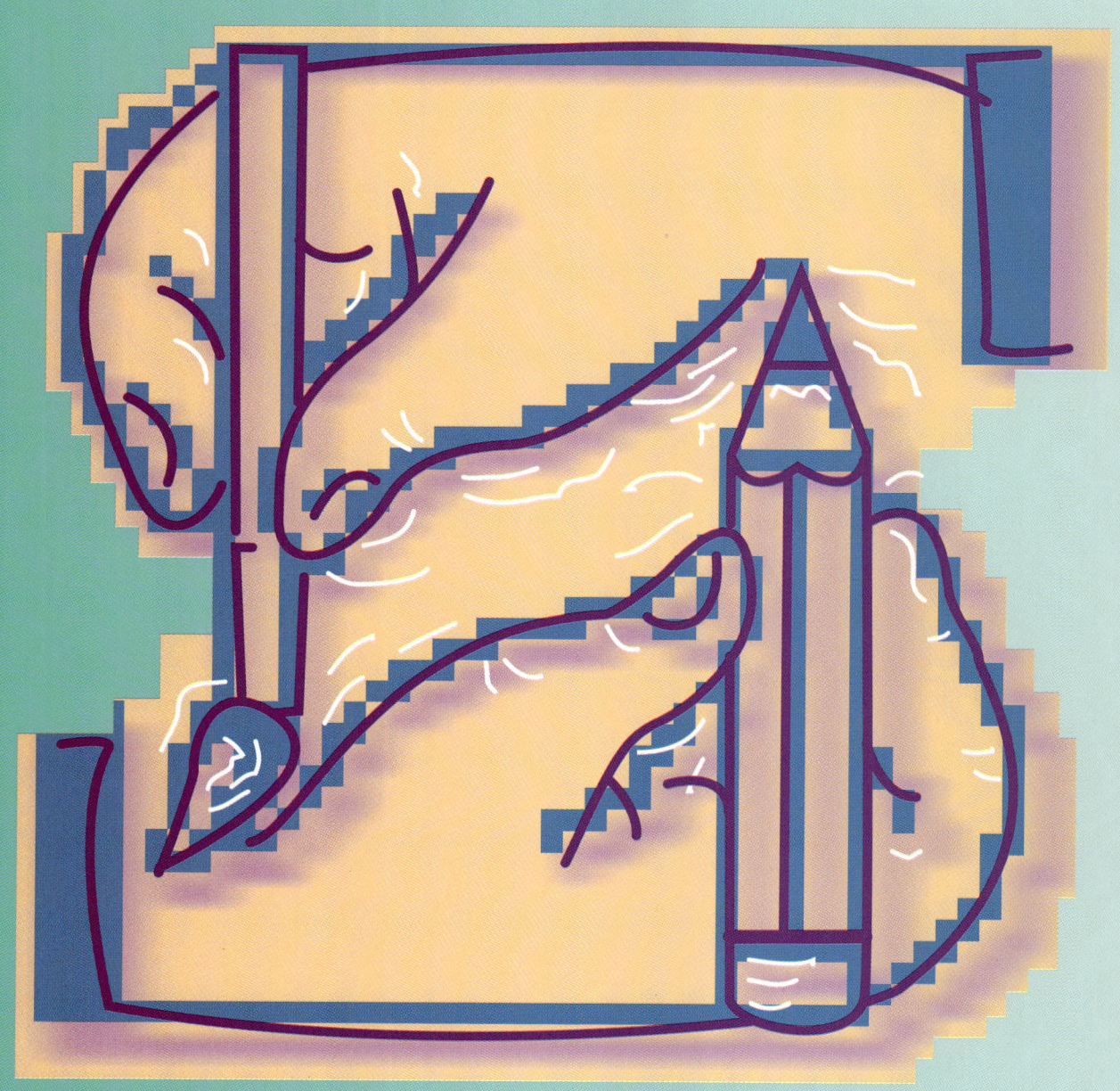

**CHAPTER 7**

# Manipulating Text and Drawings

In certain very rare cases, what you draw or what you write will be perfect, right off the bat. But most of the time, you'll want to improve or alter your first attempts; polishing and fine-tuning your work is really part of the creation process itself.

One of CorelDRAW!'s most valuable assets is that it makes it so easy to rework your text and drawings. This chapter introduces some of the basics. First you'll learn how to select shapes and text; you need to select objects as a precursor to manipulating them in any way. You'll also learn how to move objects—so you can place them exactly where you want them—and how to copy objects, in case you want multiple instances of the same image in your drawing. Finally, you'll discover how to undo and repeat certain actions. Especially when you begin manipulating objects—moving them, copying them, deleting them, and so on—being able to undo some of the things you've done will come in handy when you make that inevitable misstep or merely change your mind.

# How to Select Text and Shapes

You need to *select* text and shapes before you can perform an action—such as moving, copying, or deleting—that affects them. When you select an object, CorelDRAW! surrounds it with eight square *handles* that form a *highlighting box.* You can also select more than one object, in which case all the objects in question are enclosed within a single highlighting box.

## TIP SHEET

- If you have a drawing tool other than the Pick tool selected, you can select the Pick tool just by pressing the spacebar. You can then reselect the tool you were most recently using by pressing the spacebar again. (This doesn't hold true if you're in the process of entering text.)
- If you click on a selected object, its handles are replaced by a whole slew of odd-looking selection arrows for rotating and skewing objects (see Chapter 11). Just click on the object again to get back your normal handles, or click on a blank area of the screen or press Esc to deselect the object.
- Selecting whole blocks of text is exactly like selecting shapes. If you instead want to select just a portion of a text block, you need to use the special selection techniques discussed in Chapter 13.
- The previous chapter showed how to delete everything from your screen. To instead delete only specific objects, select them and then press Delete.
- When you first draw an object, it is selected by default, even though it's not enclosed within a highlighting box. You can tell such objects are selected because you can see their nodes, and because of the status line display.

**1** Check that the Pick tool is selected. If you're going to experiment, make sure to have a few objects on the screen so you can try selecting them.

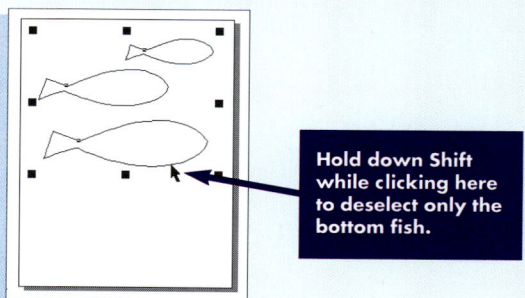

Hold down Shift while clicking here to deselect only the bottom fish.

**6** If you have several items selected and you only want to deselect a single one of them, click on it while holding down the Shift key. Repeat this process as often as you like to deselect specific selected objects.

**5** If you want to "deselect" all the selected items, just click on any blank area of the drawing window, or press Esc. Also remember that selecting a new item automatically deselects any currently selected items.

How to Select Text and Shapes  **57**

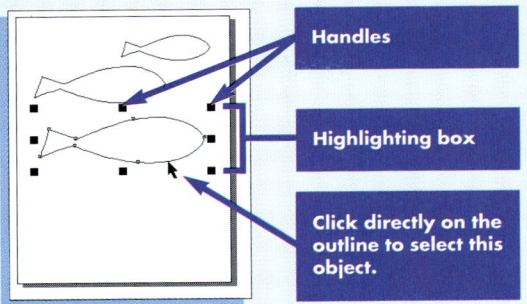

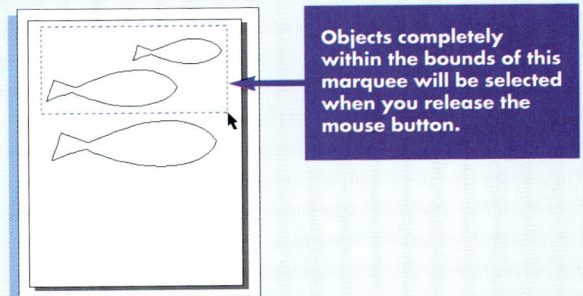

**2** To select a single object, just click on it. If the object is filled with a color or pattern, you can click anywhere within it; if not, be sure to click directly on the outline. (You'll learn how to fill and color objects in Chapter 10.) Once you select an object, you'll see the eight handles that form its highlighting box. Note that selecting an item normally deselects any other items that were selected.

**3** If you want to select several items at once, make sure the Pick tool is selected and drag to create a dashed rectangle (called a *marquee*) that completely encloses the items to be selected, as shown here. (Be forewarned that items that are only partially within the marquee will not be selected.) When you release the mouse button, all the items within the marquee will be enclosed within a single highlighting box. In addition, when more than one item is selected, the status line tells you how many items are selected.

**4** Another way to select several items is to select the first one by clicking on it, and select additional items by holding down the Shift key while clicking on them. As when you use a marquee, a large highlighting box encloses all the items you've selected. The advantage of this method is that it lets you select two or more items that may not be contiguous. The highlighting box may make it look as though more items are selected than actually are; check the status line for an up-to-the-minute report on how many items are in fact selected.

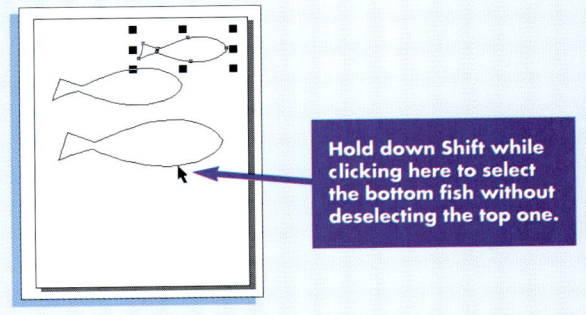

# CHAPTER 7: MANIPULATING TEXT AND DRAWINGS

# How to Move and Copy Objects

Once you've selected one or more objects, you can move them so they are precisely where you want them on the page, and copy them to make duplicates that you can either leave as is or use as a starting point for new shapes or drawings. In fact, once you've copied an object, there's a good chance that you'll then want to move it to a more appropriate spot on the page, or even to another page or a different drawing altogether. You'll learn how to do all of those things here.

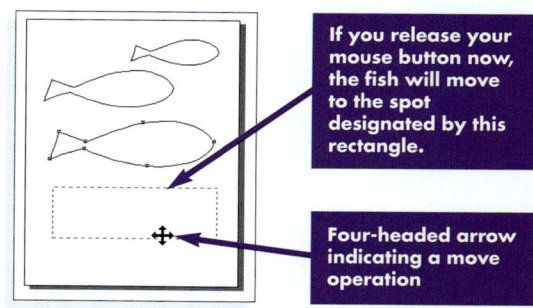

**If you release your mouse button now, the fish will move to the spot designated by this rectangle.**

**Four-headed arrow indicating a move operation**

**1** To move an object, select it, hold down the mouse button while pointing to the object (if the object is just an outline, make sure to point directly at that outline), and then drag to move the object. As you drag, the mouse pointer will change into a four-headed arrow, and you'll see a dashed rectangle indicating where the object will be repositioned if you release your mouse button, as shown here. (If you've selected more than one object, dragging in this manner will move all the selected objects.)

### TIP SHEET

▶ **You can modify the amount of offset of both duplicated and cloned objects: Simply choose Preferences from the Special menu and then change the Horizontal and Vertical settings under Place Duplicates and Clones.**

▶ **If you hold down the Ctrl (constrain) key while dragging objects to move them, you can only move those objects at 90 degree angles.**

▶ **You cannot clone a clone, although you can duplicate one.**

▶ **If you delete an original, any clones are deleted also.**

▶ **If you paste onto the same page from which you cut or copied, the image winds up in its original location. So, if you copy a shape and paste it onto the same page, it will completely cover the original.**

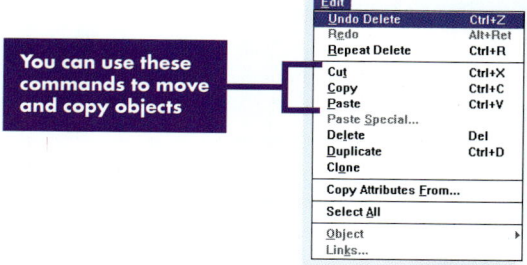

**You can use these commands to move and copy objects**

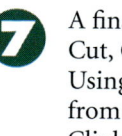

A final way to move or copy objects is with the Cut, Copy, and Paste commands on the Edit menu. Using Cut (Ctrl+X) removes the selected object from your drawing, placing it on the Windows Clipboard, a temporary storage area. Using Copy (Ctrl+C) places a copy of the selected item on the Clipboard, without removing the original from your drawing. Using the Paste command (Ctrl+V) inserts the item from the Clipboard back into your current location. With the Clipboard, you can move or copy objects to other pages in the same drawings, to different drawings, and even to different Windows applications just by moving to the desired location before issuing the Paste command—something you cannot accomplish with the methods for moving, duplicating, and cloning objects previously described.

How to Move and Copy Objects   59

❷ If you want to more precisely position objects that you are moving, here's one tack to take: First make sure the rulers are displayed. Then drag from the rulers to insert guidelines where you want to place the object. (Remember, choose Show Rulers from the Display menu to display the rulers if they're not already on the screen.) Finally, move the object as described, lining up the dashed rectangle with the help of the guidelines you just added.

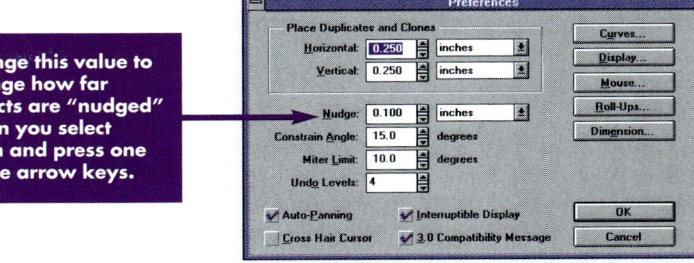

**Change this value to change how far objects are "nudged" when you select them and press one of the arrow keys.**

**Inserting guidelines can help you line up objects as you're moving them.**

❸ If you need to move selected objects in small increments, you can *nudge* them. To do this, select the object to be moved and then press the arrow key that points in the direction in which you want to move the object. (To move the object up press ↑, to move it down press ↓, and so forth.) If you want to change the amount by which objects are moved with each nudge, choose Preferences from the Special menu and, in the Preferences dialog box that appears, change the value under Nudge.

❹ One way to copy an object is to select it and choose Duplicate from the Edit menu or press Ctrl+D. This inserts an exact copy of 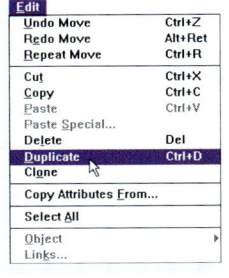 the selected object just above and to the right of the original object. Unless you want to leave the duplicate in this spot, you can now move it to the desired location using any of the methods just described. (Incidentally, you can copy several items at once just by selecting them first.)

❻ An additional way to copy objects is to use the Clone command on the Edit menu. As when you use the Duplicate command, CorelDRAW! generates a copy that it places above and to the right of the original. However, in this case the copy, or *clone*, will be affected by any subsequent changes to the original. As an example, if you color the original blue, any clones also become blue; and if you change the size of the original, any clones change size accordingly. (Note, however, that you can modify the clone without affecting the original.)

❺ CorelDRAW! also lets you copy items by holding down the plus (+) key on the numeric keypad while dragging to move the selected object. (When you use this strategy, make sure to release the mouse button *before* releasing the plus key.) This moves a copy of the object while leaving the original in place. Unlike creating duplicates, this technique lets you position your copy where you want it on the page.

# How to Change Your Mind and How to Repeat Yourself

Frequently you'll move, copy, or delete something and then wish you could change your mind. Well, you can. CorelDRAW! offers an undo feature that permits you to reverse many of the actions that you take. This is handy not only when you have a change of heart but when you punch the wrong key or otherwise take a wrong turn down the electronic road. CorelDRAW! even lets you change your mind about undo operations: You can use the Redo command to redo what you just undid. When you perform an action that you'd like to repeat rather than retract, CorelDRAW! provides a Repeat command, which is invaluable when you have to perform the same task over and over again.

**1** If you've just performed some action—such as drawing or deleting an object—that you want to reverse, choose Undo from the Edit menu or press Ctrl+Z. The full command name will depend upon the action being undone; it might be Undo Delete or Undo Duplicate, for instance. (The Undo command is not available if you haven't done anything that can be undone. For example, if you've just opened a new file, there's nothing to undo and the Undo command will be grayed.)

### TIP SHEET

- **There are certain actions that you cannot undo. For example, you can't reverse zooming and scrolling operations (you'll learn about zooming in Chapter 9); you can't undo file operations such as save and open; and, finally, you can't select an object and then choose undo to deselect it.**

- **It's a good practice to scan the full command name before performing an Undo, Redo, or Repeat command. Since the name of the command tells you which action will be undone, redone, or repeated, this can help you decide whether to go ahead with the operation.**

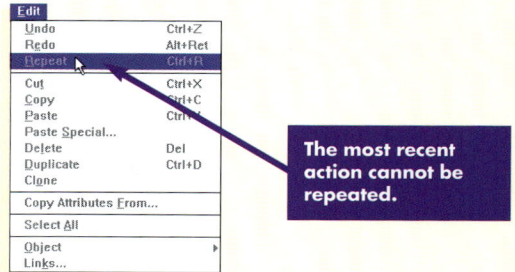

 You can repeat an action as often as you like, but you can only repeat your most recent action. (Remember, you can undo and redo several previous actions.) And if your most recent action is one that can't be repeated (say you just drew a square), the Repeat command will not be available.

# How to Change Your Mind and How to Repeat Yourself    61

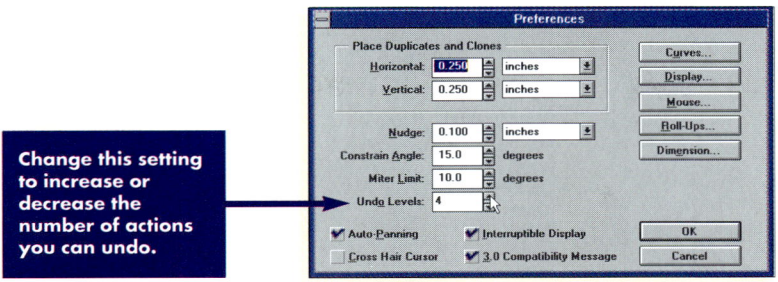

Change this setting to increase or decrease the number of actions you can undo.

**2** You can undo more than one action. For example, if you just duplicated an object and then moved it, you can undo the move operation and then the duplication, in that order, just by choosing Undo twice from the Edit menu or pressing Ctrl+Z two times. You can undo up to four actions by default. If you want to be able to undo more (or fewer) previous actions, choose Preferences from the Special menu and change the setting under Undo Levels.

**3** Once you've undone one or more operations, the Redo command becomes available. To reverse your most recent Undo command, choose Redo from the Edit menu or press Alt+Enter. As with Undo, the full name of the Redo command depends upon the action being redone; it might be Redo Duplicate or Redo Create, to name just two.

**4** You can also redo more than one action. In fact, you can redo just as many actions as you can undo. To do this, just choose Redo from the Edit menu, or press Alt+Enter, repeatedly. As with the Undo command, this redoes commands in reverse order. For example, if you undid a move operation and then undid a duplication operation, choosing redo twice would redo the duplication and then the move, in that sequence.

**5** If you decide to repeat an action instead of reversing it, you can simply choose Repeat from the Edit menu or press Ctrl+R. (This affects the currently selected objects.) You can only repeat transformations to objects; for example, you can use the Repeat command to repeat a move or copy operation. You cannot, however, draw a shape and then use the Repeat command to create another one just like it. As with the Undo and Redo commands, the full name of the Repeat command depends upon the action being repeated.

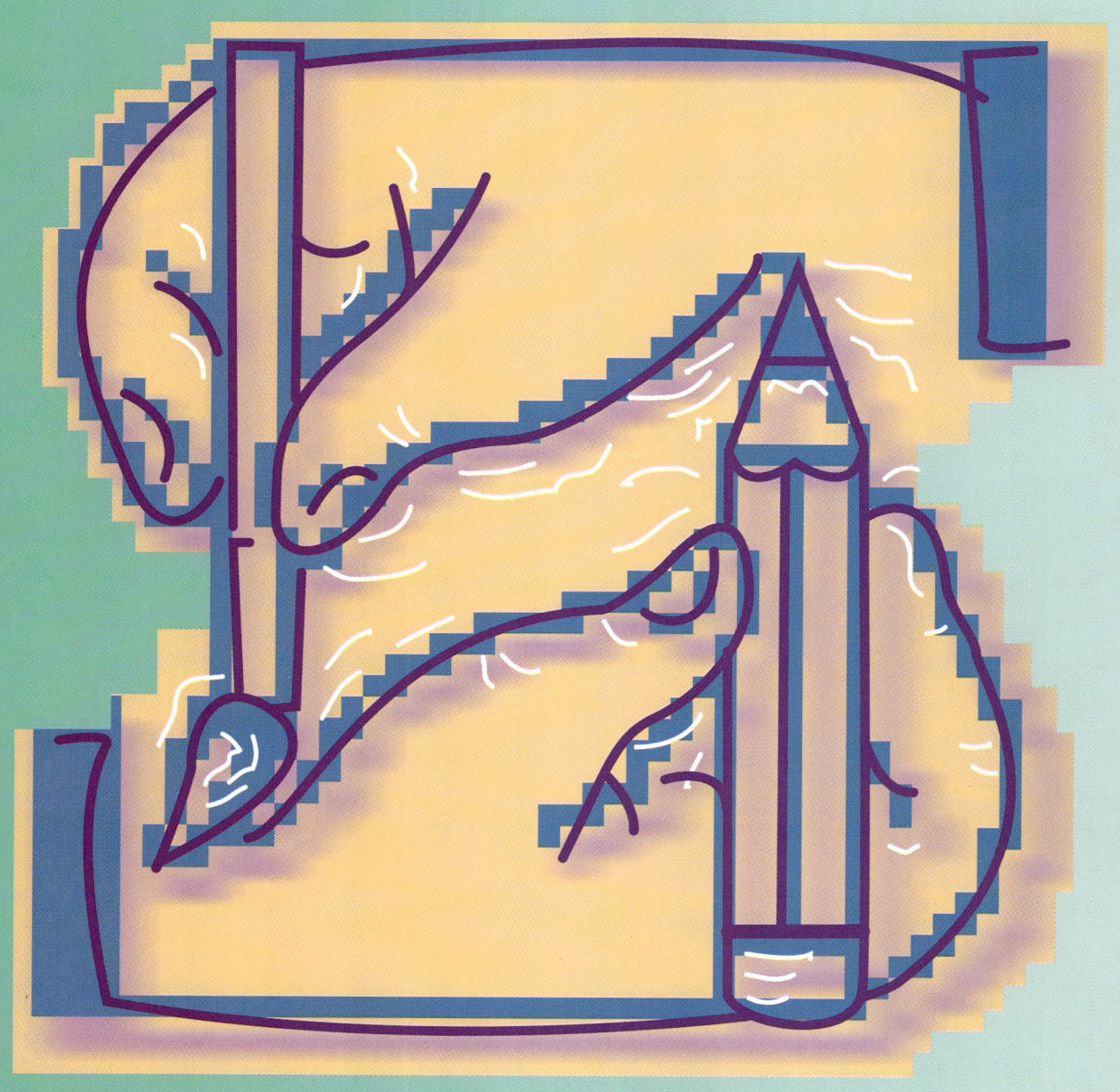

# CHAPTER 8

# Printing Your Drawings

Depending on the quality and resolution of your monitor, what you see on your screen may not be all that close to what you'll really get. For this reason, you might want to print at various stages along the way to get a more accurate idea of how your design is progressing. And once you've perfected your drawing, printing on paper is your reward for so many hours of hard work. A printed copy is also the form of output you're most likely to generate—for anything from birthday party invitations to newsletters to professionally crafted brochures. (CorelDRAW! lets you produce files that you can use to create other forms of output—including slide shows, video, and film—but those are beyond the scope of this book.)

You'll be pleased to know that the printing basics in CorelDRAW! are remarkably easy. At the simplest, it requires just three clicks to print a single copy of the drawing that's open at the moment. It takes only a little extra effort to print multiple copies, to change the size and position of your drawing before printing, and to print only selected elements or selected pages of your drawing.

# How to Print Your Entire Drawing

**V**ery often you'll want to print just a single copy of your entire drawing. This is the simplest printing option available in Corel-DRAW!. At the same time, it's extremely easy to print multiple copies, as well as to change the size and position of your printed image on the page.

**1** Look over your drawing carefully before printing, so you don't waste paper and do away with any more trees than absolutely necessary. Also turn on your printer and check that it's well supplied with paper.

Check that everything looks okay before printing.

### TIP SHEET

▶ Sometimes you'll want to take a close-up look at all or part of a drawing before printing. You'll learn how to do this in the next chapter.

▶ You can use the Print to File option in the Print dialog box to "print" the information in your drawing to a file. For example, you can save a drawing on a floppy disk and have the results printed on a high-quality printer at a service bureau. If you go this route, consult with the service bureau for details on the specific settings they require for a drawing printed to a file. (Your documentation will also include information on printing to a file.)

▶ If your drawing extends beyond the boundaries of the page, you can use the Tile option under Position and Size in the Print dialog box to have CorelDRAW! print the extra parts of the drawing on additional pages. (Your drawing will print on separate pages even though it looks like it's on a single page in the Print dialog box.)

▶ The red lines in the preview area of the Print dialog box demarcate the printable area of the page. Depending on your printer, you may not actually be able to print to the very edge of the page.

**8** When all settings in the Print dialog box look just right, click on OK to print your drawing.

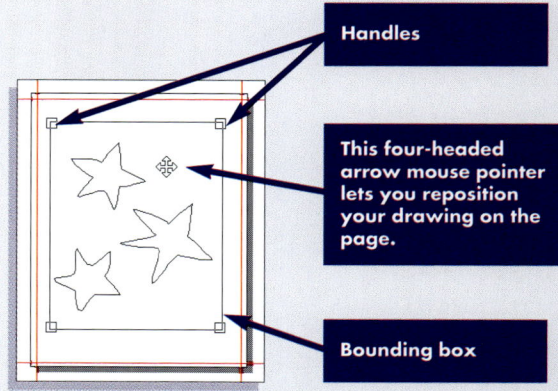

Handles

This four-headed arrow mouse pointer lets you reposition your drawing on the page.

Bounding box

**7** You can also move or resize your printed drawing by using the mouse. (Again, changes that you make in this way just affect the printed copy, not the actual drawing.) To resize your drawing, place the mouse pointer over one of the four handles on the *bounding box* enclosing the drawing, and then drag to increase or decrease the size of the drawing. To reposition your drawing on the page, place the mouse pointer anywhere within the bounding box. It will become a four-headed arrow, and you can drag in any direction to move the drawing that way. (You can't reposition your drawing if either Fit to Page or Center is selected.)

## How to Print Your Entire Drawing    65

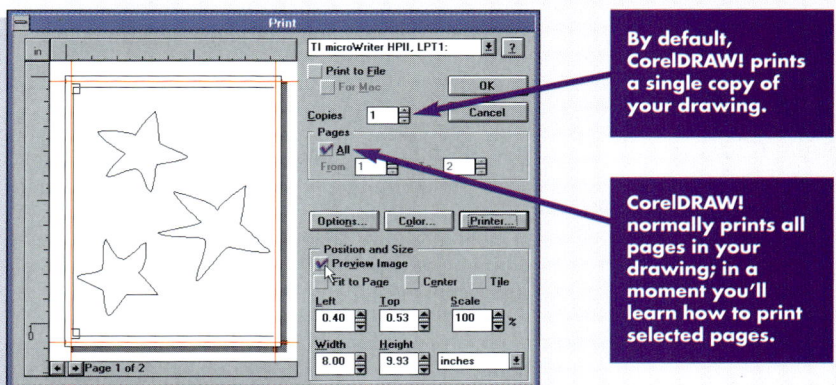

 Choose Print from the File menu or press Ctrl+P to initiate the printing procedure.

**3** You'll see the Print dialog box shown here. Notice that there's a preview of your drawing on the left side of the dialog box. (If you see a blank box rather than a preview, select the Preview Image check box.) Try not to be put off by the number of options here; basic printing is really quite simple.

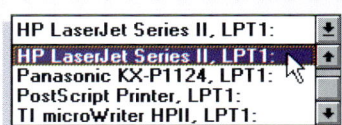

**4** Check that the correct printer name is displayed in the upper-right corner of the Print dialog box. If not, pull down the drop-down list box and select a new printer from the list. (If your printer isn't listed, consult your Windows documentation. You may need to install a printer driver so Windows can converse with your particular printer.)

 CorelDRAW! makes it easy to change the position and size of your drawing as you're printing. In the Print dialog box, select the Center check box to center your drawing on 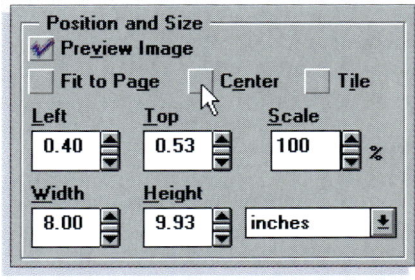 the page (CorelDRAW! will treat all objects as a single object that it then centers.) Select the Fit to Page check box to increase or decrease the size of the drawing so that it fills the entire page. And change the value under Scale to increase or decrease the size of the printed image. It's crucial to note that these options affect only the printed copy; they do *not* affect the actual drawing.

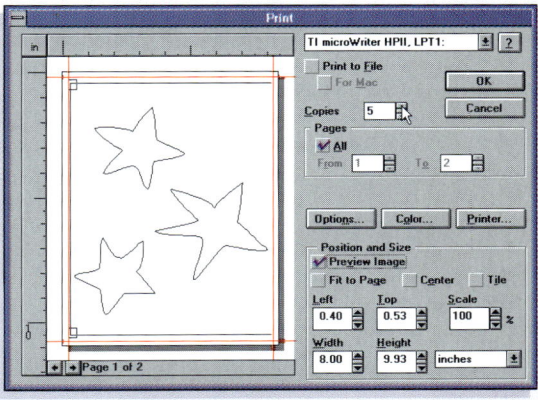

**5** If you want to print more than one copy, change the setting under Copies. You can enter any value from 1 to 999. If you need a very large number of copies, it may be more efficient to print a single one and then use your copy machine to make duplicates.

# How to Print Just a Portion of a Drawing

There will be times when you need to print only a portion of your drawing. You might have a particularly complex design, of which you only want to print selected areas or shapes. Or you may need to print only certain pages of a multipage effort. In either case, it is pleasantly straightforward to print designated portions of your drawing, as you'll learn here. Being able to print selectively both lets you proceed more quickly and permits you to hone in on the areas of your text or drawing that still need work.

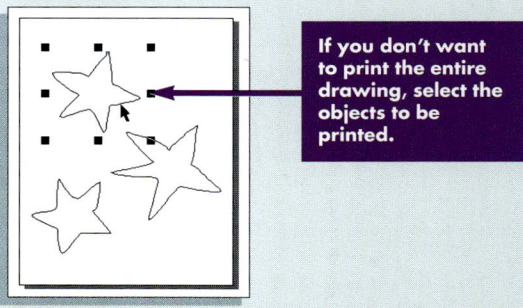

▶ ❶ If you want to print just selected items on a single page, first select those items. (You can flip back to Chapter 7 if you need to refresh your memory on this topic.)

### TIP SHEET

▶ **You can deselect the All check box under Pages only if your drawing contains more than a single page.**

▶ **You cannot print noncontiguous pages using the From and To options in the Print dialog box. For example, if you wanted to print pages 1 to 4 and pages 15 to 24 of a drawing, you'd be forced to perform two print operations: one to print the first four pages, and another to print the remaining pages.**

▶ **You can resize and reposition objects when printing selected shapes or pages, as when printing your entire drawing. Turn back to the previous two pages if you need to jog your memory on how to do this.**

❼ When you've selected the desired range of pages, just click on OK to go ahead and print those pages.

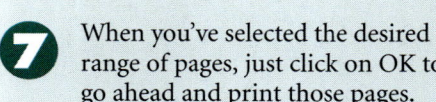

❻ Under Pages in the Print dialog box, deselect the All check box by clicking on it. The From and To boxes will become available (they'll turn black), and you can specify a range of pages to print. If you decided to print just the first three pages of a ten-page design, for instance, you'd enter 1 in the From box and 3 in the To box. If you need to print a single page, enter that page number in both the From and To boxes, as shown here.

How to Print Just a Portion of a Drawing  67

❷ Choose Print from the File menu (or press Ctrl+P) to display the Print dialog box. Notice the new check box Selected Objects Only, which hadn't put in an appearance before.

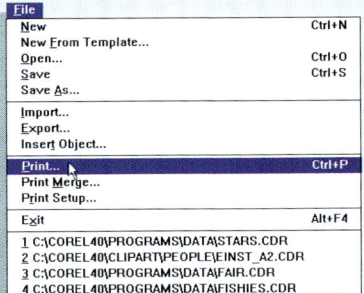

❸ As in any printing operation, check that the correct printer and number of copies are selected.

❹ Select the Selected Objects Only check box, noting that now only the selected objects show up in the preview area on the left. Make any other selections in the Print dialog box and then click on OK to print just the items you've selected.

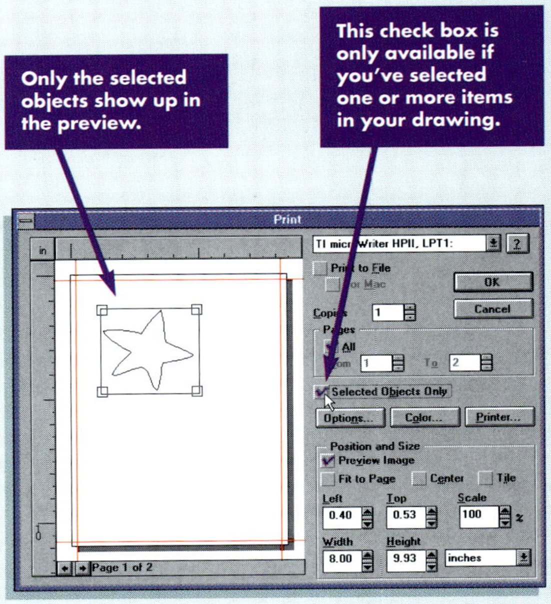

Only the selected objects show up in the preview.

This check box is only available if you've selected one or more items in your drawing.

❺ It's also simple to print designated pages of a multipage design. To do this, again choose Print from the File menu or press Ctrl+P to display the Print dialog box.

**CHAPTER 9**

# Different Ways of Viewing Your Drawings

So far CorelDRAW! has displayed the same view of all your drawings: You've seen a single page at a time, and you've seen that page in its entirety. Although this view is perfectly adequate in a wide range of situations, there will be times when you need to gain a different perspective on your work. You might want to move back and get an overview, or you may need to step in and get a close-up view. CorelDRAW! makes it exceedingly simple to do either of these things.

You can also see your drawings from several other different points of view. You can get a new view of a drawing, not just by shrinking or enlarging it, but by changing the orientation of the page from vertical to horizontal or vice versa. In addition, you can display more than a single page at once on the screen—this is particularly helpful when you're putting together multipage designs. And finally, you can see a simplified view of your drawing—called *wireframe mode*—in which only outlines are shown. When you begin to create more complex drawings, this view will speed up your work considerably.

# How to Zoom In and Out

Like a zoom lens on a camera, CorelDRAW!'s Zoom tool lets you get the right perspective on your drawing. You can zoom in to see just a small portion of a design in great detail; this will help you do fine work. In addition, you can zoom out to see a larger area of your drawing in less detail; this broader perspective can help you gain a sense of the overall composition. You can also display your drawing in the size in which it will be printed, and you can enlarge or reduce a drawing just enough so that everything you've drawn shows up on the screen.

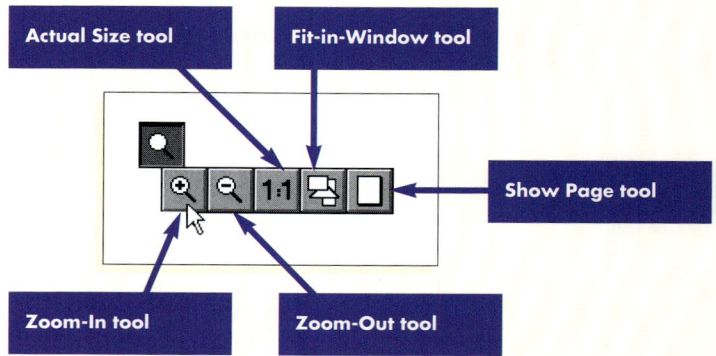

 **1** Click on the Zoom tool; you'll see the Zoom flyout menu shown here. Notice that the Zoom tool is actually five tools combined into one.

### TIP SHEET

▶ When you've zoomed in on a drawing, you may need to scroll to see a portion of the drawing that is no longer visible. If you need to jog your memory on how to scroll, consult "Maneuvering with the Mouse" in Chapter 2.

▶ You can't reverse zoom operations with the Undo command; you need instead to choose a different option from the Zoom flyout menu.

▶ If you like, you can set the right mouse button so that it lets you zoom in or out. To do this, choose Preferences from the Special menu, choose the Mouse button, and select the 2x zoom option button. Then click on OK twice to close the dialog boxes. Now you can magnify your drawings by a factor of two by clicking with the right mouse button, and you can shrink your drawings to half their size by double-clicking with the right mouse button.

**7** Finally, there will often be times when you want to get back where you started, returning your drawing to its original magnification. To do this, click on the Show Page tool to once again see the entire printable page area.

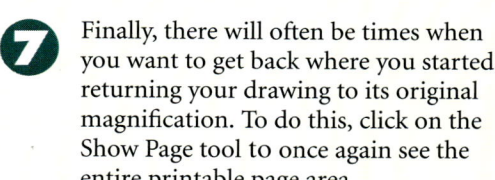

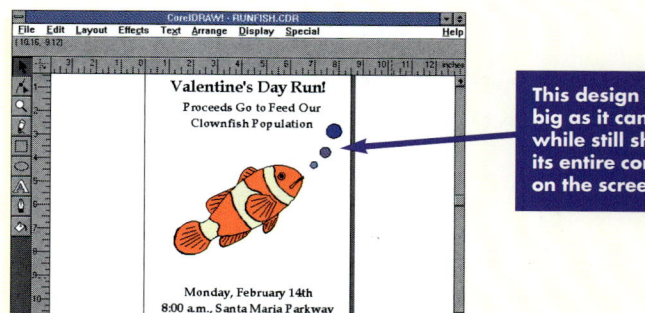

This design is as big as it can be while still showing its entire contents on the screen.

**6** Under certain circumstances you may want to see the largest possible view while still displaying everything you've drawn in its entirety. In this case, choose the Fit-in-Window tool. Your drawing will be enlarged as much as it can be and still fit on the screen. (Or, if you've zoomed in, your drawing will be reduced so that you can see all of it at once.)

## How to Zoom In and Out 71

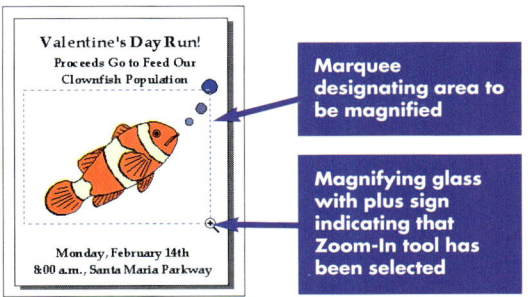

Marquee designating area to be magnified

Magnifying glass with plus sign indicating that Zoom-In tool has been selected

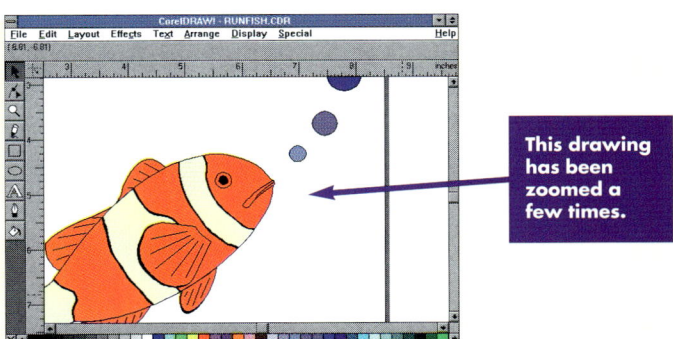

This drawing has been zoomed a few times.

**2** Click on the Zoom-In tool. The mouse pointer will change into a magnifying glass containing a plus sign. Now drag to draw a dashed rectangle, or marquee, enclosing the area of the drawing that you want to zero in on. When you release the mouse button, the portion of your drawing within the rectangle will be enlarged to fill the screen.

**3** To zoom in again, simply choose the Zoom-In tool again, and again drag a marquee around the area of the drawing that you want to enlarge. To what extent you can magnify your drawing depends on your monitor and display adapter.

**4** If you want to get more of an overview of your drawing, use the Zoom-Out tool. Selecting this tool does one of two things: If you have zoomed in, it zooms you out to your previous setting (you can even select this tool repeatedly if you've magnified your drawing quite a bit). Alternatively, if you can currently see the entire page, if you see your drawing in actual size, or if you've scaled your design to fit in the drawing window, selecting the Zoom-Out tool shrinks your drawing to half of its current size.

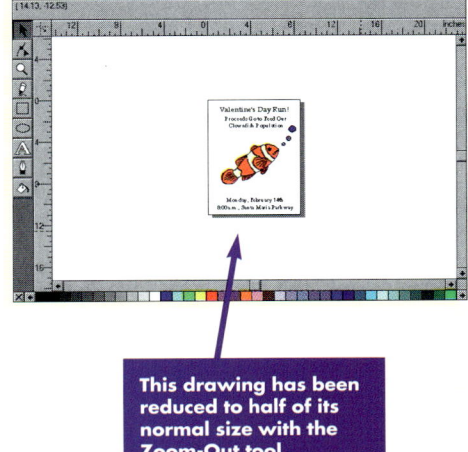

The rulers can help you gauge whether this drawing is close to its actual printed size.

This drawing has been reduced to half of its normal size with the Zoom-Out tool.

**5** If you want to see approximately what your drawing will look like when printed, click on the Actual Size tool. This enlarges or reduces the display to show the image at approximately its actual printed size. (An easy way to check its accuracy is to display the rulers and check whether they are about the right size; choose Show Rulers from the Display menu if the rulers aren't already showing.)

# How to Change the Orientation of Your Drawing

So far all the drawings you've seen have had a vertical, or *portrait*, orientation. You can easily change the orientation of your drawings, so that the long edge of the page goes from left to right rather than top to bottom. This horizontal orientation is known as *landscape* orientation. As you'll see, if you change the orientation of the printable page, you should generally ask CorelDRAW! to change the orientation of your paper when printing.

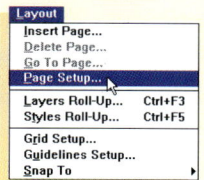

 **1** To change the orientation of the printable page, first choose Page Setup from the Layout menu.

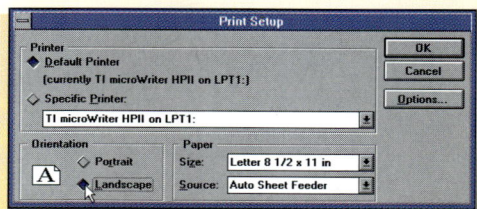

**6** You can also match up the two orientations—printable page and printer paper—ahead of time by giving instructions to the printer. To do this, choose Print Setup from the File menu, and choose the desired orientation under Orientation in the Print Setup dialog box that puts in an appearance.

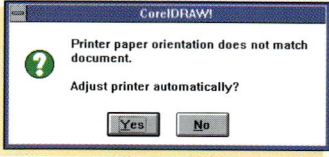

**5** If you print a drawing that you've composed in landscape orientation, you'll need to also tell CorelDRAW! to switch the paper orientation so that the drawing fits properly on the page. If the two orientations do not match up, CorelDRAW! automatically asks if you want to change the paper orientation when you choose Print from the File menu, as shown here. Simply click on Yes to have the orientation of the printable page match that of the paper in your printer. Then go ahead with the printing operation as usual. (If necessary, see Chapter 8 for the lowdown on printing.)

### TIP SHEET

- **If you start a drawing and then change the orientation of the page, the page is rotated but not the image. Be careful with this: You can wind up with an image that no longer fits on the page. It's best to change to page orientation first, and then begin your drawing.**

- **A drawing's orientation is saved with it. So, if you open a drawing that was created (and saved) in portrait orientation, it remains in that orientation, regardless of the orientation of the drawing that was on the screen previously.**

## How to Change the Orientation of Your Drawing 73

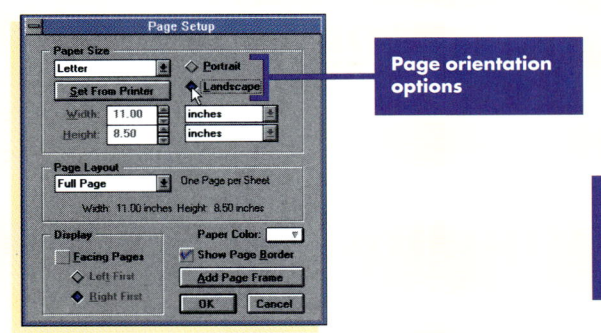

Page orientation options

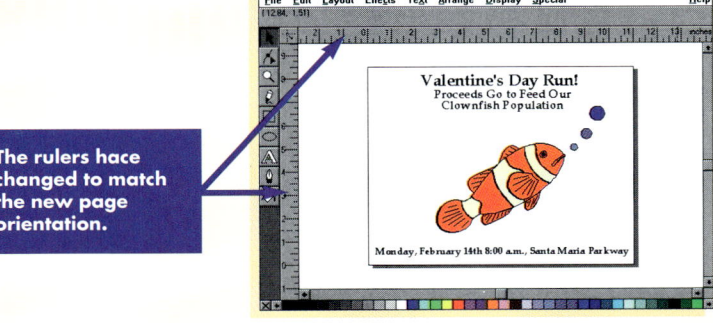

The rulers have changed to match the new page orientation.

**2** You'll see the Page Setup dialog box. This is where you can change the page orientation, the paper size, and more. To change the orientation of the printable page, click on the Landscape option button.

**3** Now click on OK. As you can see, the orientation of the printable page will flip, and the rulers (if they're displayed) will change size to accommodate the new page size and orientation.

PORTRAIT

LANDSCAPE

**4** If you were previously in landscape orientation and you start CorelDRAW! or start a new drawing, the printable page will be laid out in landscape orientation. To switch back to portrait orientation, simply choose Page Setup from the Layout menu and then choose the Portrait option button from the Page Setup dialog box that appears.

# Other Ways of Viewing Your Drawings

You've learned how to zoom in and out to magnify and shrink your drawings on the screen, and how to switch your drawings' orientation on the screen and the printed page. CorelDRAW! provides a few additional ways of taking a look at your drawing. Some of these techniques can help speed up your work, and some can also give you a much better sense of how your work will look when printed.

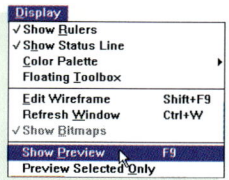

 **1** If you like, you can see a preview of your drawing. To switch to this view, choose Show Preview from the Display menu, or press F9.

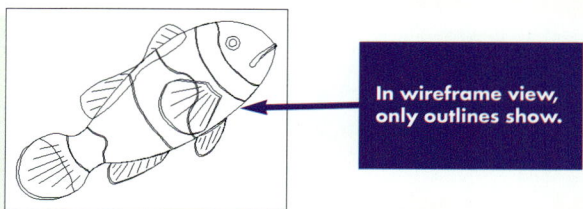

*In wireframe view, only outlines show.*

**7** Wireframe view shows only the outlines of objects; it's like seeing a sketch rather than a completed drawing. For instance, here's the fish from the previous example shown in wireframe view, with only its outlines showing. To leave wireframe view and return to the editable preview, choose Edit Wireframe from the Display menu (or press Shift+F9) a second time.

**6** When you begin to create more complex drawings—especially those with colors and fill patterns—it can take quite some time for Corel-DRAW! to draw them on the screen. So far you've seen all drawings in *editable preview,* the default view. This view shows all colors, fills, and so on—that is, it displays your drawings in complete detail. (Editable preview is *not* the same as the preview mode you experimented with a moment ago. It is simply the view you've been using all along.) CorelDRAW! also provides what's called *wireframe view*. To switch to wireframe view, choose Edit Wireframe from the Display menu, or press Shift+F9.

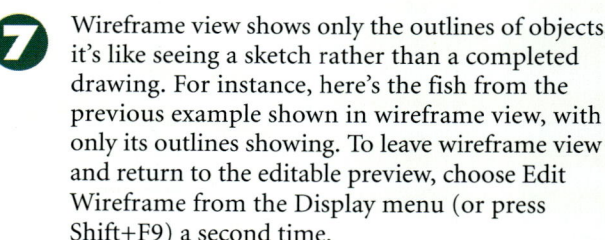

## TIP SHEET

- **You cannot edit your drawing while you're looking at a preview of it. You must first press F9 or the Escape key to leave the preview screen. Then you can go back to editing your drawing as you normally would.**

- **Displaying a preview is not the same as bringing your entire drawing into view. If your drawing had been zoomed, it remains zoomed even in the preview.**

- **You'll learn how to work with colors and fills in Chapter 10. If your drawing doesn't contain fills or colors, there's little difference between what you see in editable preview and what you see in wireframe view.**

OTHER WAYS OF VIEWING YOUR DRAWINGS **75**

 You now can see only your drawing—the screen has been relieved of the rulers, toolbox, menu bar, color palette, and so on. This preview removes from view all the potentially distracting elements that normally clutter the screen, allowing you to concentrate on the drawing itself.

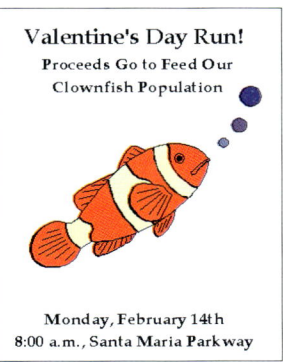

To leave the preview screen and bring all screen elements such as the menu bar and toolbox back into view, press F9 again or press the Escape key. (Remember that you can also hide selected screen items, such as the rulers, by making selections from the Display menu.)

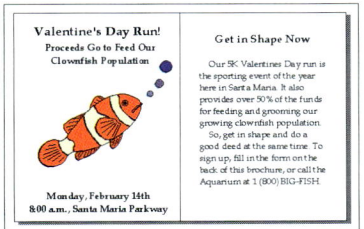

If you're working on a multipage design—one that will become a booklet or brochure, for example—you may want to see two pages on the screen at once to get a better sense of how those pages will work together as a unit. To be able to view two pages simultaneously, choose Page Setup from the Layout menu to bring up the Page Setup dialog box. Then click on the Facing Pages check box, and click on OK to close the dialog box.

At this point, you'll be able to see two pages at once. You can choose to have the first page on the right and the second page on the left. (This is the default; in most books even-numbered pages fall on the left and odd-numbered pages on the right.) Or, if you like, you can place the first page on the left and the second page on the right.

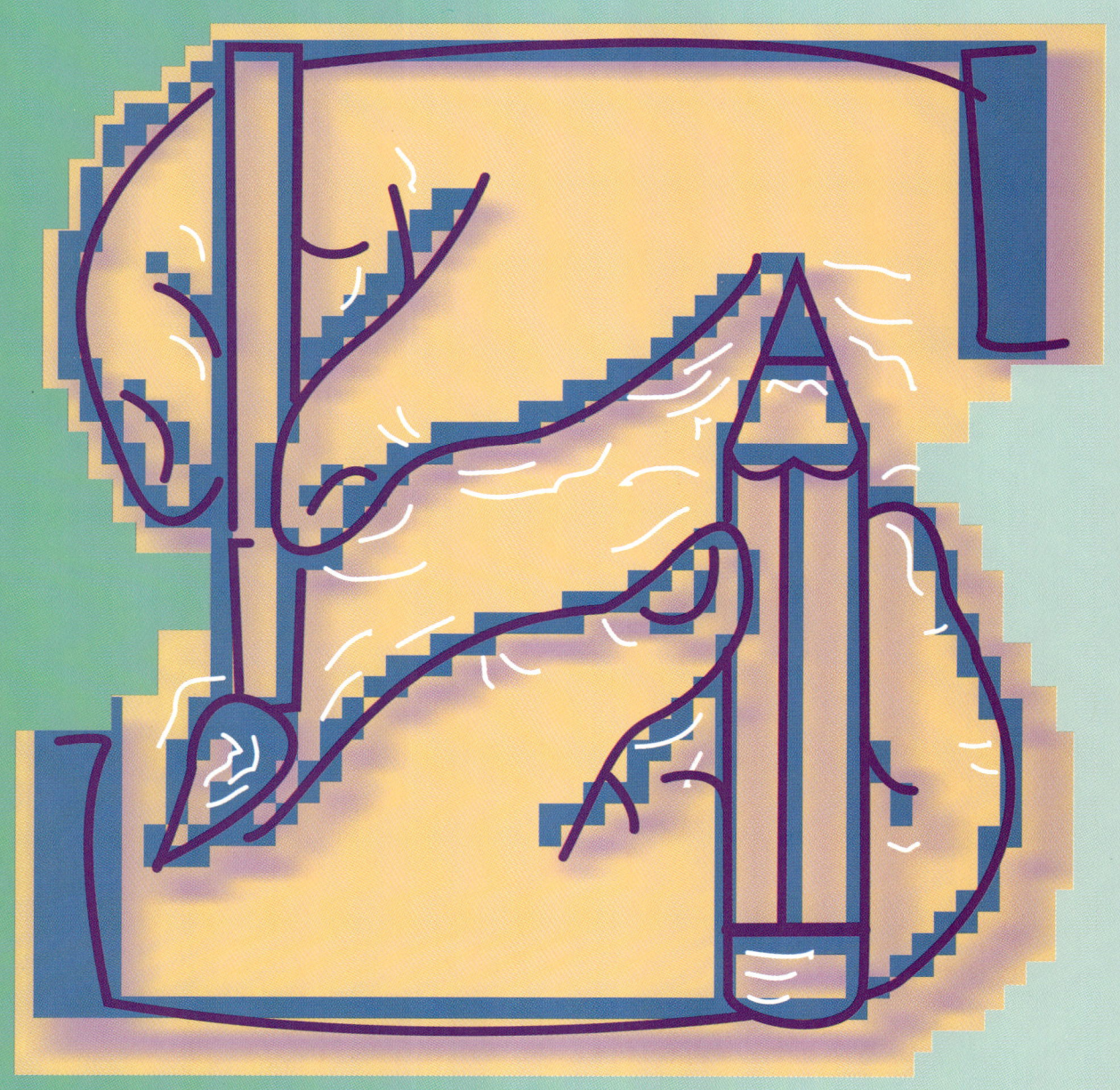

**CHAPTER 10**

# Coloring and Filling Shapes

 The shapes you've drawn up until now have most likely just consisted of outlines, containing no colors or fill patterns whatsoever. Your drawings would be awfully drab if they retained this monochrome quality, and at this point you're probably eager to liven them up with a dash of texture and color. CorelDRAW! supplies a wealth of colors, fill patterns, and textures that you can apply to the shapes that you've drawn. Once you learn the simple techniques presented in this chapter, you'll be able to produce bedazzling Technicolor designs.

At the easy end of the spectrum, it takes only a step or two to introduce solid colors and shades of gray to your drawings. And it requires just a modicum of additional effort to add textured fills; CorelDRAW! provides a spectacular library of these textures—including everything from mineral samples to cloud nebulae—which you can also modify to suit your tastes. In addition, it's not all that complicated to build fountain (gradient) fills in which two colors blend together gradually in a pattern that you determine. Finally, you can apply pattern fills—of either two colors or a full range of colors—consisting of anything from woven or crosshatched designs to tiled patterns of imported graphics. Like CorelDRAW!'s other tools, the implements for coloring and filling your drawings are well-designed and simple to master. Once you've learned the basics laid out in this chapter, only your imagination will put a crimp on what you can do.

# CHAPTER 10: COLORING AND FILLING SHAPES

# How to Apply Colors the Easy Way

Chapter 3 briefly introduced the color palette, the row of colored squares at the bottom of the screen, just below the horizontal scroll bar. This palette provides the quickest and easiest way to apply basic solid colors to the shapes that you've drawn. In addition, you can almost as easily use the Fill tool in the toolbox to color objects black, white, or one of several shades of gray.

### TIP SHEET

- If no colors show up on your screen, you may be in wireframe view. (Remember, in this view CorelDRAW! displays only the outlines of objects.) To display colors, either press Shift+F9 or choose Edit Wireframe from the Display menu to turn this option off and return to editable preview.

- You can only apply colors (or fills, for that matter) to completely enclosed objects such as squares, circles, polygons, and freehand drawings in which the beginning node is joined with the ending node. If you select an object and the status line reads "Open Path," you will not be able to color that object.

- If you don't see a color palette at the bottom of the screen, choose Color Palette from the Display menu and then choose the desired palette from the submenu that CorelDRAW! displays (Custom Palette is the default).

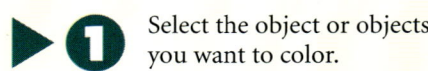 Select the object or objects you want to color.

 You can use the Fill flyout menu to change the color that CorelDRAW! uses by default when you draw shapes. For example, to automatically fill all shapes with a shade of gray, first *make sure that no shapes are selected*. (The center of the status line should be blank.) Then open the Fill flyout menu and click on the desired shade of gray; this brings up a dialog box like the one shown here. Leave just the Graphic check box selected, and then click on OK. Now any enclosed shapes that you draw will promptly be filled with the selected shade of gray. To reverse your choice—so that objects are no longer filled automatically—repeat this operation but this time choose the X (no fill) button from the Fill flyout menu.

HOW TO APPLY COLORS THE EASY WAY  **79**

**Click here to see more colors to the left.**

**Click here to see more colors to the right.**

**2** Click on the desired color in the color palette at the bottom of the screen. The selected objects will immediately take on that color.

**3** If you change your mind and decide to try a different color, just click on that color in the color palette, making sure that any objects whose color you want to change are still selected. Don't forget that you can't see all the available colors at once; you may need to scroll through the palette to find the color you need. If you click on the palette scroll arrows with the right mouse button, the palette will scroll the width of the screen instead of a single color at a time.

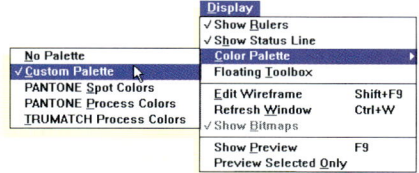

**4** CorelDRAW! actually provides a number of different color palettes, and it's easy to switch between them. To do so, choose Color Palette from the Display menu and then choose a new palette from the submenu that appears. A discussion of the different palettes—and the different color systems they use—is beyond the scope of this book. For help, consult your CorelDRAW! documentation or a more advanced book on the subject.

**Click here to remove the color from any selected objects.**

**Click here to color your object white.**

**Click here to color your object black.**

**Click on one of these four buttons to color your object a shade of gray.**

**6** It's as easy to get rid of colors as it is to introduce them in the first place. Make sure the objects in question are selected and, if the Fill flyout menu is open, click on the X at the left end of its bottom row; if the Fill flyout is not already open, simply click on the X at the far left end of the color palette.

**5** You can also use the Fill tool in the toolbox to add black, white, and a few shades of gray to your drawings. Click on the Fill tool (it looks like a bucket of paint) to open the Fill flyout menu, which is shown here. Then click on the buttons on the bottom row of this menu to color the selected objects black, white, or a shade of gray. (Although they may look the same in some cases, there *is* a difference between objects with no color and objects that have been colored white. Simply put, an object that has no color is see-through, while a white object is not.)

# How to Apply Texture Fills

CorelDRAW! provides a large number of textural images that you can use as fill patterns to add interest to your work. These images are remarkably vivid and varied, ranging from satellite photographs to cloud formations to solar flares to the surface of the moon. Of course, you have to have a good-quality monitor and—even better—access to a color printer for these images to be at their best.

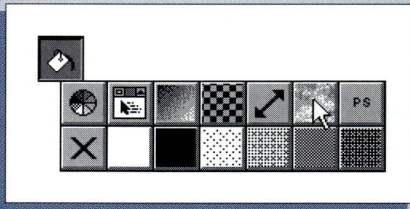

 **1** Select the object or objects you want to fill, click on the Fill tool in the toolbox, and then click on the texture fill button in the Fill flyout menu that pops out.

### TIP SHEET

- **CorelDRAW!'s texture fills are a special kind of graphic image called a *bitmap* (basically this means that they're composed of dots). These types of graphics tend to take up a lot of disk space; they'll make your files quite large and this, in turn, means that your drawings will take significantly longer to print. In other words, use these particular fills sparingly unless you have a powerful system.**
- **Texture fills may degrade in quality if you change the size of the filled object. For this reason, it's better to change the size of the shape first, and then apply the texture fill. (The same does not hold true for other types of fills.)**
- **If you alter a texture fill and want to be able to use that modified version at some later date, you can save it using the Save As command button in the Texture Fill dialog box. See your documentation for complete details.**

**7** You can make a texture fill into the default fill that CorelDRAW! uses when you draw objects. Make sure no objects are selected (check that the status line is blank) when you select the texture fill button in the Fill flyout menu. When CorelDRAW! asks whether you want to change the default, leave just the Graphic check box selected and click on OK. Then go ahead and pick out the desired fill, as just described. To get rid of a texture fill—and restore no fill as the default—again make sure no objects are selected, click on the X button in the Fill flyout menu, and click on OK in the ensuing dialog box. This technique works for all the fill types you'll learn about in the upcoming sections.

 **6** If you decide to get rid of a texture fill, make sure the filled object is selected and, if the Fill flyout menu is open, click on the X at the left end of its bottom row. Otherwise, click on the X at the left side of the color palette.

# How to Apply Texture Fills  81

**2** In the Texture Fill dialog box, you can choose different textures from the Texture List, and then scan the preview box to see what the new texture looks like. Some of these patterns are quite complex, so it might take CorelDRAW! a moment to draw the preview.

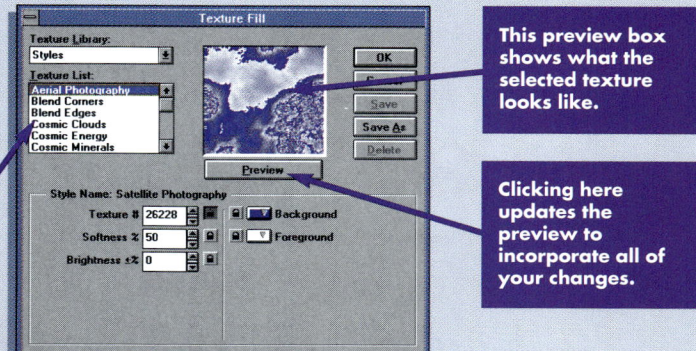

Choose new textures from this list.

This preview box shows what the selected texture looks like.

Clicking here updates the preview to incorporate all of your changes.

**3** You can choose from a different set of textures by picking a different texture library. Simply pull down the Texture Library drop-down list box and choose a different library from the list. You'll see a new set of textures under Texture List, and can browse through these choices as before.

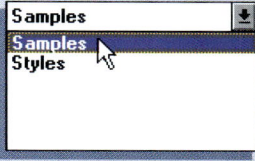

Click on one of these buttons to change one of the texture's colors.

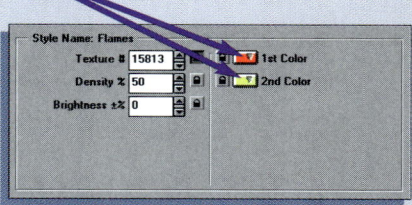

**4** When you select a texture, its parameters are displayed in the bottom of the Texture Fill dialog box. For example, here are the parameters for the Flames texture in the Styles library. The number of parameters varies with each texture. You can change these parameters to modify the texture fill. For instance, to change a color, just click on its color button and choose a new color from the list of colors that appears. Once you've made your selections, click on the Preview button to update the preview and see how your selections affect the texture.

**5** Once the preview looks the way you want it to, click on OK to apply this fill to the selected shapes. This ellipse is filled with the Satellite Photography fill from the Styles library. Don't worry about changing a texture fill's parameters, since CorelDRAW! promptly restores the default parameters as soon as you apply the modified texture fill to the selected shapes. You're applying these changes to the selected shapes, rather than to the texture as stored with CorelDRAW!

# How to Apply Fountain (Gradient) Fills

Fountain fills—also known as gradient fills—are a blend of two colors. One color changes gradually into the next in a pattern that you determine. You can create fountain fills that blend colors in a linear fashion, in concentric circles, or in a conical pattern. Fountain fills (often just called "fountains") are a sophisticated designing device that you can use to create subtle color backgrounds and even to give shapes the appearance of three dimensionality.

### TIP SHEET

- **CorelDRAW! provides a number of ready-made fountain fills.** To gain access to these fills, pull down the Presets drop-down list box in the lower-left corner of the Fountain Fill dialog box and choose a fill from the list. A sample will show up in the preview box, and you can then click on OK to apply the selected fill to your drawing.

- **To remove a fountain fill, make sure the filled object is selected and either click on the X in the Fill flyout menu or click on the X at the left end of the color palette.**

- **When choosing colors for fountain fills, keep in mind that the more similar the two colors, the more subtle the fountain.**

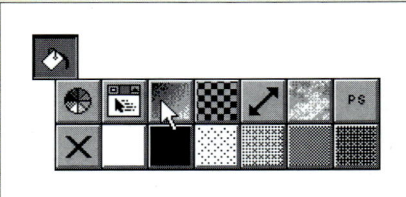

▶ **1** Select the object or objects to be filled, click on the Fill tool in the toolbox, and then click on the fountain fill button in the Fill flyout menu.

**7** Once the preview in the Fountain Fill dialog box passes your inspection, click on OK to apply the fill you've devised to the selected shapes.

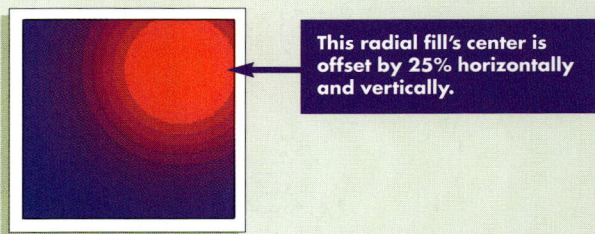

This radial fill's center is offset by 25% horizontally and vertically.

**6** Usually radial fills are blended in a concentric pattern that radiates out from the exact center of the filled shape. However, you can also change the position of a radial fill's center point. To do this, enter values under Horizontal and Vertical in the Center Offset area of the Fountain Fill dialog box. Entering negative values moves the pattern down and to the left; entering positive values moves it up and to the right.

## How to Apply Fountain (Gradient) Fills

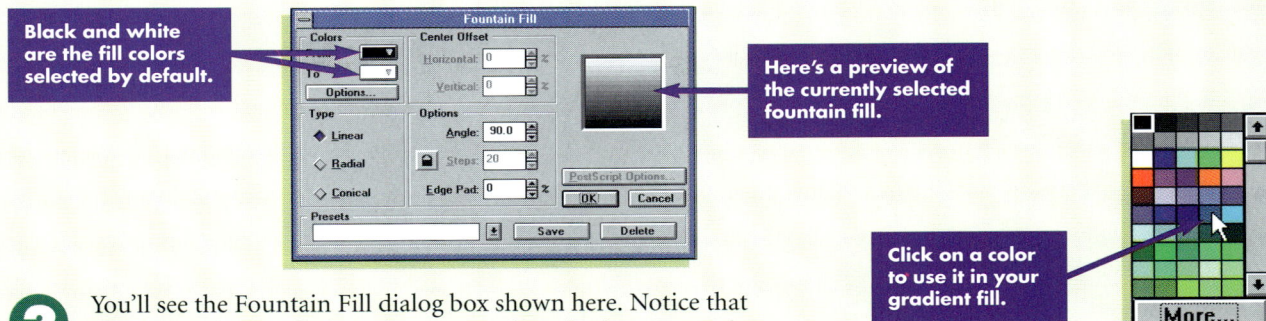

**Black and white are the fill colors selected by default.**

**Here's a preview of the currently selected fountain fill.**

**Click on a color to use it in your gradient fill.**

**②** You'll see the Fountain Fill dialog box shown here. Notice that the colors black and white show up on the color buttons under Colors; also note that CorelDRAW! automatically selected the fill type Linear under Type.

**③** Most likely you'll want something more colorful than the fountain fill that CorelDRAW! first proposes. To pick new colors for the fill, click on the button to the right of From under Colors and choose a color from the list that appears. (You may need to scroll to find the color you want.) Then do the same for To. Check the preview box at the right side of the dialog box to inspect the new fountain you've just created.

**Linear fountain fill**  **Radial fountain fill**  **Conical fountain fill**

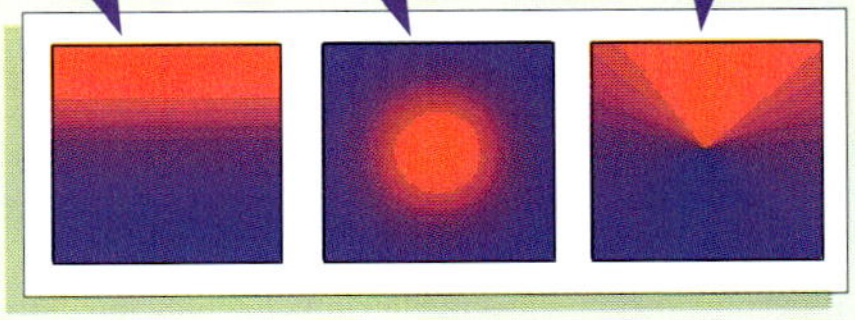

**④** In the Linear fill type, the colors are blended in a single direction, from one side to the other. Try selecting the Radial option button under Type and see how this affects the sample fill shown at the right side of the dialog box; the colors are now blended in a concentric pattern. Then try selecting Conical and see how the two fill colors merge together in wedge-shaped segments that originate from the center.

**This linear fill's angle has been changed to 45°.**

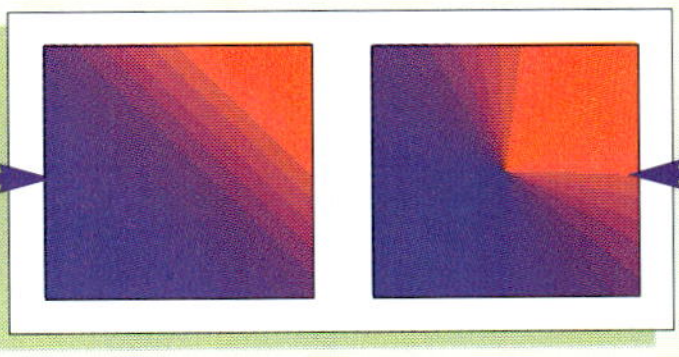

**This conical fill's angle has been changed to 45°.**

**⑤** You can also select the angle for Linear and Conical fills by typing or selecting a new value in the Angle box under Options. You could do this, for instance, if you wanted a linear fill that blended at a diagonal instead of from top to bottom.

# How to Apply Two-Color Pattern Fills

Two-color pattern fills consist of a single design or image arranged in a repeating pattern. CorelDRAW! provides a variety of ready-made patterns. In addition, you can easily devise patterns of your own using images included with CorelDRAW!, graphics from other sources, or even drawings that you've created yourself. The applications for these types of fills range from purely professional (including crosshatching for architectural or technical drawings) to truly whimsical (such as critters used as background patterns for stationery for a niece or nephew).

### TIP SHEET

- When you create a new pattern fill using the Import dialog box, CorelDRAW! adds that pattern to the end of the list of patterns that appears when you click on the pattern preview box in the Two-Color Pattern dialog box. This makes it very easy to reuse patterns that you've created. If you think you'll never have use for a particular pattern again, you can select it from the list by clicking on it, and then choose Delete Item from the File menu at the top of the list.
- The foreground (Front) and background (Back) colors that you select for a pattern fill must have sufficient contrast. If not—for example, if you use a navy blue background and a black foreground—the pattern will be hard to distinguish.
- Creating pattern fills is not unlike creating a tiled pattern of symbols, which you learned how to do in Chapter 5, under "How to Enter Special Symbols." However, in this case you can select the shape or shapes that you want to fill, whereas when you tile with symbols CorelDRAW! automatically fills the entire page.

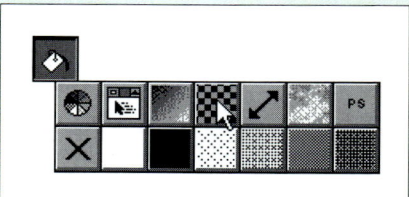

**1** As usual, select the object or objects you want to fill, click on the Fill tool in the toolbox, and then click on the two-color fill button in the Fill flyout menu.

**7** Once you've selected or created a fill pattern and made any needed changes to it, click on OK to apply it to the selected shapes. Here, for example, is a fill pattern made up of the DOLPHIN.CDR file found in the COREL40\CLIPART\CREATURE directory. Notice that the foreground (Front) color has been changed to blue.

**6** From the Import dialog box, choose a drive and directory containing an image that you want to use in your fill pattern. To experiment, you can try getting into the COREL40\CLIPART directory and then finding an interesting-sounding subdirectory, such as CREATURE or SPORTS. (Remember, double-click on a subdirectory to see a list of the files it contains; to see all subdirectories of a directory, double-click on the directory.) Finally, under File Name, click on the file you want to use and then click on OK. You'll be returned to the Two-Color Pattern dialog box, where you'll see a sample of your new fill pattern. If necessary, change the fill's colors and size as described a moment ago.

How to Apply Two-Color Pattern Fills  85

❷ In the Two-Color Pattern dialog box that appears, click on the large pattern preview box to the right of the Create and Import buttons to display a batch of patterns supplied with CorelDRAW! If necessary, scroll to find the pattern you want. Once you've found the desired pattern, double-click on it to select it. The preview box will change accordingly.

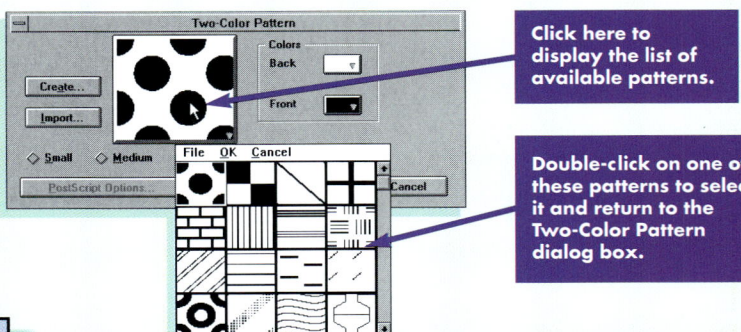

Click here to display the list of available patterns.

Double-click on one of these patterns to select it and return to the Two-Color Pattern dialog box.

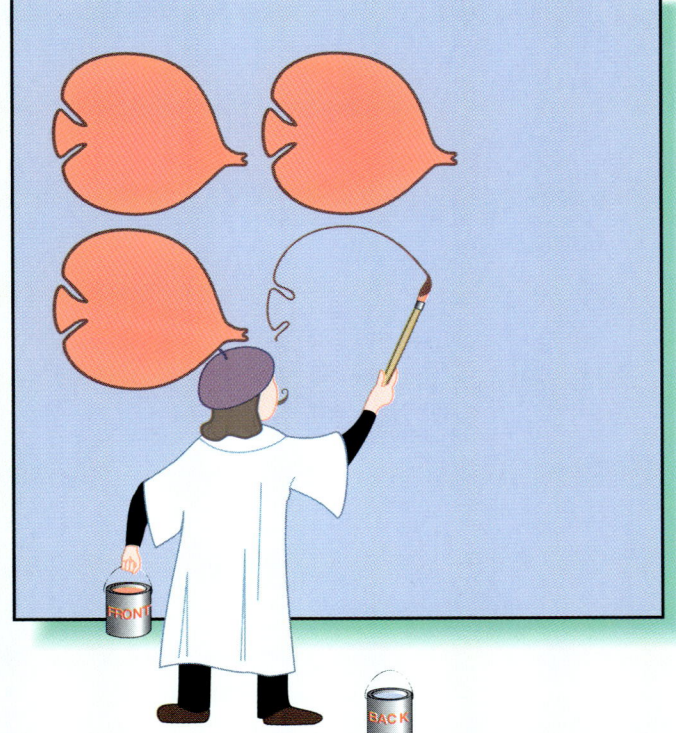

Click on these buttons to change the size of the pattern.

❸ If you want to shrink the pattern you selected, click on the Small option button in the Two-Color Pattern dialog box. If you want to enlarge the pattern, click on the Large option button. You can make additional changes to the fill pattern by clicking on the Tiling button. For example, you can click on Tiling and then enter values under Width and Height to change the size of the image or pattern that's being repeated.

❹ Very often you'll want to choose different colors for the pattern you've selected. To do this, click on the Back button under Colors to display a group of possible background colors for the pattern. Click on the desired color to select it. Click on the Front button to display the same set of colors; this time click on the color that you want to use as the foreground color—that is, the color for the pattern or image itself. In either case, you may need to scroll to find the color you seek.

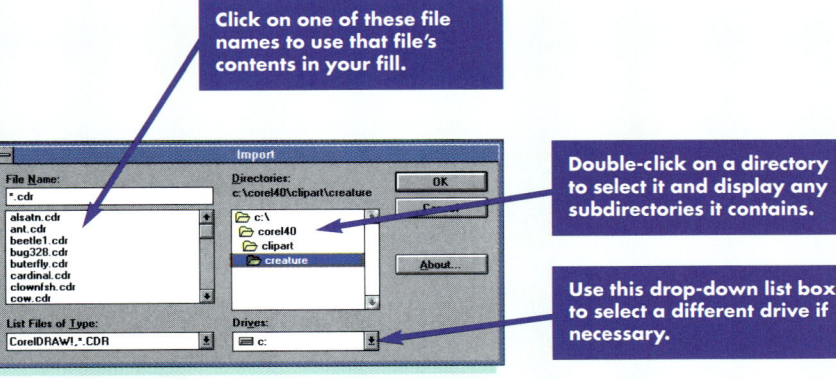

Click on one of these file names to use that file's contents in your fill.

Double-click on a directory to select it and display any subdirectories it contains.

Use this drop-down list box to select a different drive if necessary.

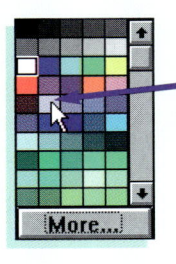

Click on a color to use it for either a foreground or background color.

❺ You are by no means limited to the fills that CorelDRAW! initially displays when you click on the preview box in the Two-Color Pattern dialog box. You can also create two-color pattern fills of your own. One reasonably easy way to do this is to click on the Import button in the Two-Color Pattern dialog box. You'll see the Import dialog box shown here; this dialog box is much like the dialog box you've already seen for opening files (see Chapter 6).

# CHAPTER 10: COLORING AND FILLING SHAPES

# How to Apply Full-Color Pattern Fills

When creating pattern fills in the preceding section, you were limited to just two colors. CorelDRAW! also enables you to create full-color pattern fills. The process is very similar to creating two-color pattern fills; virtually the only difference is that you work with multi-colored images. In addition, when creating full-color pattern fills, you don't have the option of easily regulating the foreground and background colors of the patterns you're using.

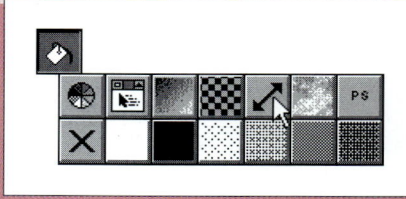

 **1** Once again select the shape or shapes you want to fill, click on the Fill tool in the toolbox, and then click on the full-color fill button in the Fill flyout menu.

### TIP SHEET

▶ When you create a new full-color pattern fill using the Import dialog box, Corel-DRAW! does not automatically add that pattern to the list of patterns that appears when you click on the preview button in the Full-Color Pattern dialog box. If you want to add patterns to that list after having imported them, just click on the pattern preview box and then choose Save Current Fill from the File menu at the top of the list of patterns. From now on, the designated pattern will be available through the Full-Color Pattern dialog box. It's a good idea to save patterns that you'll use repeatedly in your work.

▶ If you decide to delete one of these patterns that you've saved, just display the list of patterns by clicking on the pattern preview box, select the pattern from the list by clicking on it, and then choose Delete Item from the File menu at the top of the list.

**6** Once you've selected or created a fill pattern and made any necessary modifications to it, click on OK to apply it to the selected objects. As an example, here is a fill pattern made up of the LOBSTER4.CDR file in the COREL40\CLIPART\CREATURE directory.

How to Apply Full-Color Pattern Fills 87

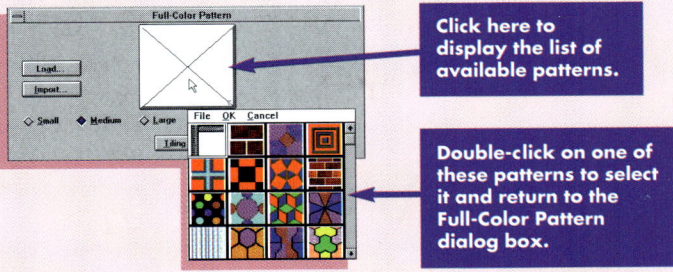

Click here to display the list of available patterns.

Double-click on one of these patterns to select it and return to the Full-Color Pattern dialog box.

**2** In the Full-Color Pattern dialog box that appears, click on the large pattern preview box to the right of the Load and Import buttons to display the patterns that CorelDRAW! furnishes. If necessary, scroll to find the pattern you want. Once you've found the desired pattern, double-click on it to select it. The preview box will change to reflect your choice.

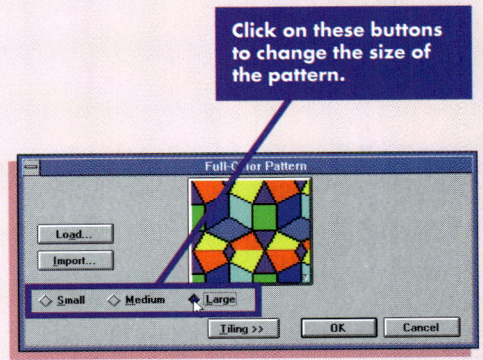

Click on these buttons to change the size of the pattern.

**3** If you want to shrink the selected pattern, click on the Small option button in the Full-Color Pattern dialog box. To enlarge the pattern, click on the Large option button. You can also click on the Tiling button to make additional changes to your fill—for example, to change the width and height of the image being used.

The image you imported shows up in the preview box.

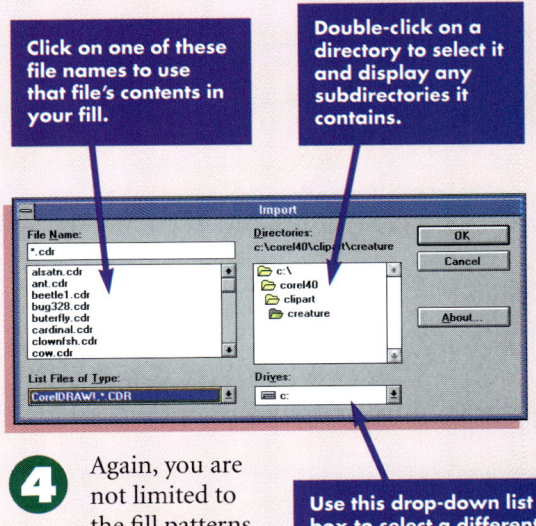

Click on one of these file names to use that file's contents in your fill.

Double-click on a directory to select it and display any subdirectories it contains.

**4** Again, you are not limited to the fill patterns that Corel-DRAW! displays when you click on the preview box in the Full-Color Pattern dialog box. One fairly easy way to create a new pattern is to click on the Import button.

Use this drop-down list box to select a different drive if necessary.

**5** From within the Import dialog box, choose the drive and directory that contain a graphic you want to use in your fill pattern. If you don't have images of your own, experiment with the graphics supplied in the various subdirectories of the COREL40\CLIPART directory. (Remember, double-click on a directory to select it and display any subdirectories it contains.) Under File Name, click on the file you want to use and then click on OK. You'll be returned to the Full-Color Pattern dialog box, which will now include a preview of your new fill pattern. If necessary, change the fill's size as described earlier.

# TRY IT!

The preceding five chapters have gone a long way toward making you self-sufficient in CorelDRAW! You learned such survival skills as how to save and open files, clear the screen, and print files. You also learned how to get various perspectives on your drawings by using CorelDRAW!'s zooming tools. Finally, you found out several ways of manipulating text and drawings—moving and copying them, for example—and discovered how to apply colors and various types of fills.

Again it's time to test out some of your new skills. Follow these instructions to construct the poster design shown here. At every step, chapter numbers indicate where the subject came up initially, so you can turn back if you need to jog your memory. Also, don't be too concerned if your results don't exactly match the ones shown here. You or someone else may have changed some of your defaults, things may look different on your monitor, or you may simply decide to go with slightly different color or font selections.

If necessary, turn on your computer, get into Windows, and open CorelDRAW! by double-clicking on its icon in the Program Manager (Chapter 2). If you're already in CorelDRAW!, you may need to clear your screen by choosing New from the File menu or by pressing Ctrl+N. If you've modified the current drawing, either save (choose Yes) or discard (choose No) the changes you've made (Chapter 6).

Choose Page Setup from the Layout menu (Chapter 9).

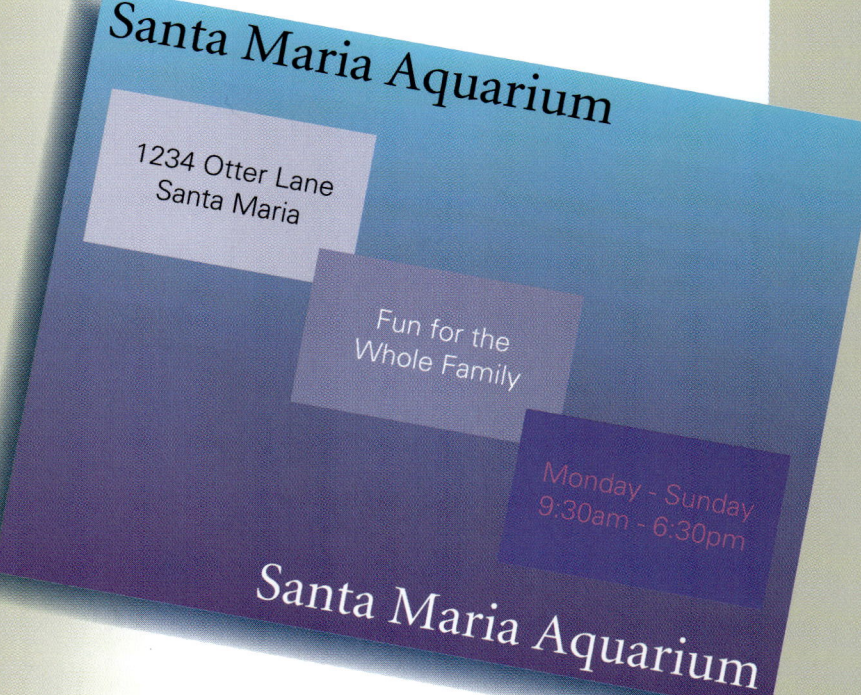

# TRY IT! 89

In the Page Setup dialog box, click on Landscape and then click on OK to change the printable page to a horizontal orientation (Chapter 9).

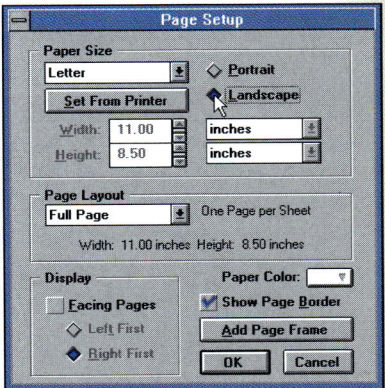

Click on the Rectangle tool and draw a rectangle that's the same size as the printable page. The nodes at each corner of the rectangle indicate that the rectangle is selected (Chapter 4).

Click on the Fill tool in the toolbox, and then click on the fountain fill button in the Fill flyout menu (Chapter 10).

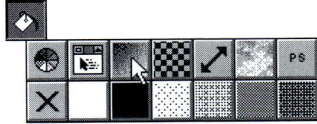

Under Colors, click on the From button to display a list of colors and choose a shade of purple from the list. Then click on the To button to display the same list of colors and pick a light shade of blue. The fountain fill you've just devised will show up on the right-hand side of the dialog box (Chapter 10).

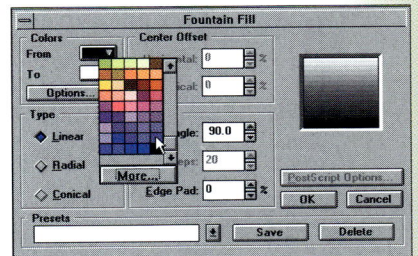

Click on OK to apply this fountain fill to the rectangle you drew a moment ago. It will look something like this, depending upon the colors that you chose (Chapter 10).

Click on the Text tool to select it. If the tool does not resemble the letter A, position the mouse pointer over the Text tool, press *and hold down* the mouse button, and select the leftmost tool from the Text flyout menu (Chapter 5).

Click in the upper-left corner of the printable page and then type **Santa Maria Aquarium**. Choose Edit Text from the Text menu (Chapter 5).

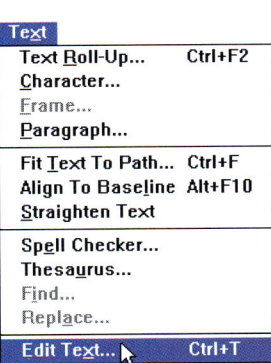

Select a point size of 60, and choose Times New Roman under Fonts. Click on OK to put these changes into place (Chapter 5).

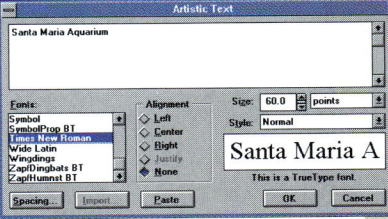

Continue to next page ▶

# 90 TRY IT!

**TRY IT!**

Continue below

**11**

The text "Santa Maria Aquarium" should be in the upper-left corner of the page. If you need to move it to place it just where you want it, click on the Pick tool, double-check that the text is selected, place the mouse pointer over the text, and then drag with your mouse. You'll see a dashed rectangle and a mouse pointer shaped like a four-headed arrow. When the dashed rectangle is in the desired spot, release the mouse button (Chapter 7).

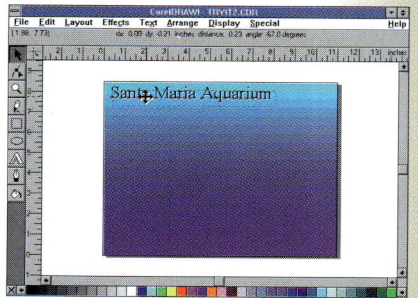

**12**

With the text still selected, choose Duplicate from the Edit menu. Notice that the duplicate copy will be selected automatically (Chapter 7).

**13**

Drag the duplicate text to the lower-right corner of the page. The text doesn't show up that well against the fountain fill, which is darker at the bottom of the page.

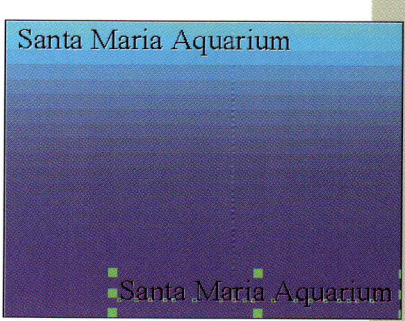

**14**

With the text still selected, click on the white square in the color palette at the bottom of the screen. The white text will stands out nicely against the purple background (Chapter 10).

**15**

Draw a rectangle of about 4 inches across and 2 inches high and position it underneath "Santa Maria" at the top of the page. Then click on a light shade of purple in the color palette to fill in this rectangle (Chapter 10).

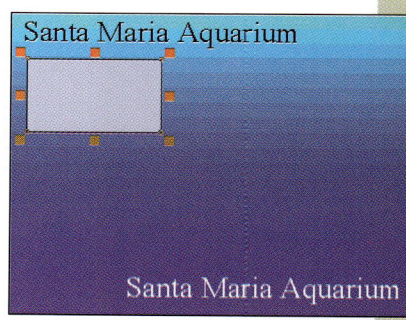

**16**

With the rectangle still selected, choose Duplicate from the Edit menu (Chapter 7). (Remember, the nodes at each corner indicate that the rectangle is selected.)

**17**

Choose Repeat Duplicate from the Edit menu to generate a third rectangle of the same size (Chapter 7).

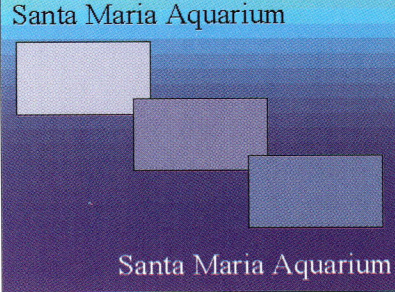

**18**

Move the top rectangle to the lower-right corner of the page, and move the second rectangle to the middle of the page (Chapter 7). Select the middle rectangle and choose a slightly darker shade of purple for it from the color palette. Select the third rectangle and assign it a bluish-purple color (Chapter 10).

**19**

Select the Artistic Text tool, click in the first rectangle, type **1234 Otter Lane**, press Enter, and type **Santa Maria**. In the second rectangle, enter **Fun for the**, press Enter, and enter **Whole Family**. In the third rectangle, type **Monday - Sunday**, press Enter, and type **9:30am - 6:30pm** (Chapter 5).

**20**

You can use the Artistic Text dialog box to edit your text. The text shown here is centered, 30-point Arial (Chapter 5). You may also have to move the text blocks to get them just where you want them within the colored rectangles (Chapter 7). Finally, select the second text block and click on the white square in the color palette; next select the third text block and click on a light blue square in the color palette (Chapter 10).

**21**

When you've got your design the way you want it, you should save it so you can use it in the future. Choose Save from the File menu (Chapter 6).

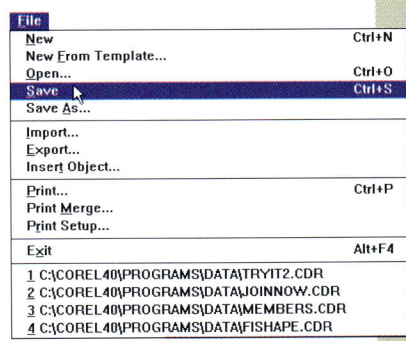

**22**

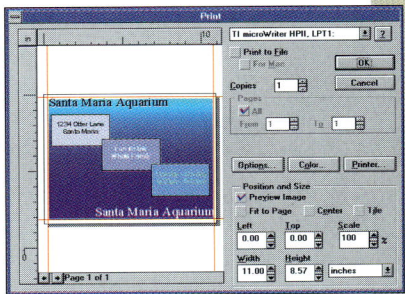

Lastly, make sure your printer is on and choose Print from the File menu. Check that the correct printer and the right number of copies are selected, and click on OK to print your drawing (Chapter 8).

# CHAPTER 11

# Reshaping Objects

Particularly when you're drawing with the Pencil tool, you'll typically need to remodel and fine-tune objects after you've sketched them initially. You've already learned an assortment of techniques for modifying existing drawings—including how to select, move, and copy them, among other things. This chapter explains several additional strategies for refining and perfecting objects that you've drawn. Far from being fancy gadgets for advanced users only, the techniques covered here are essential tools that will enable you to achieve just the design results you want. Remember, reworking and reshaping objects is an integral part of the drawing process.

When reshaping objects, you can naturally change them in varying degrees. There are a number of ways of "transforming" objects—CorelDRAW!'s term for altering an object without changing its essential shape. For example, if you enlarge a square or stretch it to make it into a rectangle, it has been transformed, but is still a four-sided object. You can transform objects by stretching them, scaling them, and creating mirror images of them. You can also transform objects by rotating and skewing them. If you decide to make more substantive changes to an object, CorelDRAW!'s Shape tool lets you manipulate the nodes of an existing drawing to alter its shape in any way at all. The Shape tool is one of CorelDRAW!'s most powerful; it furnishes you with the means to transfigure objects completely as well as to make the most subtle changes to them.

# How to Stretch, Scale, and Mirror Objects

*Stretching* an object means modifying its size in a single direction. This changes the object's proportions (its width-to-height ratio). For example, if you stretch a circle, it becomes an ellipse. If you want to alter the size of an object without changing its proportions, you can *scale* that object, changing its size in two directions at once. If you scale a circle it becomes a larger or a smaller circle, but isn't transformed into an ellipse. Finally, *mirroring* means creating a reflection of an object. This does not create a duplicate copy of a shape that mirrors the original, but instead changes the selected object into a mirror image of its former self.

### TIP SHEET

- **Clear Transformations, which reverses all transformations at once, is often superior to the Undo command, which only undoes one change at a time, and may not be able to undo all changes to an object. But if you leave the original unchanged while transforming a copy of an object, you cannot reverse the operation—get rid of the transformed duplicate copy—by using Clear Transformations. Instead you need to use either Undo or Delete.**
- **Hold down Ctrl while dragging to stretch or scale objects in increments of 100%. Hold down Shift key dragging to stretch or scale objects from the center outwards. Hold down Ctrl+Shift while dragging to do both of these things at once.**
- **When you stretch or scale an object, the status line displays the amount of the change as a percentage, making it easy to change an object to twice (200%) or half (50%) of its original size. When you mirror an object, the change shows up as a negative percentage.**
- **You can stretch and scale artistic text but not paragraph text.**

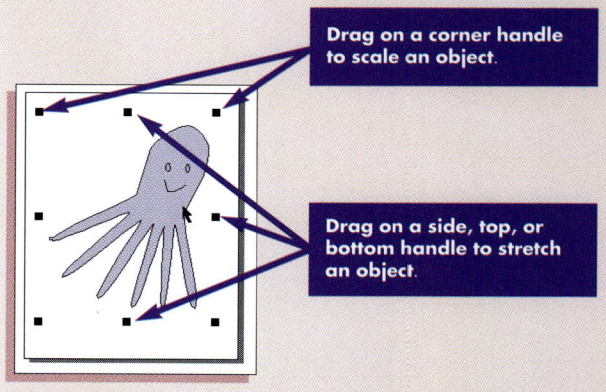

 As when moving or copying objects, you need to select a shape before stretching, scaling, or mirroring it.

**6** If you make several changes to an object and then decide to discard them all, you can restore the object to its original form by making sure the object is selected and then choosing Clear Transformations from the Effects menu. This undoes any changes you may have made by stretching, scaling, or mirroring the object. However, it may not put the object back in its original location; if necessary, move the object yourself using the methods from Chapter 7. In addition, if you left the original object intact while transforming a copy of it (as discussed in step 5) Clear Transformations returns the selected object to its original form, without affecting any other copies of the object floating around on the screen.

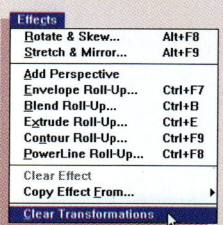

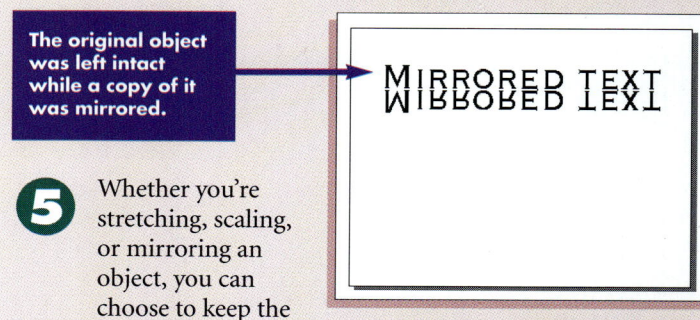

**5** Whether you're stretching, scaling, or mirroring an object, you can choose to keep the original unchanged. When you do this, you'll wind up with two copies of the object: one in its original form and one in its modified form. This technique is particularly effective with text, as illustrated here, but is by no means confined to that. To leave the original intact while transforming a copy of it, drag as usual but, at any time while the dashed rectangle is visible, either click once on the right mouse button or press and then release the plus sign on the numeric keypad.

HOW TO STRETCH, SCALE, AND MIRROR OBJECTS **95**

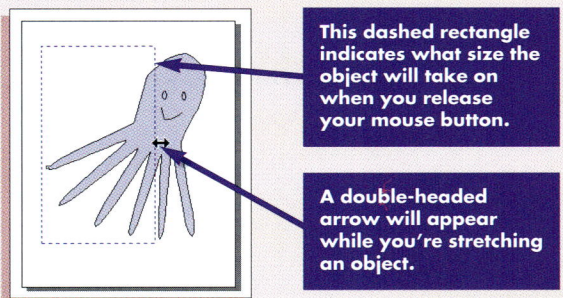

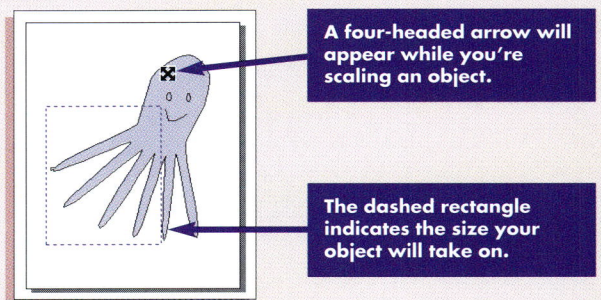

**②** To stretch an object, place the mouse pointer over one of its four side handles (avoid the corner handles). Then drag inward toward the shape to decrease its size, or drag away from the shape to increase its size. As you drag, the mouse pointer changes into a double-headed arrow. (The arrows indicate the two directions in which you can change the size of the selected shape.) A dashed rectangle indicates the size your shape will take on when you release the mouse button. Release the mouse button to finish stretching the object.

**③** To scale an object—that is, change its size but not its shape—again make sure it's selected, but this time position the mouse pointer over one of the corner handles. Then drag inward to reduce the size of the shape or drag outward to enlarge the shape. As you drag, the mouse pointer changes into a four-headed arrow. As before, you'll see a dashed rectangle that indicates the new size your shape will take on if you release the mouse button. To finish the process, go ahead and release the mouse button.

**④** Mirroring an object is slightly less intuitive than stretching or scaling, but not by much. To mirror an object, select it, and then hold down the Ctrl key as you drag *in toward* the object on one of the side handles. As you drag, the mouse pointer will change into the same double-headed arrow you see when stretching objects (mirroring is essentially reverse stretching). Once you've dragged *all the way across* the object in question, a dashed rectangle indicates where the mirror image will appear. Now you can release the mouse button to see a mirror image of the selected shape. (Make sure to release the mouse button before you release the Ctrl key if you want the mirrored object to be the same size as the original.) Note that you can mirror both shapes and text.

# How to Rotate and Skew Objects

Another way of transforming objects is to rotate or skew them. *Rotating* is pretty straightforward: It's a matter of spinning an object clockwise or counterclockwise at an angle that you settle upon. *Skewing* an object is like slanting it, again at an angle that you specify. If you rotate a square, it remains a square, even though its sides may no longer be exactly vertical or horizontal. If you skew a square, in contrast, its sides no longer meet at right angles—in other words, it's no longer a square.

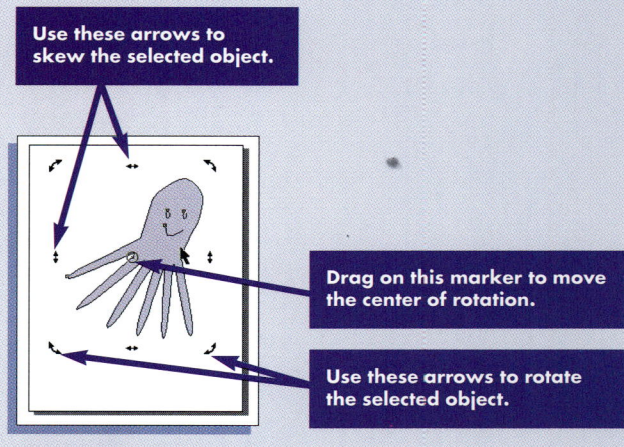

**1** Not surprisingly, before you can rotate or skew an object you need to select it. In this lone case, however, you need to select the object in a special fashion, and you have to work with a different set of handles, as shown here. To display these handles, double-click on the object you want to select. (If an object is selected already, you can click on it just once to select it in this manner.) The rounded arrows on the corners enable you to rotate the object; the straight arrows on each side permit you to skew the object.

## TIP SHEET

- After rotating or skewing an object, you can use the Clear Transformations command on the Effects menu to return the object to its original form. (Remember, this command also reverses stretching, scaling, and mirroring.) If you want to reverse one or more of the most recent changes, rather than all of them, instead use the Undo command on the Edit menu.

- If you hold down the Ctrl key while dragging the center of rotation marker, CorelDRAW! only lets you move that marker to one of the eight handles or to the center of the object.

- When you're rotating or skewing an object, the status line displays the amount of the change as an angle. This makes it easier for you to rotate a shape by 90 or 180 degrees, as an example.

- You can rotate but not skew paragraph text. You can both rotate and skew artistic text.

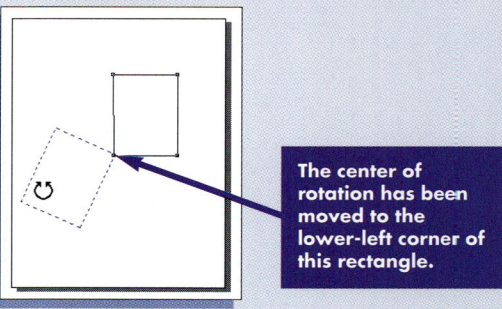

**6** You've probably noticed the circular marker in the center of shapes that you select to rotate or skew. This marker allows you to change the selected object's *center of rotation*. Normally, when you rotate a shape, it moves around a fixed point located at the center of the object. If you want to pick a different point around which to rotate the object, first change its center of rotation by dragging the circular marker to the desired spot. Then rotate the object as usual, noting that it now revolves around the newly defined center point. Here the center of rotation has been moved to the lower-left corner of the rectangle. Notice how the dashed rectangle is rotating around that point.

## HOW TO ROTATE AND SKEW OBJECTS    97

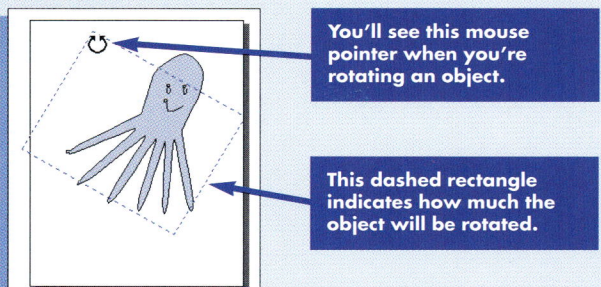

You'll see this mouse pointer when you're rotating an object.

This dashed rectangle indicates how much the object will be rotated.

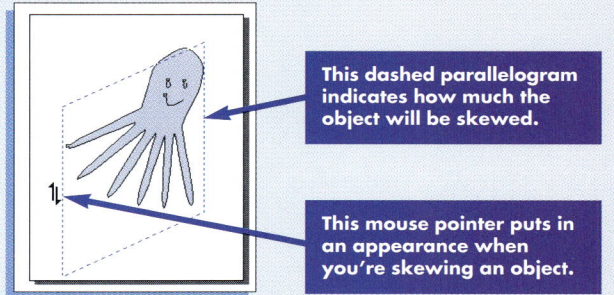

This dashed parallelogram indicates how much the object will be skewed.

This mouse pointer puts in an appearance when you're skewing an object.

**2** To rotate an object, first make sure you see the special selection handles. Then place your mouse pointer over one of the corner (rounded) handles and drag in the direction in which you wish to rotate the object. As you'd expect, a dashed rectangle indicates where the object will be positioned when you release the mouse button. Also note that, as you drag, the mouse pointer takes on the shape of a curved double-headed arrow (it's almost a full circle) that suggests the rotation process. Release the mouse button when you've got the object where you want it.

**3** If you want to skew an object, again verify that you see the special selection handles for rotating and skewing. Position the mouse pointer over a side (straight) handle and drag in one of the directions indicated by the arrow. You'll see a dashed parallelogram indicating the approximate shape the selected object will assume when you release the mouse button. You'll also see the mouse pointer for skewing, which reminds you that you can drag in one of two directions. Release the mouse button when the object has the desired slant.

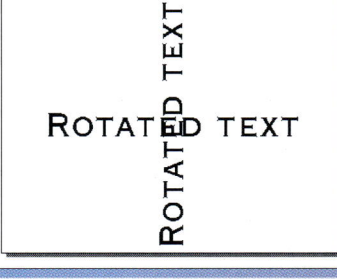

**4** When rotating and skewing objects—as when stretching, scaling, and mirroring—you can leave the original object intact and just modify a copy of it. To do this, drag as usual and either click the right mouse button or press and then release the plus key on the numeric keypad while the dashed rectangle (or parallelogram) is still displayed. As shown here, you'll end up with two copies of the object, one modified and one unchanged.

**5** You can rotate or skew an object in 15-degree increments simply by holding down the Ctrl key as you drag. In addition, you can change this angle by choosing Preferences from the Special menu and then changing the setting under Constrain Angle.

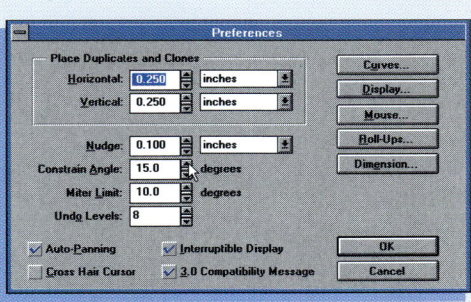

# How to Use the Shaping Tool

**W**hen you stretch, scale, mirror, rotate, or skew objects, you modify them without altering their basic shape. To exercise more complete control over the shape of an object, you should use the Shape tool. This powerful implement lets you reshape objects completely by moving their curves, repositioning the nodes that demarcate the beginning and end points of line or curve segments, and manipulating the control points that regulate the curves associated with particular nodes. Because it is so powerful, the Shape tool is not all that easy to master. Try not to get flustered if at first your curves are not cooperating and your lines become unruly. For additional information or exercises to hone your skills, consult your CorelDRAW! manual or a more advanced book on CorelDRAW!

### TIP SHEET

- ▸ If you alter an object with the Shape tool, you cannot undo your changes with the Clear Transformations command on the Effects menu. You must instead rely upon the Undo command. And remember, you may not be able to reverse all of your changes with this command.
- ▸ You can "nudge" nodes—move them in small increments—by selecting them and then pressing the arrow key that indicates the direction in which you want to move the node.
- ▸ You can get rid of nodes, add nodes, change the type of a node, join nodes together, and much more. For the facts on these important CorelDRAW! features, consult your documentation or a more advanced book on the subject.

**1** To reshape objects you must first choose the Shape tool by clicking on it or pressing F10.

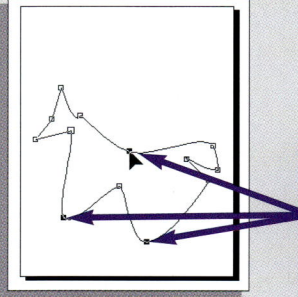

*If several nodes are selected, dragging on any one of them moves the others correspondingly*

**6** You can alter several nodes at once by first selecting them and then dragging on any one of them. (The nodes that you select needn't be adjacent.) To select multiple nodes, you can either drag to draw a marquee around them, or you can select one node by clicking on it and select additional nodes by holding down the Shift key while clicking on them. When you move one of them, all the selected nodes move accordingly. You can deselect all of them by clicking on a blank area of the screen (this does not deselect the currently selected object).

HOW TO USE THE SHAPING TOOL  **99**

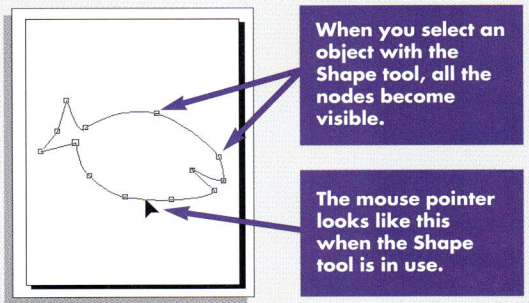

**When you select an object with the Shape tool, all the nodes become visible.**

**The mouse pointer looks like this when the Shape tool is in use.**

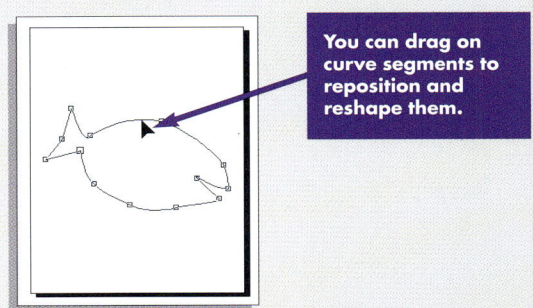

**You can drag on curve segments to reposition and reshape them.**

**2** Before you can manipulate an object with the Shape tool, you have to select the object by clicking on it. (If a single object was selected when you clicked on the Shape tool, that object will remain selected.) Notice that, in this case, you won't see the standard highlighting box composed of square black handles. Instead, all of the object's nodes become visible; they look like small hollow boxes around the perimeter of the shape. Also note that the mouse pointer changes into a heavy arrowhead.

**3** Once an object is selected, you can begin to reshape it with the Shape tool. If you like, you can drag on a curve segment itself to reposition and reshape that segment. (You cannot alter straight line segments in this way.) In certain cases, doing so may also affect the adjacent curves.

**4** Another way of modifying your shape is by moving its nodes. To move a node, just drag on it; in this case, the line or curve segments on either side of the node will also be affected. If the node you're dragging on is associated with a curve rather than a line segment, you'll see the node's control points.

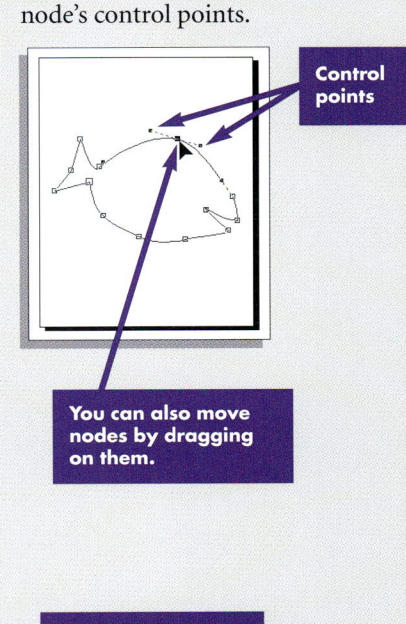

**Control points**

**You can also move nodes by dragging on them.**

**5** To make the most incremental changes to a shape, it works best to manipulate the control points associated with the shape's nodes. (You can also change curves quite radically by moving their control points.) When you click or drag on a node affiliated with a curve, it becomes selected (it changes into a solid black square) and its control points appear. As you may remember from Chapter 4, you can modify the slope and height of the curve by dragging on these control points.

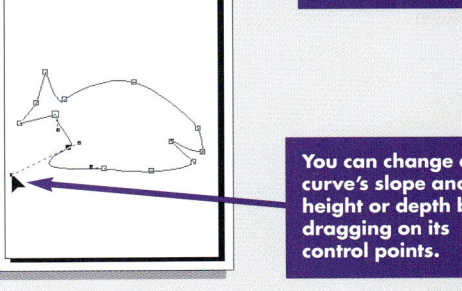

**You can change a curve's slope and height or depth by dragging on its control points.**

# CHAPTER 12

# Rearranging Objects

So far you've acquired a fairly respectable set of skills for altering objects: You can move and copy them; stretch, scale, and mirror them; rotate and skew them; and reshape them to your heart's content with the Shape tool. This chapter delves into some alternative ways to modify existing objects; you discover how to rearrange them in a variety of ways.

The first thing you learn is how to change the order in which objects overlap. Ordinarily, if you draw a small square and then draw a larger square directly on top of it, the smaller square will be concealed. (Of course, this only holds true if the squares are filled or colored.) However, if you switch the order in which those two squares overlap, the smaller one will reappear on top of the larger one. You'll also learn how to align objects—either changing their position relative to one another, or changing their position relative to the center of the page. As you'll find, this is significantly easier than trying to position objects by eye. Lastly, you learn several ways of linking multiple objects together so Corel-DRAW! treats them as a single object. This enables you to draw a complex design made up of any number of shapes, and then group those shapes together and operate on them as though they were just one item. Among other things, you'll be able to center the complete image, apply a color to the whole thing, or move the design all in one piece.

# Changing How Objects Overlap

When you produced the three identical rectangles in the preceding Try It! section, you may have noticed that they overlapped in a particular fashion. Specifically, the second rectangle was positioned on top of the first one, and the third one was on top of the second. This is often referred to as the "stacking order" of objects, and it simply means that the last object you drew will always be on top if it overlaps with any other objects; similarly, the first object you drew will always be on the bottom, and so forth. Fortunately, it's easy to change the order in which objects overlap, so you don't have to make a big production out of drawing objects in the correct stacking order right from the start.

### TIP SHEET

- **You can select several items and change their order in the stack. (Remember, you can select multiple objects by holding down the Shift key while you click on them.) This does not change their order relative to each other, but does change their order in relation to the other objects you've drawn. For example, if you select the top two items in your stack of objects and choose To Back, those two items move to the bottom of the stack, but the one that was on top initially remains on top of the other object that had been selected.**

- **If you select several objects, you can use the Reverse Order option in the Order submenu to change the stacking order of all selected objects. If you select four objects and then choose Reverse Order, the first becomes the fourth, the second becomes the third, the third becomes the second, and the fourth becomes the first.**

- **Objects that are not filled do have a stacking order, it's just next to impossible to see what it is because the objects are essentially see-through.**

 To see how a series of shapes will stack up, you first need to draw and then color or fill several objects. (If the objects are not filled, it's next to impossible to see which one's on top.) The example shown here includes two squares and two circles. They were drawn starting in the upper-left corner of the screen and progressing down to the lower-right corner, and they were filled with colors selected from the color palette. As you can see, the items drawn later are stacked on top of the items that were drawn earlier.

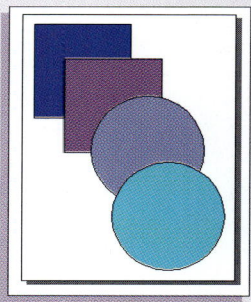

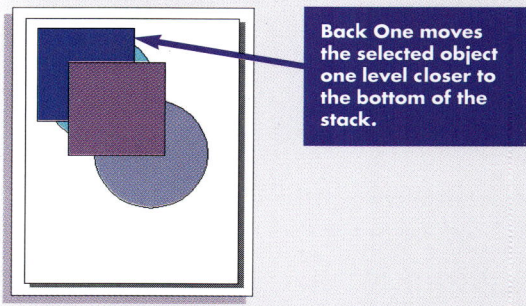

Back One moves the selected object one level closer to the bottom of the stack.

**8** As you can probably guess, you choose Back One (shortcut Ctrl+PgDn) to move the selected object down one level in the stacking order. For example, here the square that was on top was bumped down one level. Notice how it's now behind the other square, but is still on top of the two circles in the drawing.

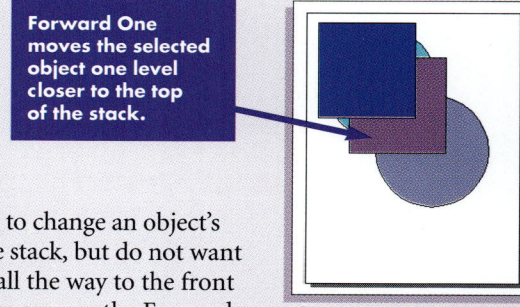

Forward One moves the selected object one level closer to the top of the stack.

**7** If you want to change an object's order in the stack, but do not want to move it all the way to the front or back, you can use the Forward One or Back One option. Choose Forward One (keyboard shortcut Ctrl+PgUp) to move the selected object up one level in the stacking order. In the illustration shown here, the second square was selected and bumped up one level. Notice that it now sits above the purple circle, but is still underneath the other square. If you left the same square selected and chose Forward One one more time, the pink square would move to the top of this particular stack of objects.

CHANGING HOW OBJECTS OVERLAP **103**

**2** The order in which shapes overlap holds true no matter where you move an object after you've drawn it initially. For example, here the circle in the lower-right corner (the one drawn last) has been moved to the upper-left corner, and it now partially covers the other shapes. This is because a shape that was drawn last will be positioned on top of any other shapes unless you explicitly instruct CorelDRAW! to change its order in the "stack."

By default, objects that were drawn last are stacked on top of objects that were drawn earlier.

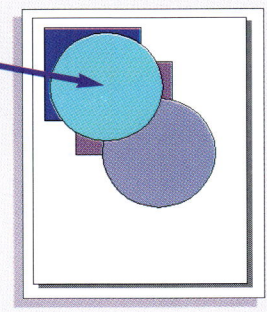

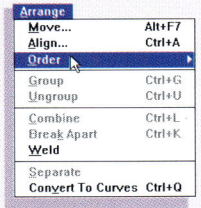

**3** Luckily for us all, CorelDRAW! makes it exceedingly easy to change the order in which shapes overlap. For starters, you select the object whose position in the stack of objects you want to change, and then you choose Order from the Arrange menu.

**4** This brings up the submenu shown here, which enables you to make five different choices for changing the stacking order of the selected object or objects. These options are described next.

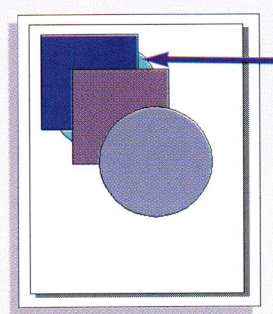

To Back moves the selected object all the way to the back of the stack.

To Front moves the selected object all the way to the front of the stack.

**6** Choose the To Front option (shortcut Shift+PgUp) to move the selected object to the very front of the stack of objects. If you selected the square in the upper-left corner and chose To Front, for example, your drawing would now look like this. Notice that the selected square overlaps all other objects in the drawing.

**5** Choose the To Back option (keyboard shortcut Shift+PgDn) to move the selected object to the very back of the stack of objects. For instance, if you selected the circle that was drawn last and chose To Back, your drawing would look like this. Note that circle is now behind all the other shapes, even though they were drawn before it was.

# 104 CHAPTER 12: REARRANGING OBJECTS

# How to Align Objects

Chapters 4 and 7 introduced a few tactics for placing objects where you want them on the page. You discovered that turning on the Snap To Grid feature can make it easier to draw objects that line up at a certain spot, and you learned how to use nonprinting guidelines as visual aids for aligning objects. In many cases, it will be sufficient for your purposes to use these techniques, or to align objects by eye just by dragging them where you want them. However, when you become a more practiced user, you'll want to be able to align objects more exactly. Not surprisingly, CorelDRAW! makes it very easy to align objects with each other, and to align objects relative to the center of the page.

### TIP SHEET

- If you like, you can choose the Align to Grid check box in the Align dialog box (one of the Horizontally or Vertically options must be selected for this option to become available). This aligns all of the selected objects to the nearest grid lines, as described by the Horizontally and Vertically settings. In many cases, the alignment may be scarcely perceptible. In addition, note that this aligns objects individually, instead of aligning them in relation to one another.

- If your drawing contains many objects, you can align just selected ones; in fact, you can align as many or as few of them as you like. (If you're aligning objects to each other, however, you must select at least two objects for your actions to have a visible effect.)

**1** Select the objects that you want to align and choose Align from the Arrange menu or press Ctrl+A. (Remember, to select multiple objects, select the first one by clicking on it, and then select additional objects by holding down the Shift key while clicking on them. You can also draw a marquee around multiple objects to select them.) Normally when operating on multiple objects, you can select them in any order. Alignment is an exception, however. When you select objects that you want to align to each other, the object you select last does not move; all other selected objects are rearranged relative to that object. If you select objects by drawing a marquee around them, the bottom object in the stacking order is treated as though it were the last selected object.

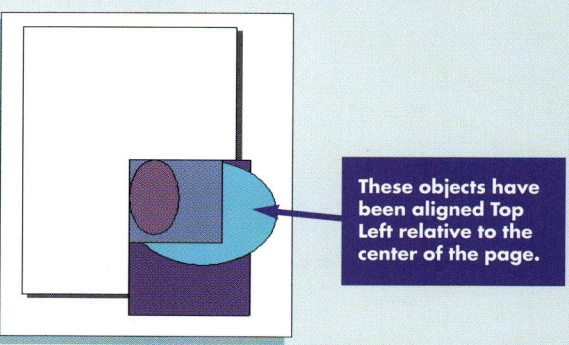

These objects have been aligned Top Left relative to the center of the page.

**7** When the Align to Center of Page check box is selected, you may not quite realize what type of alignment you'll get when selecting any option other than Center under Horizontally and Vertically. For example, if you choose the Top and Left options, you might think that the selected objects would move to the upper-left corner of the page. This is not true. Bear in mind that you are aligning objects relative to the *center* of the page. Here, for example, are the four shapes you've seen before. In this case, Align to Center of Page is selected, as are the two options Top and Left. As you can see, the top and left edges of each selected shape are positioned at the exact center of the page.

# How to Align Objects    105

**2** After you choose Align from the Arrange menu, CorelDRAW! displays the Align dialog box shown here. As you can see, there are numerous options for aligning objects. You can align objects vertically, horizontally, or both. In addition, you can align objects to the center of the page; you'll learn more about this in a moment.

*Select this check box to align objects relative to the center of the page.*

**3** 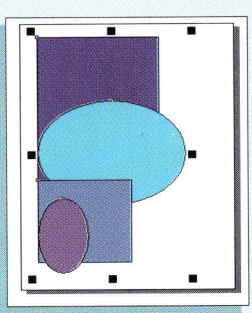 CorelDRAW! provides three options—Left, Center, and Right—for aligning objects horizontally. For example, here all four shapes have been selected and the Left option button under Horizontally has been selected in the Align dialog box. (Notice that the left edges of all the shapes now line up.) In this case, the objects were marquee selected, so the large rectangle in the upper-left corner (the bottom shape) is the object that remains stationary. If you had instead first selected the upper-left rectangle, and then selected the other shapes from top to bottom using the Shift+click method, all objects would have aligned to the lower-right ellipse (the last selected shape), which itself would have stayed put.

**4** 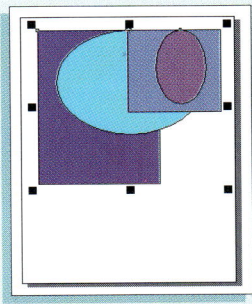 You can also align objects vertically by choosing from the options under Vertically in the Align dialog box. For example, here are the same four shapes aligned vertically at the top. (Their left alignment was reversed before they were aligned at the top.) Again notice that all of the objects aligned themselves with respect to the top of the large purple rectangle at the top of the page, since it's the bottom item in the stack of objects. (If you had not marquee selected the objects, and/or had selected them in a different order, they'd be in a different position on the page, even though their tops would still all line up.)

**6** In addition to aligning objects to each other, you can align them to the center of the page. To do this, you simply select the objects to be aligned, select the Align to Center of Page check box in the Align dialog box, and then choose the desired option buttons under Horizontally and/or Vertically, as usual.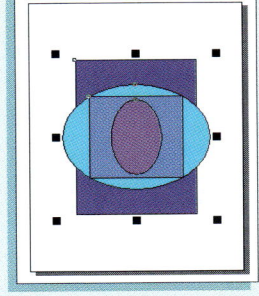
This time, however, the objects will be aligned, not to each other, but to the center of the page. As an example, here are the four shapes you've already seen, but this time they're centered around the center of the page—with the Center option button selected under both Vertically and Horizontally (when you click on Align to Center of Page initially, these two options are selected by default).

**5** A third option is to align selected objects both vertically and horizontally. For instance, in the figure pictured here, the four shapes have been aligned both to the top (vertically) and to the left (horizontally). Again, the alignment that you end up with depends on how and in which order you selected the objects being aligned.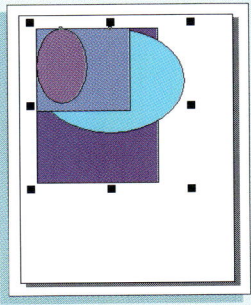
When aligning options both horizontally and vertically, you have even more options than usual, given that you can have any combination of horizontal and vertical settings (Top/Left, Center/Center, Bottom/Right, and so on). Take the time to experiment with some of these settings to get a feel for how they work and how they look.

**106** CHAPTER 12: REARRANGING OBJECTS

# How to Group Objects Together

So far, when manipulating objects in any way, you have for the most part worked with separate shapes individually. In a few cases, you've selected several shapes at once and operated on them simultaneously. Often, however, you'll want to treat a group of objects as a single item at all times. There are a few ways of telling CorelDRAW! to consider several objects as one. These techniques become especially useful when you begin creating more complicated designs made up of many component parts. Once you've told CorelDRAW! to look upon the separate parts as a single object, you'll be able to color the whole drawing in one operation, move all the elements together, resize everything proportionally, and much more.

### TIP SHEET

- As when aligning objects, you can choose to group, combine, or weld only selected objects within a batch of objects. Don't forget that you select the first object by clicking on it, and then select additional objects by holding down the Shift key while clicking on them.
- If you want to group together several items of different colors (and retain those colors), you need to use the Group command; you cannot use Combine or Weld.
- When you group, combine, or weld objects, they are aligned as a single unit rather than as component pieces.

 One way of telling CorelDRAW! to look upon several shapes as a single object is to group them together. To do this, select the objects in question and choose Group from the Arrange menu or press Ctrl+G. (Note that this option is only available if you've selected two or more objects.)

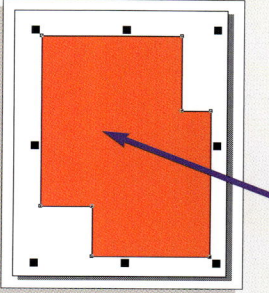

**The Weld command removes outlines where objects overlap; the welded objects only have a single outline around their perimeter.**

 A final command for combining objects is the Weld command on the Arrange menu. This command literally melds two or more shapes together into a single object with a single outline. For example, here are two rectangles that have been welded together. Notice that, where the two objects overlap, you no longer see the outlines distinguishing the two individual rectangles. Weld doesn't remove the fill from the overlapping portions of the objects, but welded objects can't include multiple colors. Although there is no command specifically for reversing the effects of the Weld command, you can undo the operation using the Undo command on the Edit menu, if you act quickly enough.

 If you change your mind after combining two or more objects, you can divide a combined object back into its component parts with the Break Apart command on the Arrange menu (shortcut Ctrl+K). The only catch is that, if the objects originally had different colors, those colors won't be restored. (If it's not too late, instead reverse the Combine operation with the Undo command on the Edit menu; this will reestablish all the combined objects' original colors.)

How to Group Objects Together  107

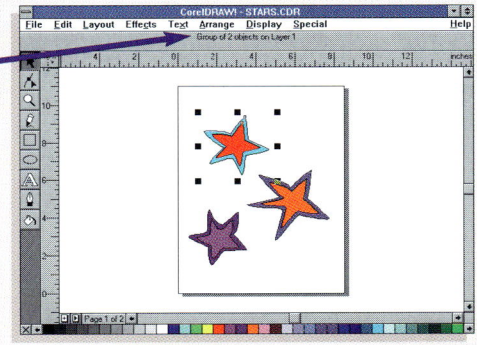

**The status line tells you that these objects have been grouped together.**

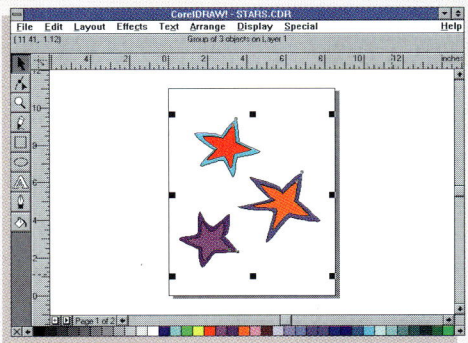

**2** Once you've grouped two or more objects, they'll generally be treated as a single object. If you select any one of the objects in the group, all of the objects will be enclosed within a single highlighting box; in addition, the status line will tell you that you've selected a group and will list how many objects it contains. For example, here each of the three sets of two overlapping stars has been grouped together—this way they'll stay in synch if moved, scaled, and so on. Note that the status line indicates that the highlighting box contains a group consisting of two objects.

**3** You can even group together objects that have already been grouped. To do this, simply select the grouped objects and again choose Group from the Arrange menu. Here, for example, each of the three stars (all of them are two stars grouped together) has been selected, and then the Group command has been issued. The status line tells you that this group consists of three objects. In other words, CorelDRAW! treats the already grouped objects as single objects.

**4** If you group objects and then change your mind, it's very easy to undo the damage. Simply select the group and then choose Ungroup from the Arrange menu or press Ctrl+U. (This option is only available if a group is selected.) The status line will indicate the number of objects selected instead of telling you that a group of objects is selected. If you've created groups within groups, you will need to ungroup each level of grouping separately. For example, in this case, you would first ungroup the group of three stars. Only then could you ungroup the individual stars that are actually made up of two stars.

**5** Grouped objects unfortunately cannot be reshaped with the Shape tool. Luckily CorelDRAW! provides another method of combining objects: the Combine command on the Arrange menu (shortcut Ctrl+L). When you combine objects with this command, you can still reshape them with the Shape tool. But the Combine command may not behave exactly as you'd expect. For example, here's a picture of two overlapping stars that have been combined. Notice that their color is the same (it wasn't originally) and that, in areas where the two shapes overlap, the fill has been removed. In some cases, you can use these features to your advantage—to produced hollowed out objects, for example. In other cases, however, you may decide to go with one of the other commands for joining objects together.

**The Combine command removes fills and colors where the combined objects overlap.**

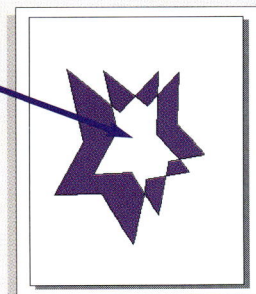

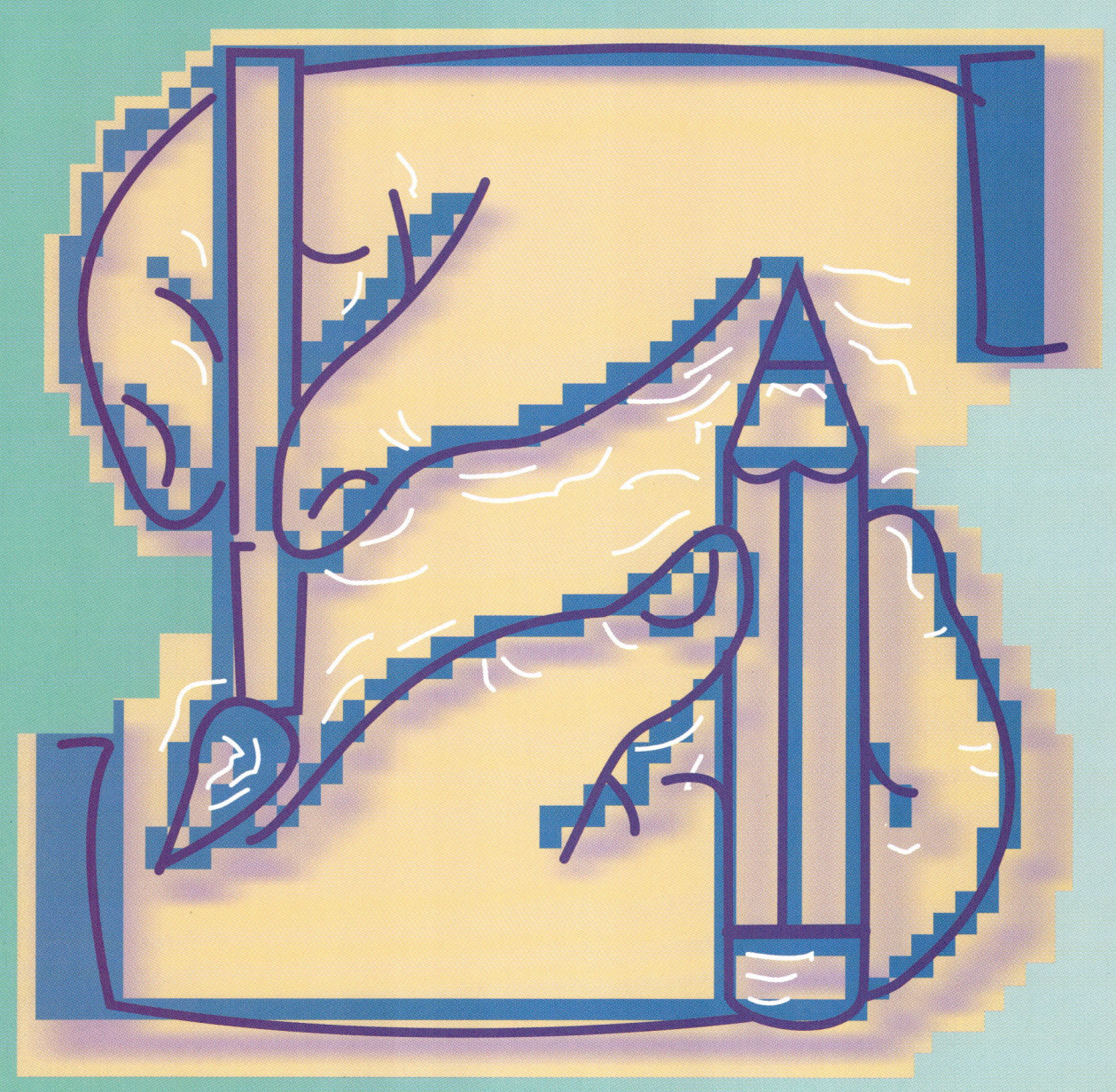

# CHAPTER 13

# Improving Your Text

You learned most of the basics about entering text in Chapter 5. However, there's a lot you still don't know about improving your text once you've entered it. With drawings, your first attempts are generally sketches that you'll want to improve upon. The same is true of text. Reworking and refining your text should be as much a part of the process as writing it in the first place.

Although it emphasizes graphics rather than text, CorelDRAW! has a remarkably wide range of text-handling capabilities, some of which you'll learn about here. First you'll discover some ways of editing your text—adding to it, deleting small and large blocks of it, moving it, and copying it. In addition, CorelDRAW! provides several implements for perfecting your writing, most notably the spell checker and thesaurus. CorelDRAW! also enables you to improve the formatting of your paragraph text by hyphenating it, altering tabs, and changing indents. You can even introduce bullet characters in front of individual paragraphs to generate bulleted lists—a perfect device for imposing some semblance of order on your text. Lastly, you'll learn how to fit text to a path. This simple but exciting technique lets you wrap text around shapes that you've drawn.

Take the time to become acquainted with the features covered in this chapter. They'll enable you to produce high-quality copy that not only looks but also sounds right.

# How to Edit Text

In Chapter 5 you learned quite a bit about entering text, but the chapter presented only the most rudimentary techniques for editing text: the Delete and Backspace keys. These tools are perfectly adequate for making minor changes—correcting typos and that sort of thing. But they begin to seem clumsy and inadequate if you want to make more extensive modifications to your text. This section presents a few tools that greatly simplify the tasks of adding text and deleting text, and even make it possible for you to copy text or move text to a new location. In most cases, you can either edit your text directly on the screen, or you can use the Artistic Text or Paragraph Text dialog boxes that were featured prominently in Chapter 5. If you're editing on screen, make sure the Text tool is selected before you begin.

### TIP SHEET

- In certain cases, your text may seem too small to edit on screen. If you prefer on-screen editing, however, there's an easy solution: Use the zoom tools you learned about in Chapter 9 to enlarge your text, and then edit it using the techniques described on these two pages.

- When adding and/or deleting artistic text, don't forget that there is no word wrap. For this reason, you may end up with lines that are either too short or too long; you'll have to adjust the length of these lines manually. You won't have this problem with paragraph text, where the word-wrap feature will readjust the length of your lines automatically when you add or delete text.

- Here's an easy shortcut for selecting a single word of text: Double-click on it.

- When you're editing text on screen, try this trick for deleting to the end of the current line: Place the insertion point where you want to begin deleting text and press Shift+End.

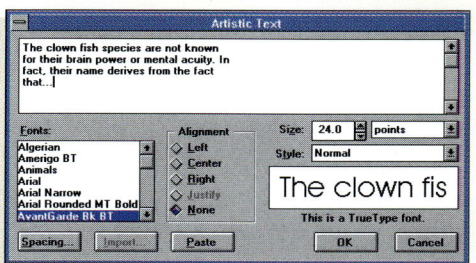

 To add text, just move the insertion point where you want to place the text and type away. (The Text tool must be selected if you're going to work on screen. To work in one of the text-editing dialog boxes, use the Pick tool to select the text block in question, and then choose Edit Text from the Text menu.) As you know, you can move the insertion point to a different place in your text block by clicking in the desired spot with your mouse; you can also use the arrow keys to move one character or line at a time in the direction of the arrow. Here are a few additional ways of moving the insertion point more efficiently: Press Home or End to move to the beginning or end of the current line, respectively; and press Ctrl+Home or Ctrl+End to move to the beginning or end of the text block, respectively.

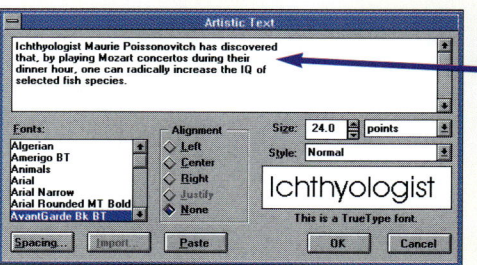

Cutting and pasting is an easy way to rephrase and improve your writing.

 You can copy or move text directly on screen or in one of the text-editing dialog boxes. This type of editing makes use of the Cut, Copy, and Paste commands on the Edit menu—you learned a bit about these commands in Chapter 7. Here's the procedure: Select the text you want to cut or copy; issue the Cut or Copy command, move the insertion point to the place where you want to insert the cut or copied text, and then issue the Paste command to insert the text into its new location. (If you're in either the Artistic Text or Paragraph Text dialog box, you must use the keyboard shortcuts Ctrl+C for copy, Ctrl+X for cut, and Ctrl+V for paste.)

 You can delete text and add text at the same time in the following way: Select the text to be deleted. Then simply begin to type; the new text you enter will replace the old.

## How to Edit Text 111

**2** To delete text, move the insertion point to the desired position and use the Delete or Backspace key to delete one character at a time, as you learned in Chapter 5. (Remember, the Backspace key deletes the character to the left of the insertion point, and the Delete key deletes the character to the right of the insertion point.) If you need to delete more than a few characters, however, there is a better way: First select the text to be deleted—as described next—and then press either Backspace or Delete.

When you place the mouse pointer in a text area, it changes into this "I-beam."

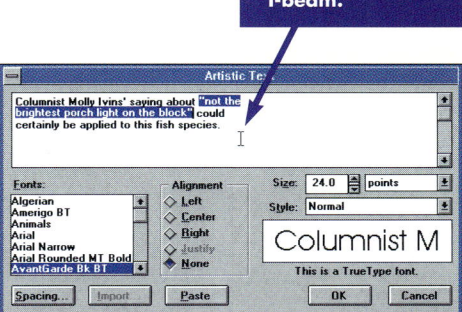

**3** One way of selecting text—either on the screen or in the Paragraph Text or Artistic Text dialog box—is to drag across it using your mouse. When you move the mouse pointer over existing text, it changes into an *I-beam pointer*. You can drag over as many characters as you like to select them. If you're on the printable page, the characters will stay black but the area around them will turn gray. If you're in one of the text-editing dialog boxes, the selected letters will be shown in *reverse video* (white characters on a dark background).

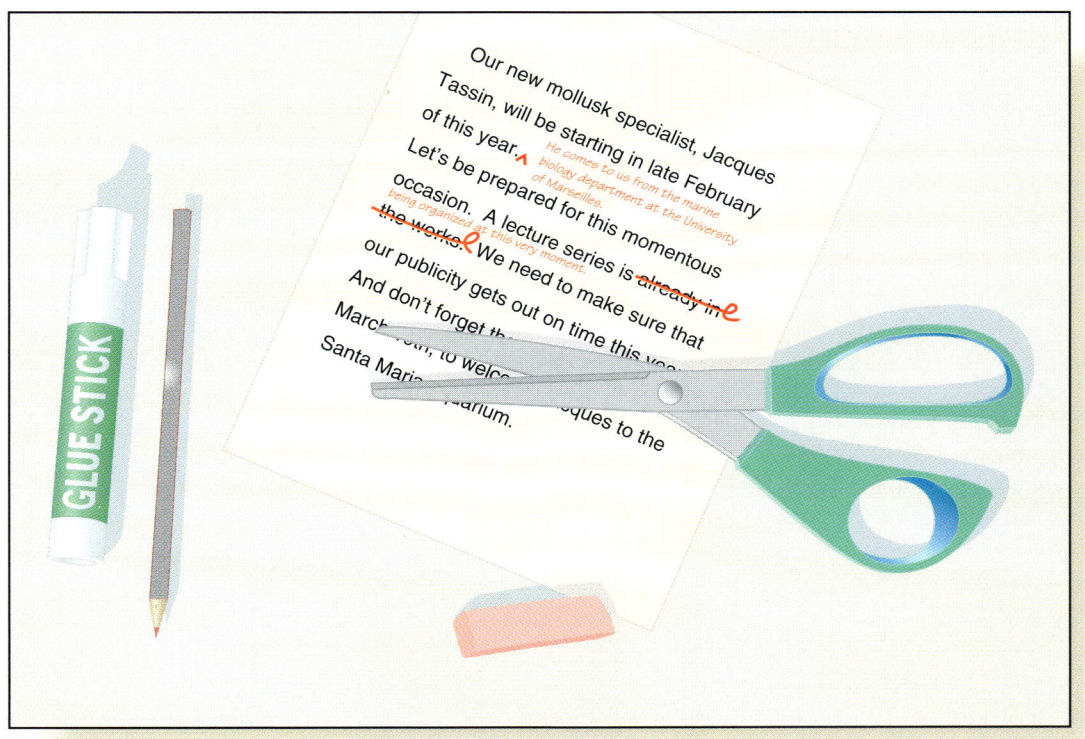

**4** If you're in one of the text-editing dialog boxes and you want to select text using the keyboard, position the insertion point where you want to begin selecting, and then hold down the Shift key while pressing one of the arrow keys (to select one character at a time in the specified direction), Home (to select to the beginning of the line), End (to select to the end of the line), Ctrl+End (to select to the end of the text block), or Ctrl+Home (to select to the beginning of the text block).

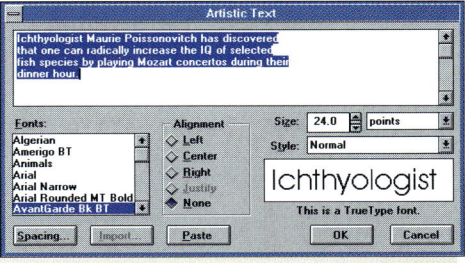

# How to Perfect Your Writing

Most modern word processors include a passel of devices that help you improve or at least mitigate your writing—everything from grammar checkers to spelling checkers to prewritten letters. CorelDRAW! comes with several of these writing accessories, perhaps the most useful of which are its spell checker and thesaurus. Used properly, these two tools can patch up your prose so that it is, at the very least, more or less error free and somewhat varied. The spell checker, in particular, can save the dyslexic or orthographically challenged from embarrassing moments.

### TIP SHEET

▶ To spell check a word before entering it, follow these steps: With no text selected, choose Spell Checker from the Text menu. Then type the word whose spelling your want to verify in the Word to Check text box and click on the Check Word button. If the word is in CorelDRAW!'s dictionary, you'll get the message "Word OK." If not, you'll get the message "Word not found." Click on OK, and, if necessary, click on the Suggest button to see if CorelDRAW! knows the correct spelling.

▶ To look up synonyms for a word that is not in your text, follow these steps: With no text selected, choose Thesaurus from the Text menu. Under Synonym For, type the word for which you want to look up alternatives; then click on the Lookup button. If CorelDRAW! knows any possible replacement words, it displays them under Synonyms. As before, you may be able to select different definitions to see different sets of synonyms.

▶ CorelDRAW! permits you to create your own personal dictionary of terms that you use frequently but that are not in the standard dictionary. Although the process is not particularly complicated, it is beyond the scope of this book.

 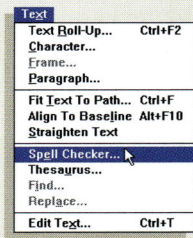

**1** To run CorelDRAW!'s spell checker, first select the text on-screen to be scanned for spelling errors. (The previous section explains how to select portions of a text block; if you want to check an entire text block, just click on it with the Pick tool to select it.) Then choose Spell Checker from the Text menu. Keep in mind that a spell checker detects words that it doesn't recognize (words that are not in its dictionary). In some cases—as with proper names and technical terms, for instance—these words may not actually be misspelled.

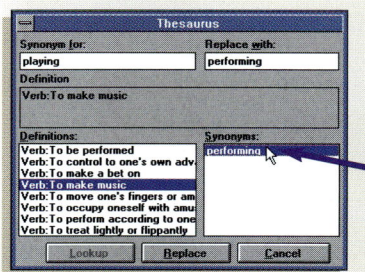

Click on a synonym to select it so you can use it as a replacement word.

 **7** If you see the word you want under Synonyms, click on it to select it; it will appear in the Replace With text box. Then click on the Replace button to substitute this new word for the old one you originally selected in your document.

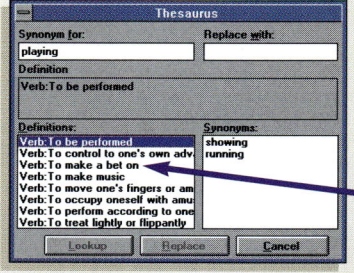

Click on a different word definition to see a different set of synonyms.

 **6** If a word has more than one meaning, these will be listed under Definitions in the lower-left corner of the Thesaurus dialog box. If CorelDRAW! knows of alternatives for the selected definition of the selected word, they'll be displayed under Synonyms in the lower-right corner of the dialog box. You can click on a different definition to display a different set of synonyms.

## How to Perfect Your Writing 113

**2** At this point you'll see the Spelling Checker dialog box shown here. To check all words in the selected text block, click on the Check Text button. If CorelDRAW! finds a word that it does not recognize, it displays that word underneath "Word not found" at the top of the dialog box. Click on the Suggest button to have Corel-DRAW! suggest replacements for the word. (Select the Always Suggest check box to have CorelDRAW! automatically suggest any possible replacement words.)

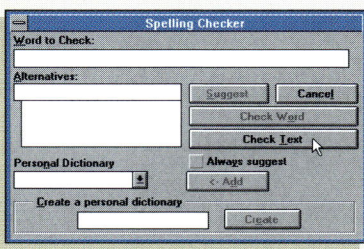

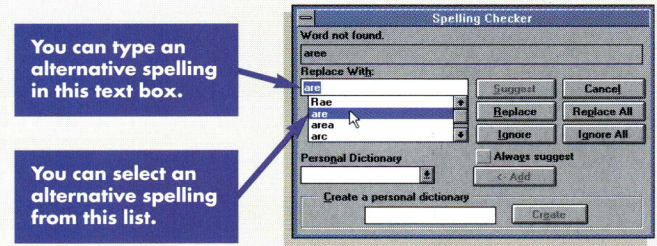

You can type an alternative spelling in this text box.

You can select an alternative spelling from this list.

**3** If the desired word shows up on the list under Replace With, click on it to select it. If not, you can type the word yourself in the text box directly under Replace With. Once the appropriate replacement word is listed under Replace With, you can click on the Replace button to replace one instance of the word, or on the Replace All button to replace all instances of the misspelled word in the current text block.

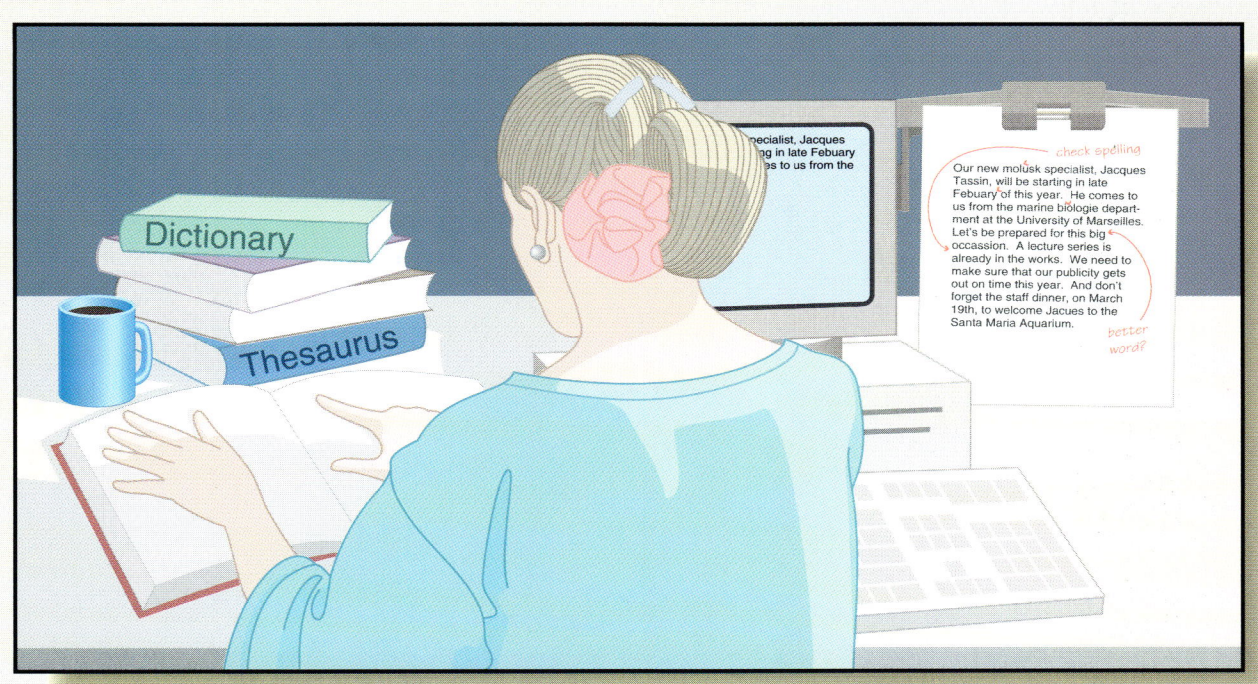

**5** CorelDRAW! also provides a thesaurus, which you can use to look up alternative words or, in some cases, to check that you're using a word correctly. To try the thesaurus, first select the word on-screen for which you want to look up synonyms. (Remember, a quick way to select a single word is to double-click on it.) Then choose Thesaurus from the Text menu.

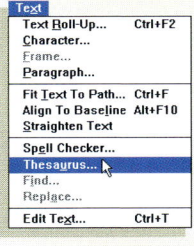

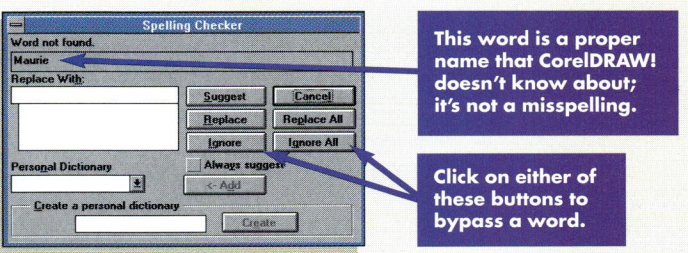

This word is a proper name that CorelDRAW! doesn't know about; it's not a misspelling.

Click on either of these buttons to bypass a word.

**4** In some cases, the word CorelDRAW! stops on is not a spelling error after all, but is just a word that's not in its dictionary. If so, you can click the Ignore button to have CorelDRAW! bypass this word, or on Ignore All to have CorelDRAW! ignore a particular word for the remainder of the current spelling check. CorelDRAW! will tell you when the spelling check has been completed. Click on OK in the message box to resume your work.

## CHAPTER 13: IMPROVING YOUR TEXT

# How to Format Paragraphs

When you enter paragraph text, CorelDRAW! does you the favor of wrapping the text within the frame that you've created. However, that's just about it for automatic formatting niceties.

In this section, you'll learn how to do somewhat more to format your paragraph text. Among other things, you'll find out how to introduce hyphenation, how to modify indents and tab stops, and how to create simple bulleted lists. These by and large easy techniques all make use of the Paragraph dialog box that comes up when you choose Paragraph from the Text menu.

### TIP SHEET

▶ The Paragraph option in the Text menu is available whether or not you have paragraph text selected. However, most of the options in the Paragraph dialog box are not available unless you've selected paragraph text.

▶ When setting indents, you can make the First Line setting smaller than the Rest of Lines setting to create a hanging indent, where first the line of the paragraph falls to the left (rather than the right) of subsequent lines.

▶ You can change paragraph text defaults (and artistic text defaults) by choosing Paragraph from the Text menu with no text selected. Then choose OK in the Paragraph Attributes dialog box that appears, and select the desired paragraph attributes.

▶ You can change hyphenation, indentation, tab, and bullet settings before you enter text to affect all subsequent text.

**1** Hyphenation is particularly suitable if you have narrow columns of text (it helps to prevent very short lines of text and ragged margins) or if you've justified your text (it should eliminate unsightly gaps between words). Here, the top paragraph has not been hyphenated and the bottom one has.

*Justified text can have unattractive gaps between words.*

*In this hyphenated paragraph, those gaps have disappeared or at least diminished.*

**7** Click on the Bullet On check box to select it. Then choose a bullet category from the list box on the left, and choose a bullet character from the list box on the right. Then click on OK to build your bulleted list; the designated bullet character will be inserted in front of all selected paragraphs.

✺ Invoice for B.W.F.M. job
✺ Go running!
✺ Call Mr. Johnson
✺ Shop for dinner
✺ Do laundry

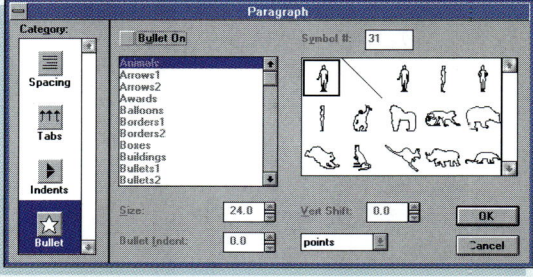

**6** A final way of formatting your paragraphs is to transform them into bulleted lists, with a bullet character of your choosing in front of each paragraph. Select the text you want to transform into a bulleted list, choose Paragraph from the Text menu, and then choose Bullet under Category in the Paragraph dialog box. You'll see this Paragraph dialog box.

# How to Format Paragraphs 115

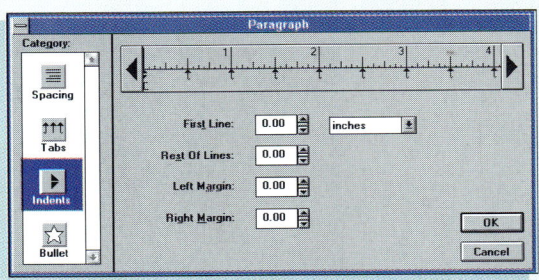

**2** To hyphenate paragraph text, select the text block in question and choose Paragraph from the Text menu. Click on the Automatic Hyphenation check box to select it, and then click on OK to hyphenate your text.

**3** In certain cases, you may want to alter the indentation of your text—that is, its distance from the right and left edges of the text frame. To modify a paragraph's indention, select it and choose Paragraph from the Text menu. Then choose Indents under Category to display this version of the Paragraph dialog box.

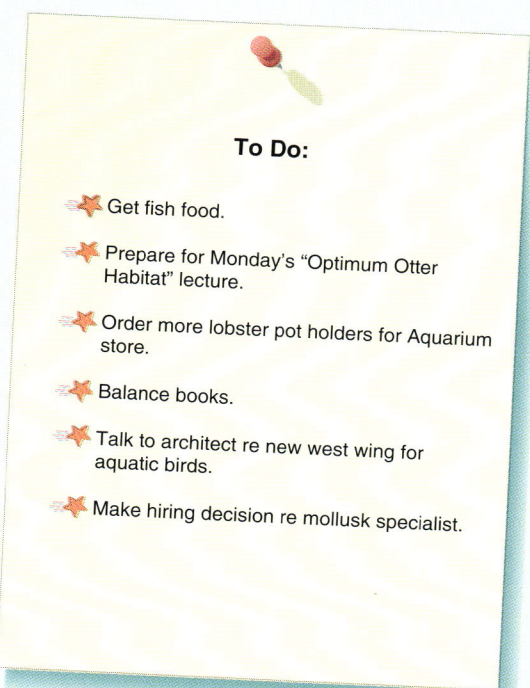

**4** To determine the indentation of the first line of the selected paragraph, alter the First Line setting. To determine the indentation of all subsequent lines in a paragraph, enter a value in the Rest of Lines box. Enter values under Left Margin and Right Margin to indent all lines in the selected paragraph from the left and right edges of the paragraph text frame, respectively. Here's one paragraph that has not been indented, followed by a second paragraph with a First Line setting of 1.00, a Rest of Lines setting of 0.50, and a Right Margin setting of 0.50.

**5** When entering paragraph text, you can use CorelDRAW!'s *preset tab stops*, which are set at every half inch. In certain cases, you may want to change these preset tab stops—perhaps you want the stops to occur at intervals of one inch instead. You can also set *custom tab stops* that fall at particular locations instead of at particular intervals. Select the text block whose tab stops you want to change, choose Paragraph from the Text menu, and click on Tabs under Category. You'll see this version of the Paragraph dialog box. From here, you can change the preset tab stops by clicking on Clear All to remove the old tab stops, entering a new value to the right of Apply Tabs Every, and then clicking on the Apply Tabs Every button. To set custom tab stops, type a position in the box to the right of the Set button and then click on Set. To remove any tab stop, click on it in the Tabs list and then click on the Clear button. In addition to left-aligned tabs, you can create right-aligned tabs, centered tabs, and decimal tabs. To do so, click on the tab stop to be changed, and then click on the appropriate option button under Alignment.

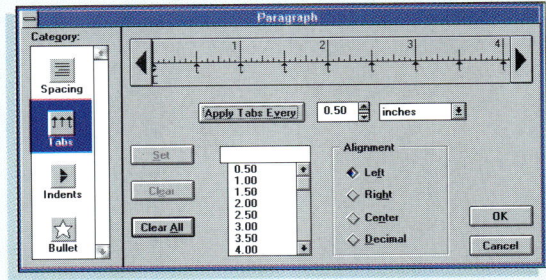

# How to Fit Text to a Path

One of the most fun and most exciting ways to manipulate text in CorelDRAW! is to fit it to a path. This simply means wrapping text around the outline of a shape that you've drawn. You can wrap text around ellipses, rectangles, and even freehand shapes. CorelDRAW! also lets you exercise a fair amount of control over how the text is "fitted" around the shape in question. For instance, you can determine how the letters are angled and which portion of the shape they're wrapped around, to name a few. And once you fit text to a path, the shape and text are linked together. If you change the shape's size, the text is rearranged to fit the new shape; and if you edit the text, it's reconfigured so that it still fits around the selected shape.

### TIP SHEET

- **Selecting Place on Other Side in the Fit Text To Path roll-up reverses the text's horizontal and vertical alignment.** For instance, if you've specified that the text should be placed below the object's outline and that it should start at the object's starting node, choosing this check box will place the text above the outline and have it end at the object's ending node.

- **Although choosing Fit Text To Path links the selected text and shape, you can delete the shape without deleting the text.** This enables you to draw a shape that you want to serve as a guideline for your text, and then to remove that guideline once you've got the text the way you want it.

- **You can fit text to shapes that you've drawn, but you can't necessarily fit text to all other images**, including the clip art images provided with CorelDRAW! (You can, however, fit text to the images available via the symbol library that you learned about at the end of Chapter 5.)

 Draw a shape around which you want to arrange some text. Then enter some artistic text. (Note that you cannot fit paragraph text to a path.) If necessary, refer to Chapter 5 and to the previous sections in this chapter for more information on entering and editing text.

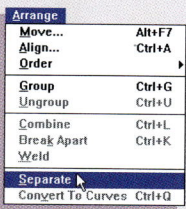

 To break the "link" that is formed when you fit text to path, you can select the text and the shape and choose Separate from the Arrange menu. Now you can manipulate each one separately again. However, note that your text still follows the shape's path. If you want to return your text to normal, select it and choose Straighten Text from the Text menu—this both straightens the text and returns it to its original location.

# How to Fit Text to a Path    117

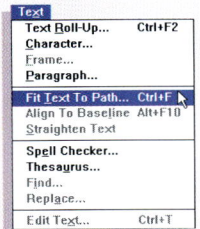

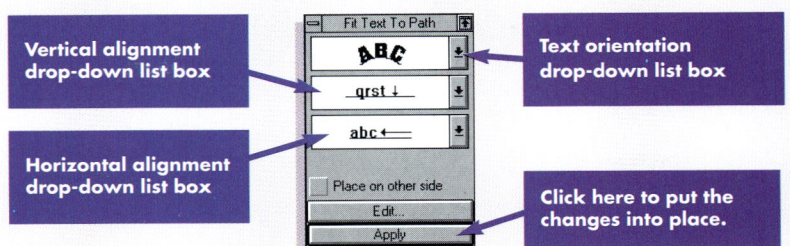

**②** Select the Pick tool and then select both the text you've entered and the shape you want to fit it to. (To select multiple items, select the first one by clicking on it, and then select any subsequent objects by holding down the Shift key while clicking on them.) Now choose Fit Text To Path from the Text menu (Ctrl+F shortcut).

**③** In the Fit Text To Path roll-up, you choose how your text is positioned as it's wrapped around the selected shape. The top drop-down list box lets you determine how the text is angled; skewed or rotated, for example. The second drop-down list box lets you determine the text's vertical alignment in relation to the selected shape's outline. With the default selection, the text's baseline will run along the shape's path. The third drop-down list box lets you determine the text's horizontal alignment—its position relative to the beginning and ending nodes of the selected shape. Text can begin at the beginning node and end at the ending node, or be centered between those two nodes.

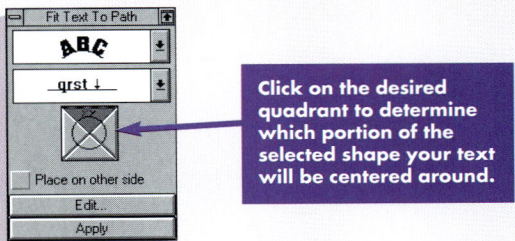

**④** The configuration of the Fit Text To Path roll-up may change, depending on which type of shape you selected. For example, if you selected an ellipse or a rectangle along with your text, the roll-up would include a square divided into four quadrants. You can select the desired quadrant to determine where to position your text. As an example, if you select a rectangle and you click on the bottom quadrant, your text will be centered around the bottom portion of your rectangle.

**⑥** Once you fit text to a path, the shape and text are linked. Now if you modify the shape, the text is adjusted to fit the new shape, and if you move the shape the text moves with it. In addition, if you edit the text, it still wraps around the shape as originally designated. To edit text that has been fitted to a path, you need to hold down the Ctrl key while clicking on the text to select it independently. Then go ahead and choose Edit Text from the Text menu and edit the text as you usually would.

**⑤** Once you've made all the desired selections in the Fit Text To Path roll-up, click on the Apply button to put the changes into place. If your text doesn't line up exactly as you want, simply make new selections from the roll-up and click on the Apply button again.

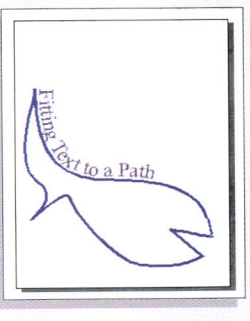

**CHAPTER 14**

# Working with Outlines

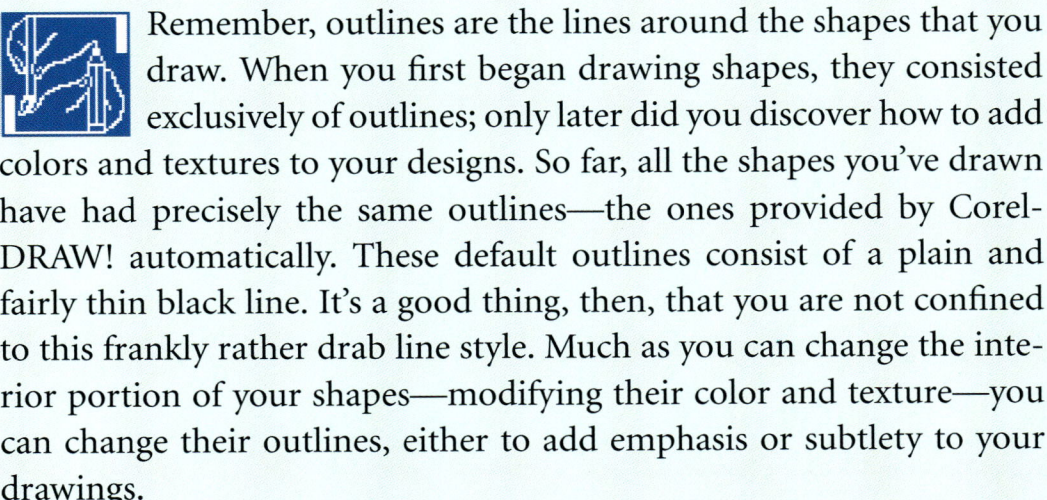Remember, outlines are the lines around the shapes that you draw. When you first began drawing shapes, they consisted exclusively of outlines; only later did you discover how to add colors and textures to your designs. So far, all the shapes you've drawn have had precisely the same outlines—the ones provided by Corel-DRAW! automatically. These default outlines consist of a plain and fairly thin black line. It's a good thing, then, that you are not confined to this frankly rather drab line style. Much as you can change the interior portion of your shapes—modifying their color and texture—you can change their outlines, either to add emphasis or subtlety to your drawings.

This chapter illustrates a variety of ways to alter the outlines of your shapes. For starters, you'll learn how to make outlines either thicker or thinner. You can use heavier outlines if you'd like your shapes to stand out, and lighter outlines for more delicate design work. You'll also learn how to change the color of an outline. This too can make shapes easier to see, especially against a background of a similar shade or color. You'll then find out how to introduce different line styles, such as dashed and dotted lines, and how to use different line endings. CorelDRAW! provides line endings ranging from arrows to airplanes, believe it or not, and you can even create your very own line endings if you're feeling adventuresome.

# 120 CHAPTER 14: WORKING WITH OUTLINES

# How to Change the Outline Size and Color

If you want a particular shape to pack a little extra punch, one way to go is to increase the thickness of its outline. By contrast, if you're doing very fine work, you'll probably want to use thin outlines. Another way to give an outline some emphasis is to change its color. This tactic can give your shape more definition, and is especially effective when the shape's color and the background color are similar. A contrasting outline color can make your shape much easier to distinguish in this context.

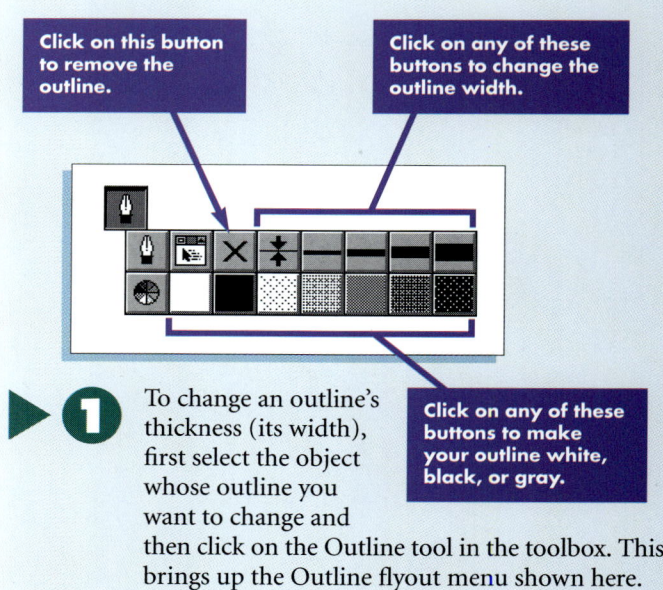

▶ **1** To change an outline's thickness (its width), first select the object whose outline you want to change and then click on the Outline tool in the toolbox. This brings up the Outline flyout menu shown here.

### TIP SHEET

▸ **If you can't see any of the changes you make to your outline, check that you're in editable preview rather than wireframe view. Wireframe view doesn't show outline attributes such as widths and colors. (If you remove a shape's outline, it still shows up in wireframe view, since you haven't actually deleted the shape itself.) Remember, press Shift+F9 to switch between these two viewing modes.**

▸ **If you alter a default outline attribute, you may later change your mind and want to switch back to the old setting. You can't use the Undo command on the Edit menu in this context. What you *can* do, however, is reverse the process. Simply make sure no objects are selected, and choose the original outline settings from the Pen flyout menu or one of its tributary dialog boxes. Just make sure to answer OK when you see an Outline Pen or Outline Color dialog box asking whether you want to change the default.**

▸ **If you're using the Outline Pen dialog box to change the width of an outline, notice that you can also change the outline color from here. Click on the button to the right of Color in the upper-left corner of the dialog box and choose a color from the list of colors that appears.**

▸ **You can change the outline width and color of text as well as shapes.**

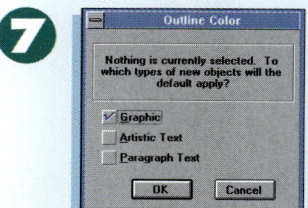

**7** You can change the default outline attributes so that subsequent shapes that you draw have the designated outline attributes—including width and color. To do this, make sure no shapes are selected, and then make a selection from the Outline flyout menu. You'll see a dialog box labeled either Outline Pen or Outline Color, asking which items you want the new defaults to apply to. Select only the Graphic check box, click on OK, and, if you selected a button that leads to a dialog box (like the Pen button), make your outline attribute selections as before. (To change the default outline color, you have to open the Outline Pen dialog box, as described in step 3, and choose a color from the color list in the upper-left corner.)

**6** You can also remove an outline altogether. (If your shape is not filled or colored, deleting its outline effectively removes it from view in editable preview.) To do this, select the object whose outline you want to remove, and then choose the X button in the Outline flyout menu. Alternatively, you can *right*-click on the X at the far left edge of the color palette. (Remember, clicking on this X with the left mouse button removes the object's fill.) Here, the lower fish has had its outline removed.

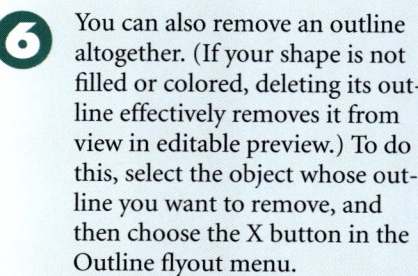

How to Change the Outline Size and Color  **121**

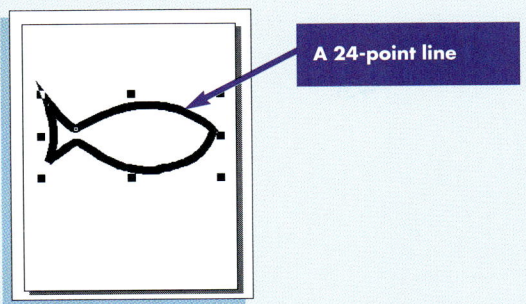

A 24-point line

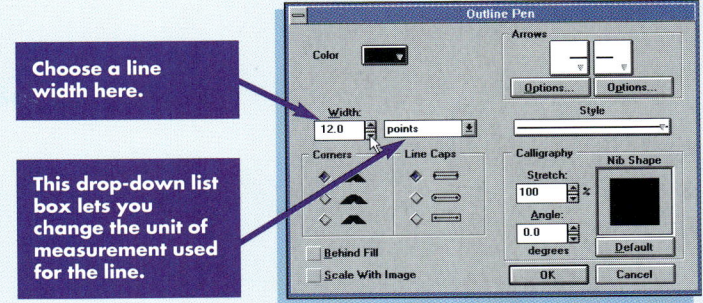

Choose a line width here.

This drop-down list box lets you change the unit of measurement used for the line.

**2** Click on any of the five rightmost buttons in the top row of this flyout menu to change the width of the selected object's outline. Here, the button on the far right has been selected for a width of 24 points; the buttons to its left are, from right to left, for 16-point lines, 8-point lines, 2-point lines (the default outline width), and ¼-point (hairline) lines, respectively. (If you're viewing an entire page, you may have to zoom in to see the difference between some of the thinner line widths.)

**3** If you want to regulate an outline's width more precisely, select the object to be affected and then click on the Pen button in the Outline flyout menu or press F12. (The Pen button is in the upper-left corner of the Outline flyout; it looks just like the Outline tool.) You'll see the Outline Pen dialog box shown here, and you can enter a new value under Width. You can enter any value between 0 and 4 inches. If you're working with points, remember that a point is 1/72nd of an inch, so a 72-point line would be one inch thick.

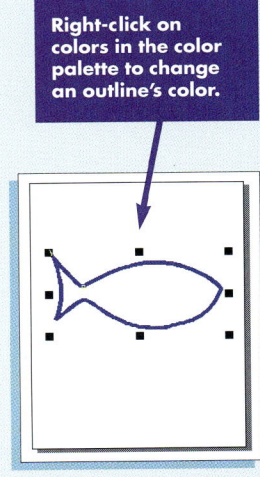

Right-click on colors in the color palette to change an outline's color.

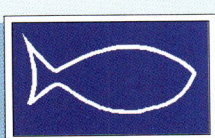

**5** You can also change a shape's outline to black, white, or a limited number of gray shades by opening the Outline flyout menu and choosing from among the seven rightmost buttons in its bottom row. A white outline doesn't show up against a white background, but it shows up very well against a dark background.

**4** Changing an outline's color is just as easy as changing its width, if not easier. Select the object in question and then *right-click* (click with the right mouse button) on a color in the color palette. (Remember, the left mouse button changes the object's fill color, not its outline.) If you don't see the color you want, you can use the arrows at either end of the color palette to bring additional color options into view.

# How to Create Different Line Styles and Line Endings

There are many types of alterations you can make to outlines aside from simply changing their width or color. The last section touched upon the Outline Pen dialog box, in which you can make very specific changes to your outline's width, as well as giving the outline a different color. This dialog box also lets you change many other outline attributes—including corners, lines styles, and line endings.

### TIP SHEET

▶ To change the defaults for these line styles, corners, and line endings, make sure no objects are selected, click on the Pen button in the Outline flyout menu, and choose OK when asked about applying the changed default. Then change the outline attributes as described here.

▶ If you're not sure which is the beginning and which is the end of a line you've drawn, here's an easy way to find out: Select the Shape tool, click on the line in question, and press the Home key to highlight the beginning node of the line, or the End key to highlight the ending node. When you select a line with the Shape tool, you may also notice that the beginning node is slightly larger than the other nodes.

▶ It's easy—and fun—to create your own line endings. Select the shape to use and then choose Create Arrow from the Special menu. Respond OK when CorelDRAW! asks if you want to make the selected shape into an "arrow" (or line ending). The shape will now show up on the list that appears when you select one of the Arrows buttons in the Outline Pen dialog box. To delete this line ending, select it, choose Options under the Arrow button, and choose the Delete From List option.

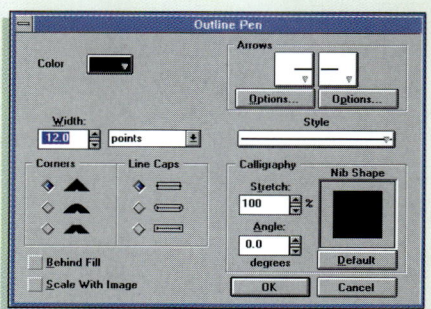

**1** Select the object whose outline you want to affect, and then click on the Outline tool to open the Outline flyout menu. In the Outline flyout, click on the Pen button in the upper-left corner to bring up the Outline Pen dialog box shown here.

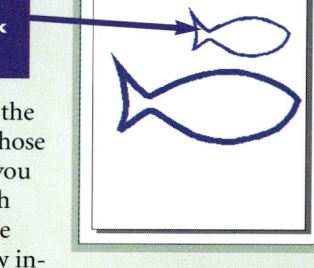

This object was scaled down and its outline width shrunk correspondingly.

**7** If you're modifying the outline of a shape whose size might change, you can select Scale With Image in the Outline Pen dialog box. Now increasing or decreasing the size of the selected shape changes the width of its outline correspondingly. If you shrink the shape, its outline will become smaller, and vice versa.

**6** To get rid of a line ending, you can pull down either list of line endings and choose the option in the upper-left corner—a line with no special ending. Alternatively, you can click on the Options button underneath the appropriate Arrows button. You'll see the menu shown here (the menu options will only be available if you've chosen a new line ending). Choose None to get rid of any special line endings. (You can also "swap" line endings in case you miscalculated which was the beginning and which was the end of the line.)

How to Create Different Line Styles and Line Endings  **123**

**Click on this button to display a list of line styles.**

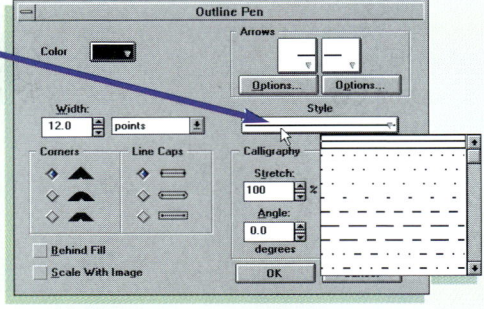

❷ To choose a new outline style, click on the button underneath Style; you'll see the list of dashed and dotted line styles shown here. Scroll through this list to get an idea of what's available. When you find the desired line style, click on it and then click on OK to put your change into place. Don't worry if your dashed or dotted outline looks somewhat jagged, or doesn't look any different from the original outline; it's most likely a display issue that will not affect your printed output. You can zoom in on your shape to check the lines' appearance.

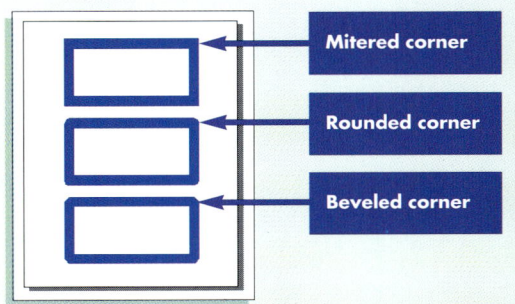

❸ If a shape has fairly sharp angles, you can change the style of its corners—that is, the way in which lines meet. Make sure your shape is selected, get into the Outline Pen dialog box, and select the desired option button under Corners. The top option is for *mitered* corners, in which the two lines' outer edges are extended until they meet. The middle option produces *rounded* corners, in which the two lines' edges are rounded off where they meet. The bottom option produces *beveled* corners, in which the two lines are beveled, or flattened, where they meet. When used judiciously, the right type of corners can make the difference between a humdrum and a sparkling design.

❺ Another way to change the line endings of shapes that are not closed is to click on either Arrows button in the Outline Pen dialog box. You'll see a list of line endings, as shown here. The available options include arrows, pitch forks, hands, and even airplanes. Click on the one you want to both select it and close the list. The left Arrows button lets you select a line ending for the *beginning* of your line; the right button lets you select a line ending for the *end* of your line. (The beginning and end of your line are not necessarily its left or right ends, but rather the places where you began drawing and stopped drawing, respectively.)

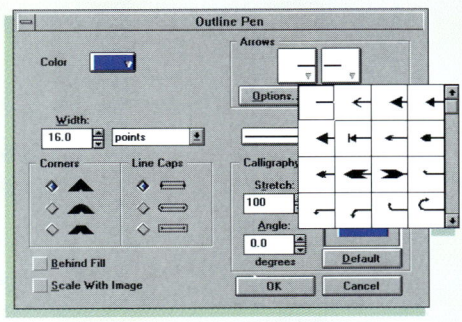

❹ There are a number of ways of altering the line endings of shapes that are not closed. You can change the *line caps* to change the way CorelDRAW! ends the line. The top option under Line Caps in the Outline Pen dialog box squares off the line exactly at its endpoint. The middle option rounds off the line, extending it a bit past its endpoint in the process. The bottom option again squares off the line, but in this case extends it a bit past its endpoint.

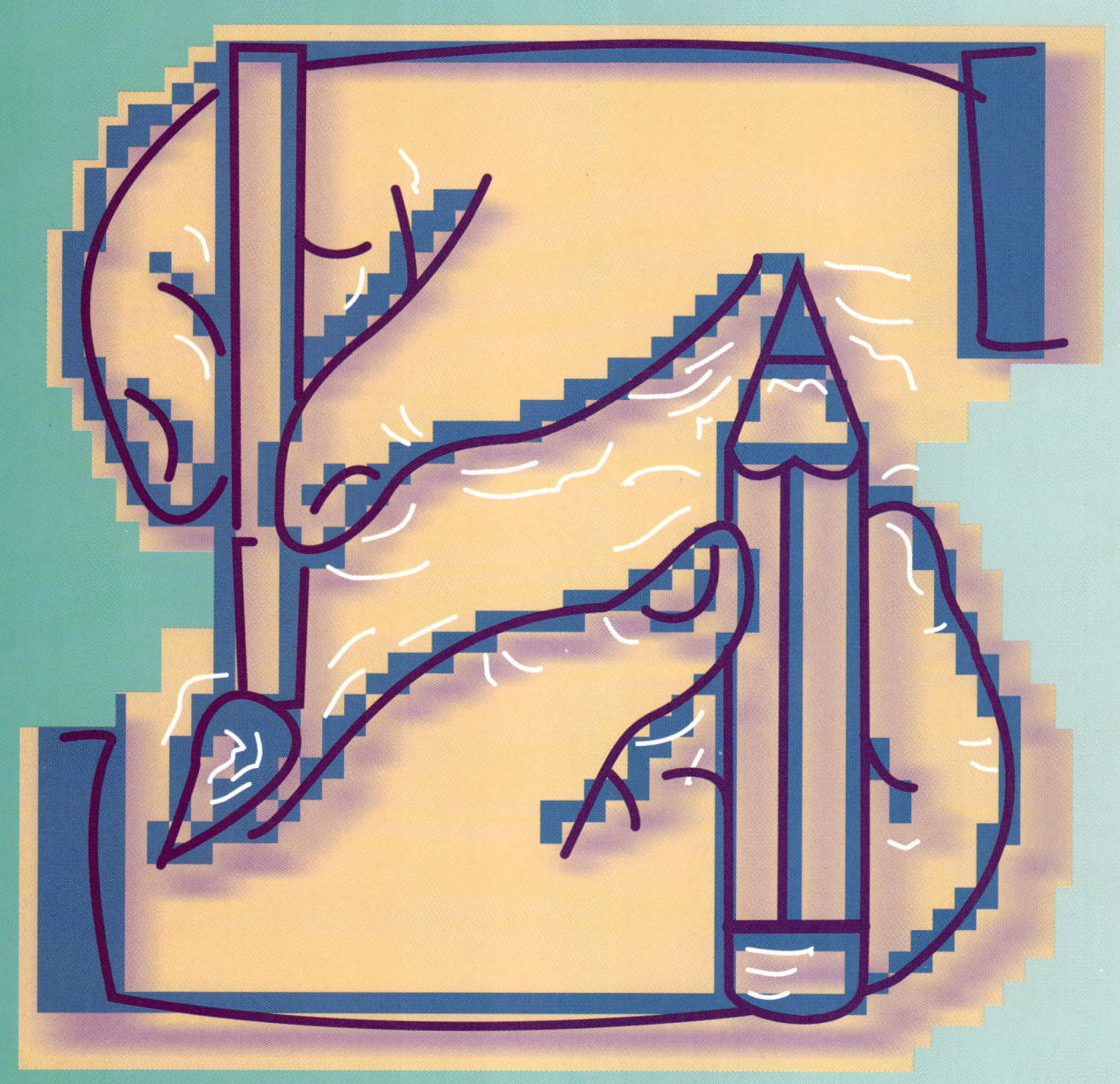

## CHAPTER 15

# Importing and Exporting Files

You can go a long way with CorelDRAW! alone. However, at some point you'll probably want to use CorelDRAW! in tandem with another software program—whether it's a desktop publishing program, a word processing program, or another graphics package. As an example, you may create an image in CorelDRAW! that you want to transfer into a Word for Windows document; or, you might want to use some text from Ami Pro in a brochure you're putting together in CorelDRAW! Whether you want to transfer information into or out of CorelDRAW!, the task is straightforward once you learn the basics outlined in this chapter.

In the first section you'll discover how to "import" files from other sources into CorelDRAW! The second section demonstrates how to "export" files from CorelDRAW!, changing their file format and/or moving them to a different location so that you can use them in another application. As you'll soon find out, CorelDRAW!'s ability to "plug into" a whole host of other programs in this way makes it an even more powerful implement. Familiarizing yourself with the techniques covered here will enable you to tap into the exciting and constantly changing array of computer tools available for work, for art, and for play.

# CHAPTER 15: IMPORTING AND EXPORTING TEXT

# How to Import Files

You may have some images or text from another program that you'd like to use in CorelDRAW!, or you might be wondering how to gain access to the many wonderful and varied clip art images that come packaged with the program. Here's where you learn how to use (*import*) text and images from other sources with CorelDRAW! As an added bonus, once you've imported some text or an image, you can in many cases modify it much as you would modify something you had drawn in CorelDRAW! itself.

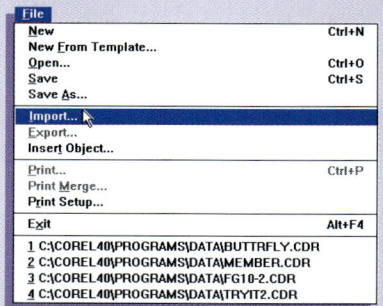

 **1** First, you need to create or open the CorelDRAW! file into which you want to import text or graphics from another source. (See Chapter 6 just in case you need any help with the details.) If necessary, move to the appropriate page of the drawing. Then choose Import from the File menu.

## TIP SHEET

▸ **Depending on how CorelDRAW! was installed on your computer, you may not have any clip art available. If you want to install some clip art, read the *Installation Guide* or consult CorelDRAW!'s help system (search for "installing CorelDRAW options"). The appendix of this book also includes information on installing CorelDRAW!**

▸ **If you want to transfer text or images from another Windows application into CorelDRAW!, you may be able to use the Windows Clipboard, the temporary storage area that you learned a bit about in Chapter 7. See your CorelDRAW! or Windows documentation if you need more details on using the Clipboard. Some objects, particularly complex graphics, may be too large to fit on the Clipboard. If you run into this problem, it's probably best to use the Import command instead.**

▸ **You can also place material from other sources in CorelDRAW! by using two techniques called *linking* and *embedding*. In either case, the material you place in CorelDRAW! maintains a connection with its application of origin. Linking and embedding are beyond the scope of this book. If you want further information, consult your CorelDRAW! documentation, a more advanced book on CorelDRAW!, or a text on Windows.**

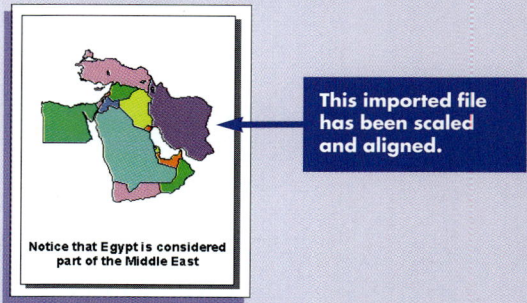

 **6** Notice that the imported object is selected—as indicated by the highlighting box's eight handles—making it easier to change right away. Once you import an object into CorelDRAW!, you can manipulate it in many ways. You can move the object, copy it, stretch and scale it, and more. Here, the map has been scaled so that it fits on the page, and has then been aligned to the center of the page horizontally (Chapters 11 and 12). In this case some explanatory text has also been added (Chapter 5). You may want to experiment with the types of changes you can make to imported text and images, especially since the allowable modifications may depend somewhat on the file format.

## HOW TO IMPORT FILES   127

**2** You'll see the Import dialog box shown here. Notice that this dialog box is fairly similar to the one you used to open files in Chapter 6. In fact, many of the skills you learned in Chapter 6 for working with files will come in handy when importing files into CorelDRAW!

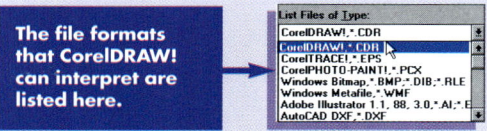

The file formats that CorelDRAW! can interpret are listed here.

**3** If necessary, choose a new file type from the List Files of Type drop-down list box. This list box includes all the types of files that CorelDRAW! is set up to import. If you're trying to retrieve some of CorelDRAW!'s clip art, choose the .CDR option, as shown here. (CDR is CorelDRAW!'s native file format.) If you're importing some other type of file, see if you can find its extension in the list. CorelDRAW! can interpret the file formats used in a wide range of applications, including word processing programs such as WordPerfect and Word, spreadsheet programs such as Excel and Lotus 1-2-3, and the formats used by many graphics programs.

Choose the directory containing the file you want to import.

Choose the drive containing the file you want to import.

**4** Now, if necessary, choose the drive and directory containing the file to import. If you don't have anything of your own, try importing a piece of clip art provided with CorelDRAW! Select the appropriate drive from the Drives drop-down list. (Choose the drive on which you installed CorelDRAW!; it's probably drive C.) Then, under Directories, choose one of the subdirectories of the CLIPART directory in the COREL40 directory. (Remember, double-click on a directory to select it and to display all subdirectories it contains.) Here the WORLD subdirectory of the CLIPART directory has been selected.

Imported objects are selected automatically so you can change them more easily.

**5** Once you see the file you want in the File Name list box, click on it to select it, and then click on the OK button to import the file into your CorelDRAW! drawing. (As a shortcut, you can just double-click on the file name.) Depending on the size of the file and the speed of your computer, you may see a progress indicator showing how much of the file has been imported. (If instead you get the message "Could not understand the file," check that you selected the correct option under List Files of Type.) When it's done, CorelDRAW! places the imported file in middle of the current page. Here, for example, is a map of the Middle East that CorelDRAW! provides.

# CHAPTER 15: IMPORTING AND EXPORTING TEXT

# How to Export Files

**E**xporting files is the counterpart to importing them; you can use this technique to transfer CorelDRAW! designs into other applications. Exporting is not much more of a challenge than importing, and can be equally invaluable. For instance, you could create a logo in CorelDRAW! and export it into your desktop publishing program for use in letterhead or a brochure. When you export a file, you are merely changing its file format and placing it in a new location. Once you've done this, you still have to get into that other program, open the exported file, and then make any required modifications to it, such as placing it in the proper place on the page. In other words, exporting from CorelDRAW! is just the first step in the process.

### TIP SHEET

- ▶ When importing a file, you have to import the whole thing. In contrast, you can export just part of a file by selecting only the portion you want to export, choosing Export from the File menu, marking the Selected Only check box in the Export dialog box, and then carrying out the export operation as usual.

- ▶ If you want to export something from CorelDRAW! into another Windows application, you may be able to use the Windows Clipboard. (See Chapter 7 or your Windows documentation for more information on the Clipboard.) Some objects are too large to fit on the Clipboard, in which case it's probably easiest just to use the Export command.

- ▶ You can also place material from CorelDRAW! into other programs by using linking and embedding, which means that the exported material maintains a connection with CorelDRAW! Linking and embedding are tremendously useful and powerful features that you may want to acquaint yourself with by studying either your CorelDRAW! documentation or a book about Windows.

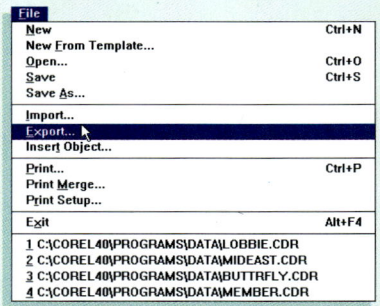

 **1** Open the CorelDRAW! file containing the text or graphic you want to export to another application, and, if necessary, go to the page containing the objects you want to export. (CorelDRAW! will only export objects on the current page.) If you want to export only certain items on the page, select them; when no objects are selected, CorelDRAW! automatically exports all objects on the current page. Then choose Export from the File menu.

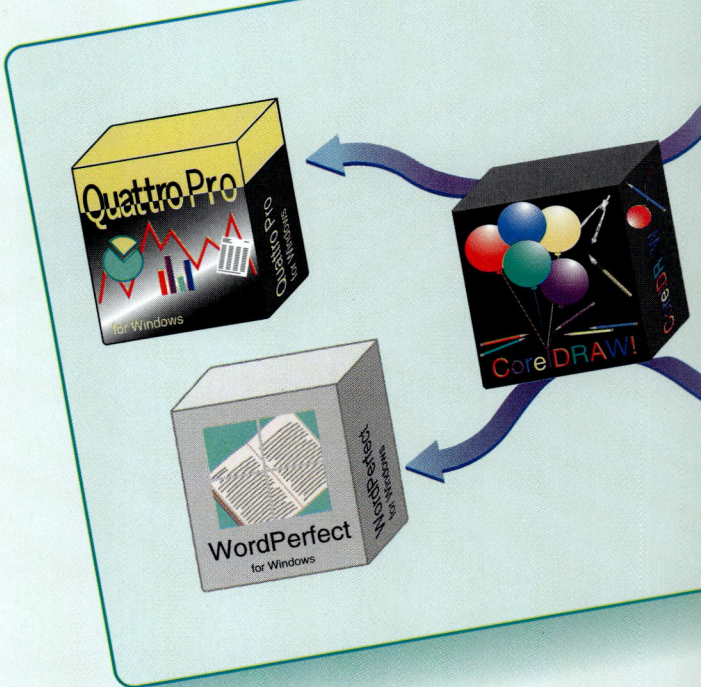

**6** Exporting a file changes its file format and moves it to the desired location. If you're not familiar with how to work with imported graphics in the other application, it's a good idea to consult the documentation. Particularly when you're working with graphics in word processing programs, you probably won't be able to use the techniques you ordinarily use to open files.

## How to Export Files 129

**2** You'll see the Export dialog box shown here. You can either accept the existing file name under File Name, or enter a new name. (If you haven't yet saved the file, you'll need to enter a name at this point.)

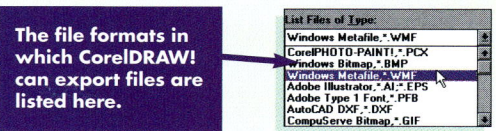
The file formats in which CorelDRAW! can export files are listed here.

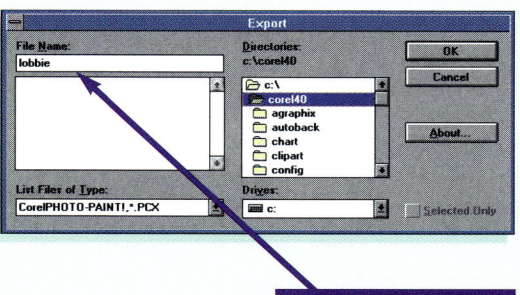

**3** Now choose a file format from the List Files of Type drop-down list box, which is shown here. You have to pick a format that the program you're exporting to can contend with; you may need to consult that program's documentation to figure this out. As an example, Word for Windows can read graphics in the .WMF (Windows Metafile) format. CorelDRAW!'s on-line help system also includes a fair amount of information on which formats work with which applications. (Refer back to Chapter 3 if you need to refresh your memory on how to use the help system.)

You can accept the original file name or enter a new one.

**4** Now choose the drive and directory to which you want to export the file. (Remember, to select a directory and display all its subdirectories, just double-click on it.) If you want to give the file to someone else or use it on another computer, you can export it to a floppy disk by choosing drive A or B from the Drives drop-

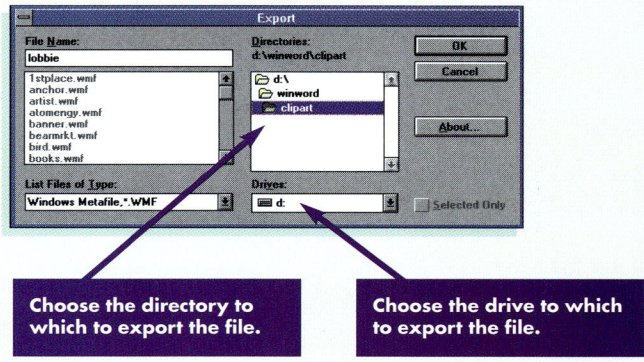

Choose the directory to which to export the file.

Choose the drive to which to export the file.

down list box. If you want to use the file with another program on your computer, indicate the appropriate drive and directory. As just one example, to use the file in your word processing program, you could place it in the directory containing graphic images for that program. Essentially what you're doing is copying the file to a different drive and/or directory, and changing its file format in the process.

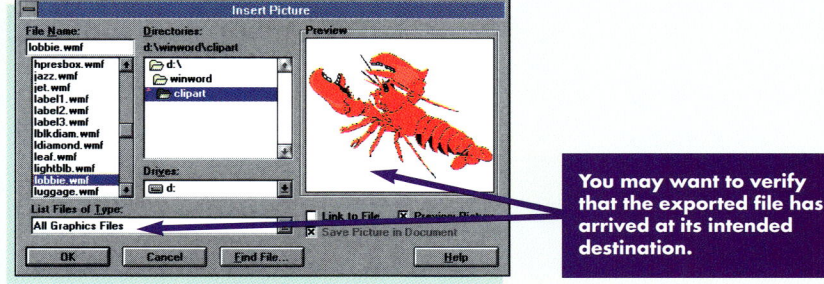

You may want to verify that the exported file has arrived at its intended destination.

**5** Once you've named your file, picked out an appropriate file format, and chosen where you want to export the file to, you can just click on OK to go ahead with the export operation. Depending on the file format you chose, you may see a dialog box asking you to make certain choices about the export format. If you need help here, consult CorelDRAW!'s on-line help system—there are a number of listings under Exporting—or the documentation for the program you're exporting to. When the export operation is completed, you'll be returned to your CorelDRAW! file. If you want to double-check that the file was exported without a hitch, switch to the application to which you exported the file, and see if it arrived safely at its destination. Here, for example, I got into Word for Windows, where I can see that my file has arrived in the designated Word for Windows directory.

# TRY IT!

Once again, it's time to put your newly acquired abilities to the test. In this exercise, you'll assemble the flyer shown here. As usual, chapter numbers indicate where topics were introduced the first time around so you can flip back if you need to refresh your memory. And if your results don't match the ones shown here all that closely, don't be too concerned. You may have slightly different defaults, things may look different on your monitor, or you might choose to use other colors, fonts, or images. Try to think of this exercise as a starting point rather than a conclusion. This book has touched upon CorelDRAW!'s most essential features, but there is much, much more. And now that you have a solid grounding in the basics, you are all set to venture off on your own and do some exploring. Have fun!

Get into Windows and then get into CorelDRAW! (Chapter 2). If you're already in CorelDRAW!, you may need to clear your screen by choosing New from the File menu. If you've modified the current drawing, either retain (choose Yes) or reject (choose No) the changes you've made (Chapter 6).

TRY IT! 131

If necessary, change the page orientation to portrait: Choose Page Setup from the Layout menu, click on Portrait, and then click on OK (Chapter 9).

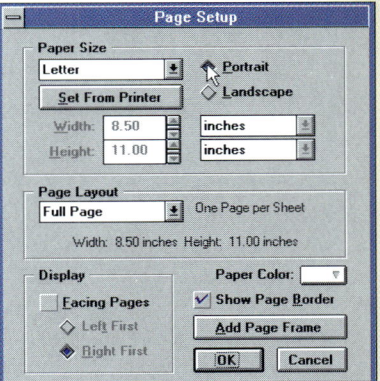

Now you'll acquire a fish image. Choose Import from the File menu. In the Import dialog box, choose the drive on which you installed CorelDRAW! (most likely drive C) and, under Directories, choose the CREATURE subdirectory of the CLIPART subdirectory (Chapter 15). If the clip art files weren't installed with CorelDRAW!, go back and install them now; if you need help, refer to Installing CorelDRAW! options in the on-line help system.

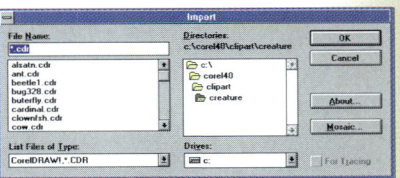

Now you should see a list of file names under File Name on the left side of the Import dialog box. If not, check that the correct file type is selected in the List Files of Type drop-down list box. In this case, select the .CDR file type. Now select a fish file from the CREATURE subdirectory and then click on OK. I've used the TROPCAL.CDR file, which may or may not be available to you, depending on your installation (Chapter 15).

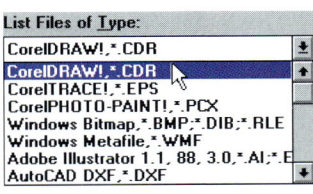

You'll see a fish on your page. Depending on its angle, rotate it so that the head is pointing pretty much straight forward. First click on the fish to introduce the special handles for skewing and rotating objects. Then drag on one of the rounded handles at the corner to rotate the fish so that its head is pointing directly forward, as shown here. Release the mouse button when the fish is at the desired angle (Chapter 11).

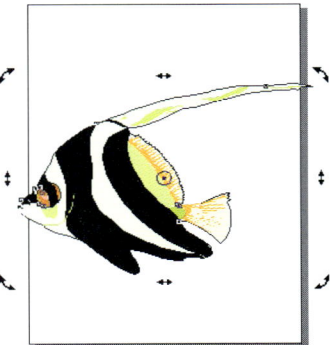

Now click on the fish once so that its handles return to normal, and then scale it down by dragging on one of the corner handles, as shown here (Chapter 11). You want the fish to fit on the page and not to take up the entire width of the page. Next drag on the fish itself to move it closer to the top of the page (Chapter 7).

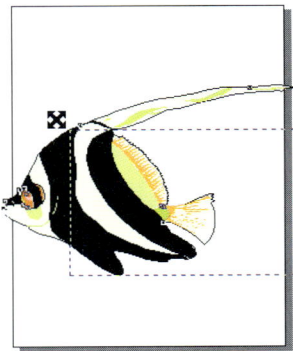

Continue to next page ▶

**132** TRY IT!

### TRY IT!

Continue below

Select the Pencil tool, switch to Bézier mode, and a draw a curve with three nodes underneath your fish, something like the one shown here (Chapter 4). If the size and shape of your curve doesn't suit you after your first attempt, select the Shape tool and modify the curve as needed (Chapter 11).

Select the Text tool, make sure you're in artistic text mode, and, anywhere underneath your fish, type **The Santa Maria Aquarium**. (You can actually type this text anywhere, but it's more convenient to type in the blank space underneath the fish.) Then choose Edit Text from the Text menu (or press Ctrl+T), and, in the Artistic Text dialog box, choose Arial under Fonts, choose a point size of 44, and then click on OK (Chapter 5).

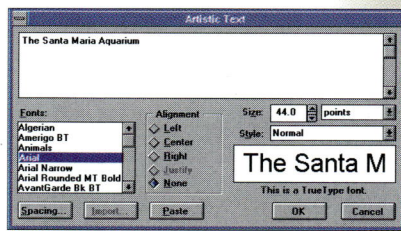

Choose the Pick tool; the text you just typed will automatically be selected. Hold down Shift and click on the curve to select it also. Choose Fit Text To Path from the Text menu. You'll see the Fit Text To Path roll-up (Chapter 13).

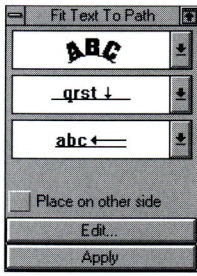

Choose the centering option from the third drop-down list box (it's the one with arrows pointing in at both the left and right side of

the letters "abc.") Then click on the Apply button to fit the selected text to the path, as in the figure. Remove the Fit Text To Path roll-up from the screen by double-clicking its Control Menu box, the dash in the upper-left corner (Chapter 13).

Select the Rectangle tool and draw a rectangle that occupies the entire page (Chapter 4). Then click on a shade of royal blue in the color

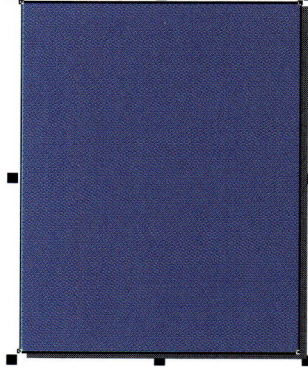

palette at the bottom of the screen. Your fish and text will be hidden behind this rectangle (Chapter 10).

To bring the hidden elements back into view, choose Order from the Arrange menu, and then choose To Back from the submenu that appears (the shortcut is Shift+PgDn). You should now see your design on a blue background, as shown here (Chapter 12).

To center the fish and your text on the page, select both objects, choose Align from the Arrange menu (or press Ctrl+A), and then click on the Align to Center of Page check box. You want to center the objects horizontally but not vertically, so deselect the Center option button under Vertically. Then click on OK (Chapter 12).

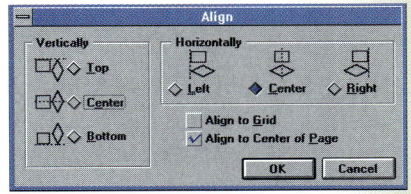

One remaining problem is that the text doesn't show up well against the blue background. To remedy this situation, make sure the text (but not the fish) is selected and then click on the yellow option in the color palette. Now your text will stand out much more clearly (Chapter 10).

Click anywhere on the blue rectangle to select it. Then, using your *right* mouse button, click on a shade of purple in the color palette to change the rectangle's outline from black (the default) to purple. (Make sure not to click with the left mouse button or you'll change the fill rather than the outline color.) Then click on the Pen tool to open the Pen flyout menu and click on the second button from the right on the top row—this assigns a line weight of 16 points to your rectangle's outline.

Now choose the paragraph text tool and draw a text frame in the bottom half of the screen, as shown here (Chapter 5).

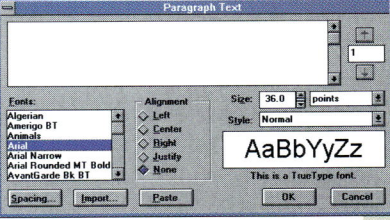

Choose Edit Text from the Text menu, and, in the Paragraph Text dialog box, choose 36-point Arial text. Then click on OK (Chapter 5).

Continue to next page ▶

**134** TRY IT!

### TRY IT!

Continue below

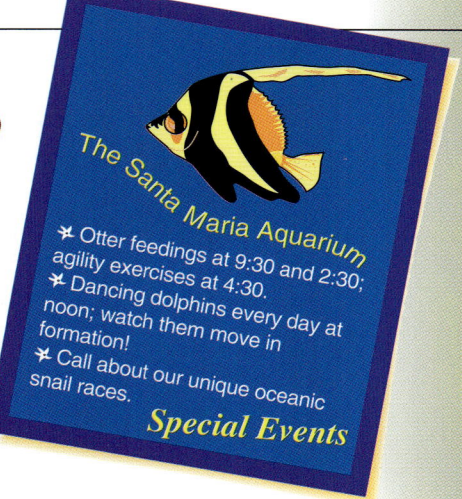

With the I-beam pointer, click inside the text frame. Then type the text shown above, pressing Enter at the end of each sentence. Make sure to include the typos; you'll ferret them out in a moment (Chapter 5).

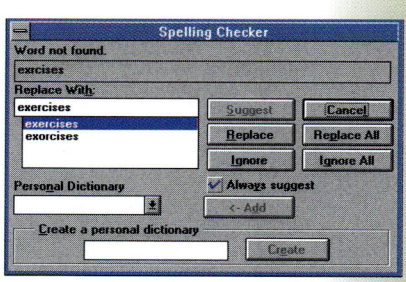

Choose Spell Checker from the Text menu. Click on the Always Suggest check box if it's not already selected and then click on the Check Text button. CorelDRAW! will stop on the word "exrcises" and suggest the alternatives "exercises" and "exorcises." Click on Replace to fix the spelling error. Next CorelDRAW! will spot the word "noone," suggesting several replacements. Click on "noon" and then click on Replace. Finally, CorelDRAW! will stop on "abot." Click on "about" and then click on Replace. Click on OK when you get the message that the spelling check is finished (Chapter 13).

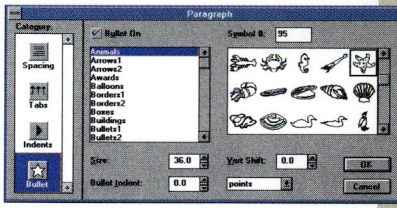

Click on the Pick tool; your text frame should be enclosed within a highlighting box. Now choose Paragraph from the Text menu. In the Paragraph dialog box that appears, click on Bullet under Category at the left side of the dialog box and then click on the Bullet On check box to select it if it's not already selected. Make sure the Animals category of bullets is selected, and then scroll through the list of symbols on the right until you find a suitable aquatic creature. Then click on it to select it—here the starfish has been selected—increase its point size to 36 to match the point size of your text, and click on OK (Chapter 13).

Notice that your black text and bullet characters don't show up well at all against the dark blue background. Make sure the text frame is still selected and then click on the white option in the color palette to make the text more clearly visible (Chapter 10).

Select the artistic text tool and, in the lower-right corner of the screen, enter the text **Special Events!** *outside* the paragraph text frame you inserted earlier. (You'll know you're outside the frame because your mouse pointer will be a crosshair rather than an I-beam.) Choose Edit Text from the Text menu, choose the Times New Roman font, pick a point size of 52, and then click on OK. (Chapter 5.) Finally, choose the Pick tool and use the color palette to change the text color to yellow (Chapter 10).

Click on the new text to introduce the special handles for rotating and skewing objects. Now drag downward on the straight handle on the left-hand side of the text to skew the text in that direction. You're simply trying to slant the text, placing it at an angle much like the one you can see here (Chapter 11).

 So you don't lose all your hard work, choose Save from the File menu to save your file. In the Save Drawing dialog box that appears, choose the drive and directory in which you want to save the file and enter **special** under File Name. Then click on OK to go ahead with the save operation (Chapter 6).

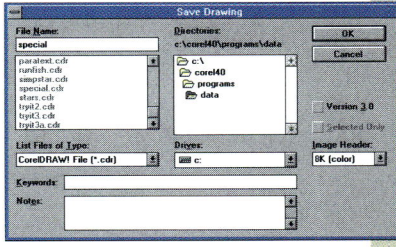

 Finally, you'll probably want to print your creation to get a sense of the finished product. Although colors won't show up unless you are fortunate enough to have a color printer, you may still may want to print a black-and-white copy to get a general idea of what the printed results will look like. Choose Print from the File menu. CorelDRAW! will display the Print dialog box. Check the preview to make sure that everything looks right, choose the desired number of copies, make any other necessary changes or selections in this dialog box, and then click on OK to proceed with the print operation (Chapter 8).

## APPENDIX

# The Installation Procedure

There's a decent chance that you've already installed CorelDRAW!, or that someone else has done the job for you. If so, you can skip this appendix. If not, however, you need to install CorelDRAW! on your computer before you can use it in any way. You may wonder what it actually means to "install" a computer program. (Don't worry; this is not a "dumb" question.) Installing simply involves transferring the program files from the floppy disks that you receive when you purchase CorelDRAW! onto your computer's hard disk. This process requires only a few fairly simple steps, and, once you get started, CorelDRAW! does an excellent job of guiding you along your way and doing most of the work on its own.

There are actually a few ways of installing CorelDRAW! You can install the entire program—a process that requires a minimum of fiddling or fuss. However, if you have less room on your hard disk, you may want to (or may have to) install just a portion of the program. This process is somewhat (but not much) more complex, involving several additional decisions on your part about what to install and what not to install. This appendix provides general instructions only. If you find that you need additional help, consult your CorelDRAW! documentation— look for the pamphlet entitled *Installation Guide*.

# Installing CorelDRAW!

If you've ever installed a program before—especially a Windows program—you'll have no trouble installing CorelDRAW! However, if you've never installed a program on your computer before, you might be a little intimidated. Don't be. Installation is a simple procedure. And once you get started, CorelDRAW! provides helpful on-screen prompts that tell you what to do next. The only hitch is that CorelDRAW! is a rather large program, and, depending on speed of your computer, the installation may take some time.

## TIP SHEET

▶ This appendix describes how to install from floppy disks. There's also a CD-ROM version of CorelDRAW! that includes more clip art, more fonts, and so on. If you have a CD-ROM drive and want to install the CD-ROM version of Corel-DRAW!, consult the *Installation Guide* provided with your CorelDRAW! documentation.

▶ If an earlier version of CorelDRAW! is already installed on your computer (that is, a version with a number less than 4), see the CorelDRAW! *Installation Guide* for advice on how to proceed.

▶ Even if CorelDRAW! is installed on your system, it may not have been installed in full. If so, you might decide to install something that wasn't installed the first time around—some clip art or some help files, for instance. Although this process is not complex, it is beyond the scope of this appendix. For instructions, turn to Corel-DRAW!'s on-line help system. From within CorelDRAW!, choose Search For Help On from the Help menu, type install, double-click on "installing CorelDRAW options" in the list of topics at the top of the Search dialog box, and then click on Go To. See Chapter 3 of this book—or the help system itself—for the details on using CorelDRAW!'s help system.

▶ **1** Open your CorelDRAW! box, pull out the floppy disks, and check whether they're 5¼-inch disks or 3½-inch disks. If your computer has both types of floppy drives, you can use either size of disk. If not, you need to make sure that the disk size matches the size of your drive. Otherwise, you won't be able to go ahead with the installation. (If your disks are not the appropriate size, call CorelDRAW! or consult your retailer about exchanging the disks.)

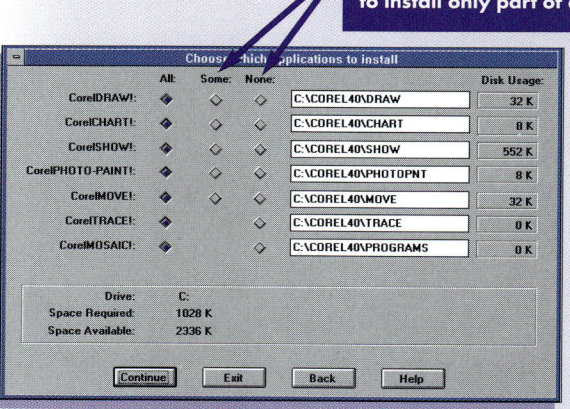

 **7** To use up less hard disk space, do a Custom Install instead of a Full Install. First click on the Custom Install button and choose Continue to confirm that you want to install into the COREL40 directory. You'll see this dialog box, which lets you choose which portion of CorelDRAW! to install. If you want to save the maximum amount of disk space, just leave CorelDRAW! selected, and click on the None option buttons to the right of all other items (CorelCHART!, CorelSHOW!, and so on). These are *add-on programs*—extra programs provided with CorelDRAW! that allow you to do things such as create charts, slide shows, and more. If you choose the Some option button to the right of a program name, you'll see an additional dialog box asking which files you want to install. Choose the desired files—the program files are the only essential ones—and then click on Continue to proceed. When you're done choosing which add-ons to include, again click on Continue to go ahead with the installation.

### Installing CorelDRAW! 139

**2** Check how much space is available on your hard disk. (Consult your DOS documentation or a knowledgeable friend if you need advice on this front.) Especially if you install the program in its entirety, CorelDRAW! takes up a significant amount of space on your hard disk (up to 37MB!).

**3** Since CorelDRAW! is a Windows-based program, you must have Windows installed on your computer before you can install CorelDRAW! If your computer has Windows installed, get into Windows now. You should wind up in the Windows Program Manager; you'll see the words "Program Manager" at the top of the screen, as shown here. (Refer to Chapter 2 of this book or a Windows text if you need any help with Windows.) If you don't have Windows installed, find out about buying and installing it; you'll need to do so before you can proceed.

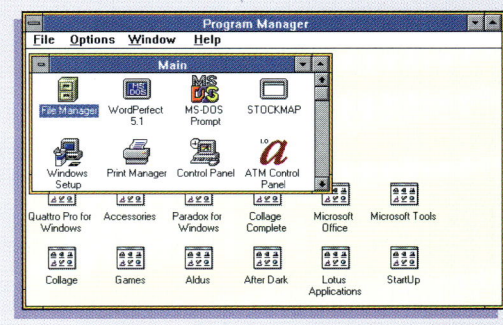

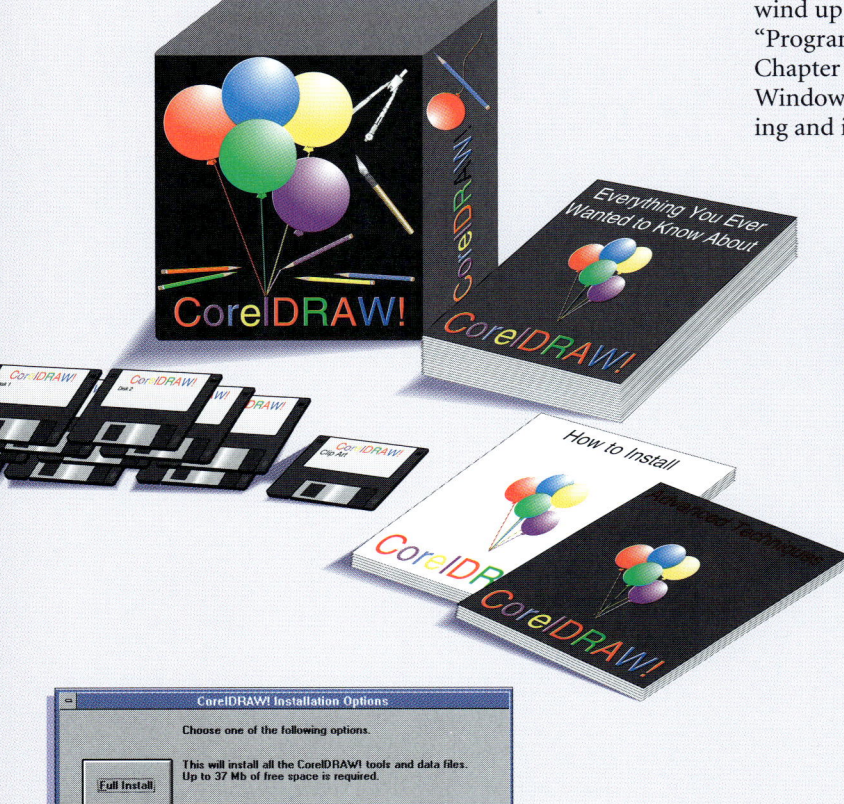

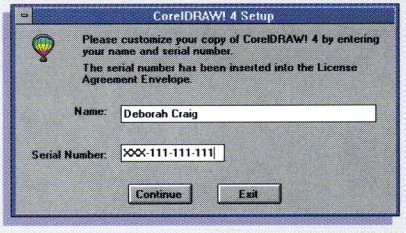

**4** Put the CorelDRAW! floppy disk labeled "Disk 1" in your floppy drive. Then choose Run from the Program Manager's File menu. In the Run dialog box that appears, type **a:\setup** if you placed the floppy disk in drive A. (Generally floppy drives are called either drive A or drive B. If you have two floppy drives, drive A is the top or leftmost drive.) If your floppy drive has a different name, substitute the appropriate drive letter. Then click on OK to start the installation program.

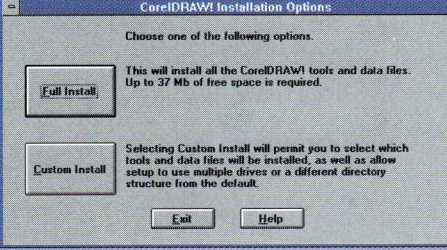

**5** You may have to wait a while as CorelDRAW! initializes the setup program. When you see a Welcome prompt, click on the Continue button. (You'll see such Continue buttons throughout the installation procedure. Just click on them to proceed. If you decide not to go forward with the installation, you can instead click on the Exit button.) In the next dialog box, provide your name, press Tab, and type your serial number (it's in the box that CorelDRAW! came in). Make sure to type the serial number exactly, including any hyphens. Then click on Continue to proceed.

**6** At this point you'll have a choice between a Full Install or a Custom Install. As mentioned, a Full Install is easier. To do this type of installation, click on the Full Install button, click on Continue to accept COREL40 as the default directory, and click on Continue again to accept the defaults when asked which fonts, filters, and scanner drivers to install (*filters* are programs that enable you to work with files from other sources). Then click on the Install button. When prompted for additional program disks, simply take out the disk currently in the drive, insert the requested disk, and click on OK. At any time, you can discontinue the installation by clicking on the Cancel button.

# INDEX

## A

active windows, 11
Actual Size tool, 70, 71
add-ons to CorelDRAW!, 2, 138
aligning objects, 101, 104–105, 106, 133. *See also* centering objects; grid; guidelines
    to center of page, 104, 105
    selection techniques and, 104
aligning text, 37, 39, 45, 132, 133
Alt key, 14, 15
angle of fountain fills, 83
animation, 2
application programs, 7
application windows, 10, 11, 12
arranging objects. *See* aligning objects; reordering objects
arrow keys, 14, 15
artistic text, 35, 36–37, 44, 91, 94, 96

## B

background color, in pattern fills, 84, 85, 86
Backspace key, 16, 37
beveled corners, 123
Bézier mode, 26, 28–29, 132
bitmaps, 80
bold, 5, 37
bulleted lists, 38, 40, 114, 134

## C

Cancel button, 16
CD-ROM version of CorelDRAW!, 138
centering objects, 133. *See also* aligning objects
centering text, 45, 132
center offset, for fountain fills, 82
center of rotation, 96
charts, 2, 138
check boxes, in dialog boxes, 16, 17
circles, 3, 25, 32–33. *See also* ellipses
clearing the screen, 42, 52–53, 88, 130
Clear Transformations, 94, 96, 98. *See also* undoing actions
clicking, 13
clip art, 1, 2, 126, 127, 138
    installing, 131
    using in pattern fills, 84, 86, 87
Clipboard, 58, 126, 128
cloning objects, 58, 59
close-up view, 70–71
closing files, 51, 53
closing programs, 10, 15
closing windows, 10, 15
color palette, 19, 21, 120–121, 132
    displaying, 75, 78
    removing, 20, 75
    switching between palettes, 79
colors, 3, 74, 77–87, 90, 91, 132. *See also* fills
    background, 85
    changing default, 78
    foreground, 84, 85
    in fountain fills, 83, 89
    of outlines, 120, 121
    in pattern fills, 85
    removing, 78, 79
    of text, 90, 133–35
columns, 5, 36, 38
combining objects, 107. *See also* grouping objects; welding objects
command buttons, 16
commands, issuing, 13, 15, 16
constrain key, 31, 33, 58. *See also* Ctrl key
Control menu, 15
Control Menu box, 10, 11, 21
control points, 28, 29, 98, 99. *See also* nodes
copying objects, 55, 58–59
corners, styles of, 122–123
creating files, 52–53
Ctrl key, 14, 15
cursor, 16, 36, 37, 110
curves, 2–3, 25
    control points and, 28, 29
    deleting, 26
    drawing in Bézier mode, 28–29
    drawing in Freehand mode, 26–27, 28, 29
    moving, 99
    nodes in, 26, 28, 29
    reshaping, 28, 99
cutting objects, 58. *See also* copying objects; moving objects

## D

dashed lines, 119, 123
Delete key, 16, 37
deleting objects, 52, 53, 56, 58
deleting text, 16, 37
deselecting objects, 56, 57, 60
desktop publishing programs. *See* exporting files; importing files
dialog boxes, 14, 16–17, 19. *See also* roll-up windows
dictionary, 4, 112, 113. *See also* spell checking
dimension lines, 26
directories, 49, 51
disk drives, 48, 49, 51

disk operating system. *See* DOS
disk space, saving, 138
document windows, 10–13
DOS, 7, 8–9
dotted lines, 119, 123
double-clicking, 13
dragging, 13
drawing, 1, 25–33
    in Bézier mode, 26, 28–29
    circles, 32–33
    with a computer, 1
    curves, 25–26, 28, 29
    ellipses, 32–33, 44
    in Freehand mode, 26–29
    lines, 25–26
    rectangles, 30–31
    squares, 30–31
drawing tools, 2, 19, 26. *See also* toolbox; tools
drawing window, 20, 21
drives, 48, 49, 51
drop-down list boxes, 16, 17
duplicating objects, 58–59, 90

## E

editable preview, 74, 78, 120
ellipses, 2–3, 21, 25, 26, 32–33, 44. *See also* circles
Ellipse tool, 21
embedding, 126, 128
enlarging drawings, 70–71
enlarging shapes. *See* scaling objects; stretching objects
erasing. *See* clearing the screen; deleting
Escape key, 14
exiting programs, 10, 15
exiting windows and dialog boxes, 14
exporting files, 125, 128–129. *See also* Clipboard

extensions, 49, 50

## F

facing pages, viewing, 75
file extensions, 49, 50
file formats, 127, 128, 129
file names, 48, 49
file name specification, 50
files
    closing, 51, 53
    copying with new name, 48
    creating new, 52–53
    defined, 47
    discarding changes to, 50, 51, 53
    exporting, 125, 128–129
    importing, 125, 126–127
    opening, 50–51
    printing, 63–67
    saving, 48–49, 50, 51, 53
Fill flyout menu, 20, 79
fill patterns. *See* fills
fills, 3, 74
    changing the default, 78, 80
    deleting pattern, 84, 86
    fountain (gradient), 77, 82–83, 89
    full-color pattern, 86–87
    pattern, 77, 84–87
    removing, 78, 79, 80, 82
    saving, 80, 86
    texture, 77, 80–81
    two-color pattern, 84–85
    using clip art in, 84, 86, 87
Fill tool, 21
filters, 139
Fit-in-Window tool, 70
floppy disk
    installing CorelDRAW! using, 138–139
    saving to, 49
    opening files on, 51

floppy drives, 48, 138, 139
flyout menus, 20
fonts, 4–5, 37, 38, 39
foreground color, in pattern fills, 84, 85, 86
fountain fills, 77, 82–83, 89
frame, text, 38, 39, 45
Freehand mode, drawing in, 26–27, 28, 29, 44
full-color pattern fills, 86–87
function keys, 14, 15

## G

Go To Page command, 52
gradient fills, 77, 82–83, 89
grid, 30, 32, 43, 104
Grid Setup command, 30, 32, 43
grouping objects, 101, 106–107
guidelines, 30, 32, 59
gutters, 5, 36, 38

## H

handles, 53, 56, 57, 64, 96
hard disk space, 139
hard drive, 48
help, 19
    backtracking, 22
    context-sensitive, 23
    definitions, 23
    exiting from, 22
    help on, 22
    on installing, 138
    jumps, 23
    search feature, 23
    table of contents, 22
highlighting box, 53, 56, 57, 134. *See also* selecting objects
horizontal orientation. *See* orientation

horizontal scroll bar, 13, 21
hyphenation, 4, 36, 38, 114–115

**I**

I-beam pointer, 111
importing files, 125, 126–127, 128, 131. *See also* Clipboard
indents, 38, 114, 115
input device. *See* keyboard; mouse
insertion point, 16, 36, 37, 110
installation, 1
   aborting, 139
   custom, 138, 139
   defined, 137
   full, 138, 139
   partial, 138
italic, 5, 37

**J**

joining objects, 101, 106–107
justification, 38, 39

**K**

keyboard
   navigating with, 14, 15
   starting programs with, 10

**L**

landscape orientation, 72, 73, 89
lines, 2, 25, 45. *See also* outlines
   beginning of, 122
   color of, 3, 119, 120–121, 133
   constraining to particular angle, 26
   corners of, 122–123
   dashed, 119, 123
   deleting, 26
   dimension, 26
   dotted, 119, 123
   drawing in Bézier mode, 28–29
   drawing in Freehand mode, 26, 27–29
   endings of, 3, 119, 122–123
   multisegment, 27, 29
   nodes in, 26, 29
   reshaping, 28
   styles of, 3, 119, 122–123
   thickness of, 3, 119, 120–121, 133
linking, 126, 128
linking objects, 101, 106–107
list boxes, in dialog boxes, 17

**M**

magnification, 70–71
margins, 38, 114–115
marquee, 57, 71. *See also* selecting objects
maximize button, 12, 20, 21
maximizing windows, 12, 15, 20
memory, computer, 48
menu bar, 11, 15, 16, 19, 21, 75
menus, 11, 16, 19
   CorelDRAW!'s, 21
   using, with the keyboard, 14, 15, 21
   using, with the mouse, 13, 21
minimize button, 12, 21
minimizing windows, 12, 15
mirroring objects, 93, 94–95
mitered corners, 123
mouse
   clicking with, 13
   double-clicking with, 13
   dragging with, 13
   left button, 12
   pointer, 12
   pointing with, 12
   right button, 12, 70
moving objects, 2, 55, 58–59
   while printing, 64
   and stacking order, 103

**N**

network, 9
new drawings, creating, 52
nodes, 26, 28, 29, 56, 93, 132. *See also* control points
   beginning, 122
   ending, 122
   moving, 98, 99
   nudging, 98
   selecting, 98, 99
numeric keypad, 14
nudging objects, 59, 98
Num Lock key, 14, 15

**O**

OK button, 16
on-line help. *See* help
opening files, 50–51
operating system, 7
option buttons, 16, 17
ordering objects. *See* reordering objects
orientation, 69, 72–73, 89, 131
Outline flyout menu, 20, 120
outlines, 3, 69, 77
   changing the default, 120, 122
   color of, 119, 120–121, 133
   corners of, 122–123
   dashed, 123
   default, 119
   dotted, 123
   endings of, 119, 122–123
   removing, 120
   style of, 119, 122–123

of text, 120
thickness of, 119–122, 133
Outline tool, 21
overlapping. *See* reordering objects
overtype mode, 36

## P

page counter, 52
page orientation. *See* orientation
pages
   adding, 53
   moving between, 52
   multiple, 69, 75
   printing selected, 66
palettes. *See* color palette
paragraph text, 35, 38–39, 94, 96. *See also* bulleted lists; hyphenation; indents; tabs
   formatting, 114–115
pasting objects, 58. *See also* copying objects; moving objects
pattern fills, 77, 84–87
Pencil tool, 21
photographs, 2
Pick tool, 21
pointing, with the mouse, 12
point size, 5, 38, 39. *See also* text, size
   of bullet characters, 134
portrait orientation, 72, 73, 131. *See also* orientation
preview, 51, 65, 74–75
printable page, 20, 21, 26, 43
   orientation of, 72–73
   displaying, 70
printer, selecting, 65
printing, 63–67, 91, 135
   multiple copies, 65
   on multiple pages, 64
   and paper orientation, 72
   selected objects, 66, 67
   selected pages, 66, 67
   to a file, 64
program group windows, 10, 11
program items, 10, 11
Program Manager, Windows, 8, 9, 10–11, 139
   mouse pointer, shape of within, 12
   starting programs from within, 10
programs, 10, 15

## R

radio buttons, 16, 17
rearranging objects. *See* aligning objects; reordering objects
rectangles, 2–3, 25, 26, 30–31
Rectangle tool, 21
redoing actions, 60–61. *See also* undoing actions
reducing drawings, 70–71
reducing shapes. *See* scaling objects; stretching objects
reordering objects, 101, 102–103, 133
repeating actions, 55, 60–61, 91
reshaping objects, 2, 93–99, 132
resizing objects, 64. *See also* scaling objects; stretching objects
restore button, 12, 20, 21
restoring objects, 94
restoring windows, 12, 15, 20
reversing actions. *See* undoing actions
right mouse button. *See* mouse
roll-up windows, 20, 40
rotating objects, 56, 93, 96–97, 131
rounded corners, 123
rulers, 20, 21, 73

## S

saving, 48–49, 50, 51
scale, changing, 70–71
scaling objects, 93, 94–95, 131
scroll arrows, 13
scroll bars, 13, 17
scroll box, 13
scrolling, 60, 70
selecting objects, 53, 55, 56–57, 96. *See also* Pick tool
selecting text, 55, 56–57, 111
setup program. *See* installation
Shape tool, 21
shaping objects, 93, 98–99, 132
Shift key, 14, 15
Show Grid option, 30, 43
Show Page tool, 70
skewing objects, 56, 93, 96–97, 135
slide shows, 138
Snap To Grid option, 30, 43, 104
spacing, 36, 38
spell checking, 4, 112–113, 134
spreadsheet programs. *See* exporting files; importing files
squares, 3, 25, 26, 30–31
stacking objects. *See* reordering objects
stacking order, 102
starting CorelDRAW!, 20
starting programs, 10–11
status line, 20, 31, 33
stretching objects, 93, 94–95
subdirectories, 49, 51

symbols
  changing the size of, 41
  creating your own, 40
  tiling, 40, 41
Symbols Library, 35, 40
synonyms. *See* thesaurus

# T

tabs, 36, 38, 114, 115
text, 4–5, 35–41, 109–117
  adding, 110
  aligning, 36, 39, 45
  artistic, 35, 36–37, 44, 45, 94, 96, 110
  centering, 45, 132
  coloring, 4, 35, 90
  columns, 5, 36, 38
  copying, 35, 55, 110
  defaults, 114
  deleting, 35, 110, 111
  duplicating, 90
  editing, 110–111
  entering, 35–41, 44, 45, 89, 91
  fitting to a path, 116–117, 132
  formatting, 114–115
  justification, 38, 39
  mirroring, 4, 95
  moving, 4, 35, 55, 90, 91, 110
  outlines of, changing, 120
  paragraph, 35, 38–39, 45, 94, 96, 114–115
  reshaping, 35, 94, 95
  rotating, 4, 96
  scaling, 94
  selecting, 55, 56–57, 111
  size, 5, 37, 38, 89, 132–134
  skewing, 96, 135
  spacing, 36, 38
  spell checking, 112–113, 134
  stretching, 4, 94
  style, 5, 37, 39
  wrapping, 4, 36, 37, 38, 39
text boxes, in dialog boxes, 16
Text flyout menu, 36, 38
text frame, 38, 39, 45
Text tool, 21
texture fills, 77, 80–81
thesaurus, 4, 112–113
tiling
  pattern fills, 85, 87
  symbols, 40, 41
title bar, 11, 21, 48
toolbox, 21
  removing, 75
tools, 21, 27
two-color pattern fills, 84–85

# U

undoing actions, 22, 52, 55, 60–61, 70, 94, 96, 98
ungrouping objects, 107

# V

vertical orientation. *See* orientation
vertical scroll bar, 13, 21
viewing drawings, 69–75

# W

welding objects, 106. *See also* combining objects; grouping objects
windows, closing, 10, 15
Windows, 7
  Clipboard, 58
  closing windows in, 10
  commands, issuing, 11
  exiting programs in, 10
  installing, 139
  opening multiple programs within, 10
  Program Manager, 8, 9, 139
  starting, 8, 9
  starting programs in, 10–11
  switching between open programs in, 10
  windows, 10, 11
wireframe view, 69, 74, 75, 78, 120. *See also* outlines
word processing programs. *See* exporting files; importing files
word wrap, 4, 36, 37, 38, 39
wrapping text. *See* word wrap; text, fitting to a path

# Z

Zoom flyout menu, 70
zooming, 70–71
Zoom tool, 21

# Ziff-Davis Press Survey of Readers

Please help us in our effort to produce the best books on personal computing.
For your assistance, we would be pleased to send you a FREE catalog
featuring the complete line of Ziff-Davis Press books.

1. How did you first learn about this book?

Recommended by a friend ............... ☐ -1 (5)
Recommended by store personnel ........ ☐ -2
Saw in Ziff-Davis Press catalog ........... ☐ -3
Received advertisement in the mail ....... ☐ -4
Saw the book on bookshelf at store ....... ☐ -5
Read book review in: _____ ☐ -6
Saw an advertisement in: _____ ☐ -7
Other (Please specify): _____ ☐ -8

2. Which THREE of the following factors most influenced your decision to purchase this book? (Please check up to THREE.)

Front or back cover information on book ... ☐ -1 (6)
Logo of magazine affiliated with book ...... ☐ -2
Special approach to the content ........... ☐ -3
Completeness of content ................. ☐ -4
Author's reputation ..................... ☐ -5
Publisher's reputation .................. ☐ -6
Book cover design or layout ............. ☐ -7
Index or table of contents of book ........ ☐ -8
Price of book .......................... ☐ -9
Special effects, graphics, illustrations ...... ☐ -0
Other (Please specify): _____ ☐ -x

3. How many computer books have you purchased in the last six months?  _____  (7-10)

4. On a scale of 1 to 5, where 5 is excellent, 4 is above average, 3 is average, 2 is below average, and 1 is poor, please rate each of the following aspects of this book below. (Please circle your answer.)

| | | | | | | |
|---|---|---|---|---|---|---|
| Depth/completeness of coverage | 5 | 4 | 3 | 2 | 1 | (11) |
| Organization of material | 5 | 4 | 3 | 2 | 1 | (12) |
| Ease of finding topic | 5 | 4 | 3 | 2 | 1 | (13) |
| Special features/time saving tips | 5 | 4 | 3 | 2 | 1 | (14) |
| Appropriate level of writing | 5 | 4 | 3 | 2 | 1 | (15) |
| Usefulness of table of contents | 5 | 4 | 3 | 2 | 1 | (16) |
| Usefulness of index | 5 | 4 | 3 | 2 | 1 | (17) |
| Usefulness of accompanying disk | 5 | 4 | 3 | 2 | 1 | (18) |
| Usefulness of illustrations/graphics | 5 | 4 | 3 | 2 | 1 | (19) |
| Cover design and attractiveness | 5 | 4 | 3 | 2 | 1 | (20) |
| Overall design and layout of book | 5 | 4 | 3 | 2 | 1 | (21) |
| Overall satisfaction with book | 5 | 4 | 3 | 2 | 1 | (22) |

5. Which of the following computer publications do you read regularly; that is, 3 out of 4 issues?

Byte ................................... ☐ -1 (23)
Computer Shopper ....................... ☐ -2
Corporate Computing .................... ☐ -3
Dr. Dobb's Journal ...................... ☐ -4
LAN Magazine .......................... ☐ -5
MacWEEK ............................. ☐ -6
MacUser .............................. ☐ -7
PC Computing ......................... ☐ -8
PC Magazine .......................... ☐ -9
PC WEEK ............................. ☐ -0
Windows Sources ...................... ☐ -x
Other (Please specify): _____ ☐ -y

**Please turn page.**

*Cut Here*

PLEASE TAPE HERE ONLY—DO NOT STAPLE

6. What is your level of experience with personal computers? With the subject of this book?

|  | With PCs | With subject of book |
|---|---|---|
| Beginner............... | ☐ -1 (24) | ☐ -1 (25) |
| Intermediate........... | ☐ -2 | ☐ -2 |
| Advanced.............. | ☐ -3 | ☐ -3 |

7. Which of the following best describes your job title?

Officer (CEO/President/VP/owner)........ ☐ -1 (26)
Director/head........................... ☐ -2
Manager/supervisor..................... ☐ -3
Administration/staff..................... ☐ -4
Teacher/educator/trainer................ ☐ -5
Lawyer/doctor/medical professional....... ☐ -6
Engineer/technician..................... ☐ -7
Consultant............................. ☐ -8
Not employed/student/retired............ ☐ -9
Other (Please specify): _____ ☐ -0

8. What is your age?

Under 20............................... ☐ -1 (27)
21-29.................................. ☐ -2
30-39.................................. ☐ -3
40-49.................................. ☐ -4
50-59.................................. ☐ -5
60 or over............................. ☐ -6

9. Are you:

Male................................... ☐ -1 (28)
Female................................. ☐ -2

Thank you for your assistance with this important information! Please write your address below to receive our free catalog.

Name: _____
Address: _____
City/State/Zip: _____

**Fold here to mail.**                                            2214-03-14

---

**BUSINESS REPLY MAIL**
FIRST CLASS MAIL    PERMIT NO. 1612    OAKLAND, CA

POSTAGE WILL BE PAID BY ADDRESSEE

**Ziff-Davis Press**

5903 Christie Avenue
Emeryville, CA 94608-1925
Attn: Marketing

NO POSTAGE
NECESSARY
IF MAILED IN
THE UNITED
STATES